GOOD GUYS FINISH FIRST

GOOD GUYS FINISH FIRST:

REFLECTIONS OF A CEO AND HOW TO START A

DE NOVO COMMUNITY BANK

ANDY.

THANKS FOR THE

GREAT INPUT -

Paul

C. PAUL JOHNSON WITH JIM BOWMAN

To order additional copies of this book, contact:
Xlibris Corporation
1-888-795-4274
www.Xlibris.com
Orders@Xlibris.com
23881

CONTENTS

Part IV-B: Outside Experts: Regulators

DEDICATED TO

MY GRANDFATHER,
WHO INSPIRED ENTREPRENEURSHIP, AND

MY FATHER,
WHO TAUGHT ME COURAGE

Acknowledgments

It's impossible to list everyone who contributed to First Colonial's success and helped make this book possible, but some do rise to the top.

- ☐ J. Russell Duncan, my mentor and the person who got me into banking
- ☐ Allen Stults, the risk-taker who lent me the money to buy my first bank
- ☐ Bill Duquaine, my close friend who was fundamental in our success. He died too young.
- ☐ Donald P. Jacobs, immediate past dean of the Kellogg School of Business, Northwestern University, who encouraged me to write this book
- ☐ Alan Schwartz, chairman of the First Colonial executive committee, to whom I turned with the big decisions
- ☐ Ron Aronberg, the steady counsel on the board
- ☐ Bob Leander, the conscience of the board
- ☐ Tom Maier, my brilliant CFO
- ☐ Pat O'Malley, our own St. Patrick
- ☐ Bob Sherman, our president and my right-hand man
- ☐ Congressman Mike Thompson, a friend and strong supporter
- ☐ Commissioner Don Meyer, who opened doors for me

- ☐ My wife Debra, who built the bank's Doers Club, a key to our profitability
- ☐ Lois Panozzo, my loyal secretary of sixteen years
- ☐ Dona Bakker, my stenographer, who put many hours into the book
- ☐ Steve Bagby, my friend, for the splendid dust cover
- ☐ Jim Bowman, my great editor
- ☐ Chauncey and Jonathan, with love
- ☐ And particularly Annie and my daughters in appreciation for their love and support

Foreword

Paul Johnson and first-class community banking were virtually synonymous in the Chicago region for many years. He developed from scratch a $2 billion company with seventeen banks operating from thirty-six locations. Having been involved in the banking industry in my entire adult life, I can really appreciate that achievement. Not many have done it. It requires knowing the banking needs of your community and developing cost-effective ways to serve them. And it requires maintaining good relationships with the various regulatory agencies that supervise virtually every aspect of banking. I am glad Paul has decided to share his recipe for success.

> — William M. Isaac
> Chairman, The Secura Group
> Washington, DC
> Former Chairman,
> Federal Deposit Insurance Corporation

Foreword

This is the perfect time for a book from a highly successful "good guy" CEO about how to succeed in business. Our recent business scandals have left America's business students wondering if integrity and character have any role in business today. Paul Johnson's book about building a highly successful and ethical bank business will be a rich resource for today's students. He brings more than technical advice and expertise to the subject—he brings real experience and a life of honesty and integrity that earned the trust of his employees, customers, and competitors. If Paul Johnson is the role model for today's business students, American business has great days ahead.

— Congressman Dick Gephardt
Missouri, 3rd District

Foreword

Mark Twain said that a banker is a fellow who lends you an umbrella when the sun is shining, but he wants it back the minute it begins to rain. He obviously never met Paul Johnson.

I first met Paul in the mid-1990s when he moved from Chicago's skyscrapers to the vineyards of California's Napa Valley. He thought he was leaving behind an extremely successful thirty-one-year career in community banking to pursue his passion in winemaking. Our community had other plans for him. Our local bank had just sold and a group of community leaders did not want to leave our Valley's financial interests to the mercy of large, distant banks with no sense of where we live and work. We put together the plans for a new community bank, but couldn't push the ball the last ten yards. I called on Paul for help, and before we knew it, Napa Valley was once again being served by a successful and personal full-service community bank.

Paul Johnson's success in community banking is an extension of his commitment in small communities and the people who live in them. He and his wife Debra wasted no time in taking an immediate interest in lending their support to a broad spectrum of programs that continue to strengthen and improve our community. His integrity, compassion and trust are pure. These are the keys to his success. This is the reason why everything he touches turns to gold.

Twain also said that the man who doesn't read good books

has no advantage over the man who can't read them. This is a good book by a good man. It should be required reading for business students, bankers or anyone who may be losing faith in our institutions and truly wants to learn how good guys can and do finish first.

— Congressman Mike Thompson
California, 1st District

Foreword

Paul Johnson and I met some thirty years ago during a very unusual weekend. I was a relatively young NASA astronaut serving as a support crew member to the Apollo-Soyuz Test Mission, the only mission to dock in the earth's orbit, an American Apollo spaceship with a Soviet Union Soyuz spaceship.

In preparing for this mission, cosmonauts came for the first time to the United States. Except for occasional news articles from Soviet sources, we, astronauts, knew little about them and virtually nothing, save lingering suspicion, about the Soviet Union. Nonetheless, the mission had been agreed to by our respective leaders; and we, astronauts, wanted to be gracious, even innovative, hosts to our counterparts—the Russian space flyers.

We soon learned that the most famous of the cosmonauts, General Vladimir Shatolov, head of the cosmonaut office, and General Aleksei Leonev, the first human to walk in space, were avid hunters. To extend a hospitable hand, we organized a trip to Lander, Wyoming, for the famed One-Shot Antelope hunt held there every year and entered an astronaut and a cosmonaut team.

The experience was memorable for all parties, perhaps because of the wide spectrum of individuals attending the One—Shot event—cosmonauts, astronauts, senators, governors, assorted celebrities, and local ranchers. But of the many new acquaintances I made during that weekend, Paul Johnson stuck most in my mind.

From our brief conversations over two evenings, I found him to be an experienced jet pilot and a rancher. But unlike the others, he seemed far keener on Western history and archeology than on hunting. Moreover, he was surprisingly passionate about young people and their education. I had that same interest, having come from a family of teachers and having once taught physics.

Paul and I became friends. Months later I learned that in addition to his many hobbies and interests, he was a successful Chicago banker. His "excuse," as he put it, for being a banker was that it took Johnson the banker to support Johnson the rancher, historian, and archeologist.

In December 1984, after my second space shuttle flight, Paul invited me and my wife to a holiday party with his First Colonial Bank employees. It was in one of the larger First Colonial Banks on a bitter cold Chicago December night. As cold as it was, my wife and I feared being coldly received, being strangers in a strange land—the business world—we two having worked only at universities and in the federal government. Our fears were totally unfounded. We spent a wonderful evening with people who seemed like members of a congenial extended family. First Colonial obviously was made up of people who enjoyed and respected each other, even if they were business colleagues.

When I resigned from NASA a few months later to join a start-up technology company in Houston, Texas, I immediately thought of that evening and of Paul and his colleagues. With a family to support and no savings to speak of, I could not attend a business school to prepare me for this work. Perhaps without realizing it, my new employer was taking a chance on me as an executive because I almost knew nothing about business. Maybe Paul, with his wide business experience, including being founder and CEO of a robustly growing bank, would be someone I could turn to for advice. This was nearly twenty years ago.

Not only did he do that, he invested in our young company, generously serving as an advisor to me on basic business principles. As the business grew, I was increasingly surrounded by colleagues (and competitors) with advance degrees from prestigious business schools. I realize now that I, in contrast, was a graduate of the lesser known but nonetheless excellent C. Paul Johnson School of Common Sense and Applicable Business Advice.

My lessons ran the gamut from a simple "Don't ask your barber if you need a haircut" to a complex "The secret of business is that there is no secret: success comes from unwavering attention to detail" to Paul's deeply felt philosophy of doing business. I summarize it this way: "Do the right thing, consistently and over the long term, for customers, coworkers, and communities." Paul was convinced that an enterprise based on these values would succeed and return substantial rewards to its shareholders.

What you are about to read spells out that philosophy and gives it flesh, blood, and bottom lines. First Colonial's success is detailed here. It is powerful evidence that Paul is right. I know it from my own experience, having applied his values to our business, Veridian Corporation, for twenty years. Ours is a business far removed from banking—bringing to government agencies concerned with national safety and security advanced technologies and teams of engineers and scientists. It didn't matter. Our success depended on what Paul had depended on at First Colonial. Our sale a few months ago at a 30 percent premium to our valuation is strong evidence that Paul is right when it comes to nonbanking business too.

This book is full of lessons taught at the C. Paul Johnson School. They are fun to read even for those not greatly interested in the world of business. As a bonus, the book has a happy ending. For those interested in business and thinking boldly about (gulp!) starting a business yourself, the book is a must. As you read, give the advice you found here your most serious attention. I assure you, it is a very good advice.

— Joseph P. "Joe" Allen, PhD
Former Astronaut
Chairman of the Board of Veridian
Corporation, sold to General
Dynamics in 2003 for $1.5 billion

Introduction

Surprised By Cynicism

I have been surprised at the cynicism of many, particularly the younger generation and students, about morality in business. There is a widespread belief that to be successful you have to bend rules and even be ruthless and devious. This is inaccurate in my experience. It is virtually impossible to rise to the position of CEO and stay there while being dishonest or vicious. The type is weeded out quickly. Indeed, publicity about such wrongdoers ironically contributes to the cynicism.

I say this in the face of recent indictments of corporate executives from Tyco, WorldCom, Adelphia, Enron, and other companies. These situations, in my opinion, are aberrations and not endemic to the corporate world. There will always be a few greedy and unethical executives who take advantage of the system and succeed for a time. But such executives are nowhere near as common as many think. The vast majority of executives are people of integrity.

Indeed, in my experience, successful CEOs are almost all honest, compassionate, contributing members of society, seldom driven by greed. They compete instead because of their desire for success for its own sake, not primarily for money and prestige.

Executives do not usually become wealthy at the expense of staff and shareholders, no matter what you hear. They learn early in their careers that they need people and have to rely on others who trust them. Such trust cannot be achieved by being ruthless or deceptive.

Trust is fundamental. Business depends on it. Deals are agreed on first by a handshake, then by a written contract. Reputations are built on honesty and the knowledge that the executive's word is beyond reproach. One learns to waste no time with someone known for reneging on deals.

I am writing this book out of concern about these misconceptions and in the hope that I reach some young people as they start their careers. I want to present a more accurate concept of business.

I do this as a financially successful former CEO of a Chicago bank that my associates and I built into a bank holding company with value far exceeding what we found there. From its sale came substantial profit to us all. And we did it with integrity and compassion.

How successful? The bank I bought in 1972—Colonial Bank and Trust Company, on Chicago's Northwest Side—had $60 million in assets. I paid $4.5 million, which I borrowed from the American National Bank in Chicago, to buy a controlling interest in the bank. It grew into seventeen banks in thirty-six locations—a $1.8 billion holding company with four financial subsidiaries. In 1995 we sold the holding company, First Colonial Bankshares Corporation, to Firstar Corporation in Milwaukee for over $350 million.

We started First Colonial with sixty employees. There were about eight hundred when we sold. We had $8 million in capital in 1980, about $120 million in 1995. Our initial public offering (IPO) in 1984 raised $9 million. We had institutional investors for it in England, Scotland, France, and Switzerland, which was unusual at that time for a smaller Midwestern bank.

In 2001, six years after our sale to Firstar at about 250 times book value and nearly twenty times earnings, we shareholders enjoyed a "triple dip." Firstar sold to Star Banc of

Cincinnati at another good premium. Then Star Banc, having assumed the Firstar name, bought U.S. Bancorp at yet another good premium.

Each sale increased our shareholder value significantly, our dividends dramatically. Our shareholders did very well. My family's charitable foundation, funded with bank stock, gives substantial sums annually to various charities, most of them science—and education-oriented.

That's the financial side of our success. The early investors and those who bought at the IPO did very, very well, including most of our senior staff and directors, many of whom became wealthy because of their long tenure with the company and our generous stock option program.

But that's only half the story and, in my opinion, the less important. A lot of CEOs and companies have been more successful, including dot-com and high-tech instant millionaires, some of whom amassed fabulous fortunes. As I write this in 2004, however, many of those fortunes have been diminished or erased, and, in any case, none of those instant "successes" will have known the satisfaction of building an organization as we did at First Colonial.

The more important part of our experience is how we built our company and what we built. It's how we treated staff and customers—with dignity and respect—as we built our "First Colonial family."

We became the quintessential community-bank group, entrepreneurially driven with a strong esprit de corps and camaraderie, known for innovations in products, services, and financing. Our seventeen banks were managed by seventeen presidents, each of whom gathered a board composed of people who lived in the area and knew the community.

When we bought a bank, we kept most of its directors and staff, and very few of them left over the years. We received extraordinary loyalty from our people. Everyone helped others when they needed help. The First Colonial family flourished.

It was a rarity in the business community, but one that can be replicated with the right ingredients and proper leadership.

First Colonial's achievements are epitomized in the words of a long-serving director, who told me just after the sale, "Paul, that was a great trip!"

Indeed it was. It ended when First Colonial was bought by a bank which was bought by yet another, which was merged with a third, namely U.S. Bancorp, which recently bought yet another, bringing its total assets to $189 billion, making it the eighth-largest bank in the United States and one of the most profitable. It's no First Colonial, however, as many of our staff who remained through the changes testify.

In its first part, this book will tell the First Colonial story—about good guys who finished first and were in a sense heroes, not just for their business prowess but also for their intelligence, compassion, and integrity.

In its later parts, it will tell how other banks and other bankers also exemplify the good-guy thesis and why and how yet others can do the same.

PART I-A

THE COLONIAL STORY: GOOD GUYS

Chapter 1

The Start of It All:

Buying Colonial Bank and Trust

One day in early 1970, I received a phone call from Jim Howard, a business acquaintance from Chicago and president of Meister Brau Brewery. I knew him through a trade organization, the National Association of Small Business Investment Companies (NASBIC). We had both formed companies under a 1959 congressional act to assist small businesses by providing government and private investment money.

Jim had gotten a state banking charter for the North Bank at Lake Point Tower in Chicago, a 718-unit building near Navy Pier where he owned a huge condo on the top floor. He told me he was having a difficult time getting the bank started. He had a fine board of directors, including Ralph Metcalfe, a state representative, who had run on the relay team at the 1936 Berlin Olympics with Jesse Owens, and Dan Edelman, president of a large Chicago PR firm. He had hired the affable Jerry Specht as president. Specht was long on personality and Notre Dame connections but had little talent in corporate finance or management and was ineffective in the position.

Jim asked me to move to Chicago from Milwaukee and help him get North Bank off the ground. I would put together a "one-bank holding company" and expand by buying an insurance agency, a leasing company, and a travel agency, all under Jim's Growth Capital company, of which I was to be president. I had been urging my mentor, J. Russell Duncan, owner of the Milwaukee Western Bank in Milwaukee, to do this sort of expansion into other financial areas in Milwaukee, but he was reluctant.

I was on the board of directors of Milwaukee Western, a $60 million bank, and was its senior vice president, having put together the deal for its purchase and financing for Russ. It was my success with that deal that attracted Jim Howard. Wanting to expand my horizons and get into a more vigorous business environment than Milwaukee offered, I jumped at Jim's offer and moved to Chicago in 1970 as president of Growth Capital.

I put together a fairly innovative financial package for the $9 million we needed to start the bank, including a loan from Michigan Avenue National Bank, which First Colonial Bankshares was to purchase fourteen years later. We then bought an insurance agency, formed a small business investment company (SBIC), and bought a travel agency.

It didn't take long for me to recognize the tremendous potential in Chicago for an innovative and creative banking organization. Commercial banking at that time in Chicago was neither competitive nor innovative. Banks were open four days a week and closed early, leading to the well-worn joke, pretty close to the truth, that all you had to do in banking was to observe the 3/3/3 rule—borrow at 3 percent, lend at 3 percent more, and be on the golf course by 3:00.

Illinois had no branching laws and no multibank holding company legislation. One could have only one bank in a holding company with no branches. Bank executives were, let's say, pretty sluggish, more concerned with their Wednesday morning tee—off time than with building anything significant or maximizing earnings. It was a comfortable way to make a living. There was little competition and a virtually protected anticompetitive radius within which to operate.

I sensed a huge potential in building a banking group, particularly if we could change archaic Illinois banking laws. This would give us better opportunity to grow and increase profitability, which would give us a great opportunity to sell out at higher multiples of book value and earnings.

I told Jim that, to vitalize our group, we should buy a community bank of some size, probably in the $50-million-asset range, and with good earnings. North Bank was a de novo (new), very small bank with meager earnings. Jim agreed and I started looking for a bank in mid-1971.

Jim Howard had come to me one day several months before that and said, "Paul, I've got some problems with the board of directors of Meister Brau, and I think I'm going to have a board fight and possibly some legal problems. Do you know a lawyer who could help me?"

I said, "Yes, Jim Modrall at Foley and Lardner in Milwaukee . . . a friend and a really smart guy, a Harvard Law School graduate . . . but I think he's pretty entrenched in Milwaukee, with a family, a nice home with horses, a country club, etc., but I think I can help convince him to come to Chicago."

It took several months of urging, but finally Jim Modrall joined Jim Howard at Meister Brau as senior counsel and moved to a Chicago suburb. He helped Jim Howard put down the board insurgency, only to see Howard's business decisions bankrupt Meister Brau in 1973. Jim Modrall also got involved with the bank I was about to buy.

In July 1971, after some intensive searching and several unsuccessful investigations and negotiations, I found the $60—million-asset Colonial Bank and Trust located on the Northwest

Side of Chicago in a stable and middle-class ethnic neighborhood—just what I was looking for. The area had many Italian and Polish households, a good savings ethic, and an old-world respect for sound financial practices.

The Colonial directors had formed two warring camps. One was led by the alcoholic and increasingly ineffective president, Clayton Hall, and included several cronies of his, one of whom turned out to have very close connections with the mob. The other was led by the bank's founder, Clarence Beutel, and directors Bob Leander and Bill White, who thought the bank should be sold. White and Leander were on the search committee established to find a buyer. They were to become two of my most trusted directors of First Colonial Bankshares and were with me for twenty-five years.

Clarence Beutel, the founder, told me he could assemble a majority of the stock for us to buy, perhaps 55 percent. He owned only about 14 percent, but he said his family and friends would be willing to sell us some of their stock. This would give us the controlling block we needed. He warned us, however, that we would have a fight with the other group, who were determined to keep control.

Clarence's secretary and associate, Irmgaard Kaak, worked closely with me to obtain agreements to purchase stock from the shareholder list they had. We negotiated the price at $65 a share, which for 55 percent would amount to about $4.5 million, a fairly daunting figure at that time for me, particularly since my net worth wasn't much more than $100,000. I was convinced, however, that somehow I could be creative enough to put together a successful package.

We started with Beutel's list. We would make a tender offer for all the stock, limiting the amount we would accept. Clarence, Irmgaard, and I assembled about 45 percent of the stock we needed, close enough, I thought, to gather another 7 or 8 percent in order to get control. The Hall group knew we were assembling shares but didn't think we could get 51 percent, so they didn't mount their own drive and probably weren't capable of raising the necessary $4.5 million anyway.

Now it was time for me to raise $4.5 million that Jim Modrall and I didn't have. (Jim Howard had bowed out because of his problems at Meister Brau.) I went to LaSalle Bank first. I walked into the correspondent banking department, introduced myself, and applied for a $4.5 million loan. Incredulous at what I guess they considered the audacity of my request, they turned me down.

However, I had heard that Allen Stults, chairman and CEO of American National Bank, was attracted to entrepreneurs and made more "character loans," depending more on the borrower's integrity and ability to pay back the loan than on collateral. The rule of good lending revolves around the three Cs of lending—character, collateral, and capacity. Character is integrity; collateral is the sum of assets you had to put up against the loan; capacity is expected cash flow.

I called and got an appointment with Mr. Stults, and on a Monday morning in September 1971, I walked into his very imposing office with its antique furniture and huge desk and chair, looking out over La Salle Street. Allen came out of his office to meet me after his secretary told him I was there—as it was his habit to greet all customers. He was an affable man, a real gentleman with a great, quick smile. But you knew right away he was a very bright, no-nonsense guy and that you would not want to waste his time.

Our discussion was direct and fairly short. I said, "Mr. Stults, I have found a very nice solid bank with good earnings, the Colonial Bank at Belmont and Central, and I can buy control of it for four and a half million dollars. I can buy the stock for book value and about seven times earnings." He asked about my experience in banking and my background. I said I had a good deal of experience in investment banking but only about four years experience in commercial banking.

He asked how much I would be putting up. "I can't put

anything into the purchase," I told him. "My net worth is only about $100,000." He looked at me incredulously and said, "Paul, you know that bankers expect some equity to be put up against a loan," and I said, "I know that, but I don't have anything to put up. But you'll have the collateral of 55 percent of the stock of the bank and you'll have my word that you'll get your money back." He chuckled and said, "Do you have a business plan on how you intend to pay the interest and principal?"

"Yes, sir," I said, and presented my plan and talked about my strategy to grow the bank, in earnings and assets.

We talked about thirty minutes. He doubled back and asked to hear more about my experience, values, and education. He wanted to hear more about me than the bank. "Paul, do you really think you can do this?" he finally asked me.

"Absolutely," I said, "and furthermore I'll become your biggest depositor someday." He laughed and said, "Okay, we'll lend you the four and a half million dollars. I'll introduce you to Marty Noll, one of our correspondent bankers, and he'll work with you."

I put the deal together, and while it did take twelve years, my company did become American National's biggest depositor in 1984.

Marty Noll and I worked more than thirty days accumulating the stock we needed, many times well into the night. Marty was bright, dedicated, and tireless. Our relationship working on this deal would result in my hiring Marty some years later to be president of our bank in Oak Park. He did a splendid job for First Colonial Bankshares, and when Firstar bought it, all seventeen of our presidents were riffed so Firstar could turn our banks into branches, at which point Marty and several top local directors from our Oak Park bank had opened a bank just blocks from Firstar's location.

Toward the end of accumulating the stock in December 1971, I saw that two of the larger shareholders, Clayton Hall and a man I will call Jack M., had not committed to selling their stock. We were short by 4 to 5 percent of the required 51 percent. So I went to Clayton and bluffed him. "We're over the top, with commitments for 51 percent. We don't need your stock anymore, but if you're inclined to sell it, we'll buy it." The next morning, he and Jack M. arrived at American National and tendered their shares. This took us from about 48 percent to 55 percent ownership. We had control of the bank.

But I had to deal with Jack M. right away. While at Growth Capital with Jim Howard, I had made contact with the organized crime strike force of the Chicago Police Department—the Chicago Police Intelligence Department— whose office was at the nearby Navy Pier. To check out mob affiliations, I would call Mike O. or Bill R., who were senior agents of the Organized Crime Squad, and they would come to my office to talk—never on the telephone.

I had asked them about Jack M. and had been told he had mob affiliations. They showed me news clippings and passed on other information that had Jack M. as president and treasurer of an Oldsmobile dealership in Chicago. Among its salesmen in 1964 was one who they said was "a well-known crime syndicate hoodlum." Seen visiting this location was another "crime syndicate hoodlum."

Jack M. was also president of a company in suburban Skokie that, I was told, "leases cars to high-echelon crime syndicate hoodlums Anthony Accardo, Paul 'the Waiter' Ricca, and 'Milwaukee Phil' Alderisio." Ricca was "considered head of the Mafia in Chicago" at the time. Police showed me newspaper pictures of the alley behind Jack M.'s dealership where bodies of two Greek holdup men killed gangland style were found with bullets in their throats.

Jack M. had sold me his stock, but he still had several accounts at the bank and some fairly substantial loans. I wanted him as neither shareholder nor customer. After the purchase I called and asked to have lunch with him. At his request, it was at the Hilton Hotel in Skokie, a known mob gathering place at the time, the hotel where several years later they found the body of mob boss Alderisio in the trunk of a car at the parking lot.

At lunch I informed Jack M. that we now controlled the bank and said we didn't want him as a customer. I wasn't sure how he would react, but he reacted in a gentlemanly way. He said he "completely understood" and that this would be "no problem." He congratulated me on getting control of the bank. I was relieved. In a week he had his loans and deposits out of our bank.

The bank had several other mob affiliations to which we were alerted several months before we bought it, when then Illinois Senator Charles Percy conducted hearings in his Senate Finance Committee about mob infiltration of banking. Some of the hearings were leaked. A story appeared in *The Chicago Tribune* naming a mob member who banked at Colonial Bank! We had an immediate run of several million dollars in deposits because of Senator Percy's handling of his "closed-door" hearings. We had been concerned about other possible mob affiliations but had been assured there weren't any.

But there were. After the purchase, when I had become the bank's chairman, I was sitting in the office of Clayton Hall, who had remained president, with its view of the Central Avenue entrance. Tom Szar, our installment lender, came in and pointed to a small, rotund man leaving the bank. "You want to see one of the top loan sharks in the city?" he said. "There he goes!" I asked why we had a "top loan shark" as a customer and told Tom to get rid of him. We already had enough mob-related public relations problems!

Not long after that, I learned from my police connection that a contractor for our new building on Central Avenue, at the time under construction, might have mob connections. They said he knew some members of the mob, but they didn't think he was affiliated. Just in case, though, I asked him out to lunch and asked him straight out if he was affiliated with the mob in any way.

His name was Frank. Frank quietly but firmly said, "No, but I went to high school with Sam Giancana," who had become a top mob boss. He had gone to Giancana's daughter's wedding because of their high school friendship and knew at the time that the FBI was taking pictures of license plates to see who was attending the wedding. Frank said if I thought he was a problem, he would leave the bank. I liked his straightforwardness, believed him, and I told him he could stay.

Frank was our concrete contractor. He helped us a lot in getting the work done on time. For instance, one day, Joe Nasca, who worked for the general contractor, came to Frank and said the "steel union" steward had just told him they were going to close the job down because Frank wasn't using enough "union boys."

Frank was a big, tough-looking guy with slicked-back black hair. He went out to the parking lot, went up to the steward and said, "Buddy, get off this property, now, and don't give us any more problems, or you'll end up in a trunk!" The guy turned white and left quickly. We never had any more problems.

While still in our original location, we'd have board meetings in Clayton Hall's very small office. Several times during a meeting, Clayton would get up to "go to the bathroom." We thought he just had a short tank. We did not realize he was going for several pops of his stash of booze that he kept there. By the end of the meeting, he was not as coherent as he had been at the start.

Clayton would also disappear for an hour every morning and for another hour every afternoon on work days to go down the street to the Candy Store, the local bar. I asked Bob Leander if he was aware that Hall was an alcoholic. He wasn't and didn't believe it at first—amazed that Clayton had hidden it from them for so many years.

In any case, we made a nice severance package for Clayton and relieved him of his duties, and I became president as well as chairman.

Soon after we took control of the bank, we had our first holdup. About midafternoon on a bright January day, a short, chunky man came through the front door, walked up to our youngest teller, and laid a note in front of her which said, "Give me all your money in a hurry. I have a gun in this paper sack and it's pointed at you."

Tellers are taught that in this event they are to (1) step on the alarm button, several inches from their right foot, (2) pull the money drawer open slowly, (3) start laying out the money, dollar bills *first*, then fives, tens, twenties, etc., and (4) take a good look at the person for later identification.

Our teller (1) did not step on the alarm button, (2) opened her money drawer quickly, (3) handed the money over in reverse order from what she'd been taught—hundreds first, then fifties, twenties, etc., and (4) did not take a good look at the robber so that later she had little recollection of what he looked like. To top it off, as soon as he went out the door, she screamed and fainted.

Fortunately, an older, experienced teller beside her had seen what was happening and had hit her button, sending a signal to the nearby police station. The police were there, sirens wailing, in minutes, led by Detective Gene Nicoletti, a tall, slender man with piercing eyes and slicked-back black hair, a veteran of the narcotics squad.

While Nicoletti and the others tried to get a description from our hysterical teller, the police sent out word of the robbery. An elderly lady who had just made a deposit and left minutes before the robbery came rushing back in, telling Nicoletti that she had seen a car "speeding away from the bank" and described the make and model and had the first three numbers of the license plate!

What a break! The police quickly identified the car and owner through records in Springfield and found the man lived only blocks away!

Nicoletti and two uniformed policemen sped to the suspect's house in an unmarked car and waited. Sure enough, down the street drove the suspect. He stopped at his house and stepped out. The three policemen got out of their car, picked him up, threw him into their car, and drove back to the bank, informing him he was under arrest. They led him in handcuffs into my office at the front of the bank, a terrified twenty-something—year-old, and pushed him into a chair in the corner of the room.

Then they brought in the young teller, who had regained her composure, to identify the robber. She looked carefully, then left the office and told Nicoletti, "He's not the man." Then they brought in the older teller, who also told Nicoletti, "He's not the man." Nicoletti came up to my desk, leaned over and whispered, "He's not the man."

I suggested they consider releasing him. Nicoletti went over, took off the handcuffs, and said, "Okay, fella, you can leave now."

The young man, still shaken, asked, "What was I supposed to have done besides cash a check here?"

Nicoletti told him, "Never mind. Have a good day." The still shaken supposed robber asked as he left my office, "Anyone got an antacid pill?"

Notwithstanding this misadventure with the customer cashing a check at our bank at the wrong time, then "speeding away" from the bank under the watchful eye of one of our senior citizens, we did track down and apprehend our robber. He had looked directly into our surveillance camera while waiting for our teller to put the money in large bills on the counter. The camera got a perfect mug shot for Nicoletti and his group.

Using the picture, they quickly identified a convict, a Mr. Johnson, who had just been paroled from the Joliet prison after serving a term for armed robbery. Prison officials, who had kept a log on incoming mail, had Johnson's girlfriend's name and Chicago address.

Nicoletti and others staked out her house and saw Johnson entering. Armed with a search warrant, they got into the house and arrested and handcuffed Johnson and put him in the police car. Johnson asked why he was being arrested. Nicoletti said, "For robbing the Colonial Bank."

"I didn't rob any bank," said Johnson. Nicoletti pulled out his picture standing at the counter with his paper sack and note to the teller.

"Then who's this?" asked Nicoletti.

Johnson paused and then said, "That's me robbing the Colonial Bank."

Nicoletti then asked, "Where's the $20,000?"

"It wasn't $20,000," said Johnson. "But what there was, I spent."

"You couldn't have spent $20,000 in two days," said Nicoletti. "And we're sure it's in your girlfriend's home. So don't make us rip the place apart looking for it. And if you don't tell us now, we're taking your girlfriend downtown and charging her for harboring a fugitive!"

"Don't do that," said Johnson. "It's under the sofa."

Eighteen thousand of the $20,000 was recovered.

At a ceremony at the bank several weeks later attended by Detective Nicoletti and a police chief, I presented a $5,000 check to the police benevolent fund for the work the department had performed on our behalf.

We at Colonial Bank became friends with Gene Nicoletti and stayed in touch for years. His daughter worked for us. Many policemen lived in our area, and many became customers. We became known as the "policeman's bank."

Meanwhile, Colonial Bank became the "earning engine" of our holding company, First Colonial Bankshares, which over the next twenty-three years grew into a highly profitable, seventeen—bank organization. Almost all the staff and directors of our flagship Colonial Bank stayed with the organization, forming the core of what we all called "the First Colonial family."

Chapter 2

Milt Hayes:

A Friend Indeed

Not long after we acquired Colonial Bank and Trust, I made the worst loan of my career, to several individuals who used the money to buy American City Bank in Milwaukee. It was the worst because it was out of our area, it was a very large loan for a bank of our size, and we knew well only one of the principals—Ray Callen.

We also hadn't done a very good job in our due diligence examination of American City. But we didn't realize this until later, when we discovered the bad condition of its fundamentals—its investment and loan portfolios and asset-to-liability ratio, which was unbalanced.

Indeed, American City soon had liquidity problems, increasingly large loan charge-offs, and earnings problems, and the Illinois Banking Commission and the Federal Deposit Insurance Corporation classified our loan as substandard. We weren't alarmed, but we were concerned.

We informed American National Bank in Chicago of the bank examiners' write-up of the American City loan. A write-off by us of the American City loan would cut into our capital and thus lessen the value of the collateral held by American

National. The news caught American National's attention and prompted a call from its chairman and CEO, Allen Stults.

Allen asked me to come downtown and talk about the American City loan. At the end of our discussion, he asked, very nicely, if I would mind having an American National representative on our First Colonial board—frankly, to monitor our investment and loan portfolio.

I said, "Of course not." He recommended a longtime American National employee and officer, currently a consultant to the bank, Milton Hayes. It was one of the best things that ever happened to us at First Colonial.

Milt had chaired American National's investment committee after a long career in its investment business. A University of Chicago graduate, he had joined American National in 1935 in its investment analysis division. He had retired from the bank in 1978 as a senior vice president. He was a director of the Independent Bankers Association of America and a frequent contributor to several bank investment magazines. He traveled periodically to London and Zurich for American National, to keep up to date on the bond markets—in the latter city to meet with "the gnomes of Zurich," he'd tell us.

As a First Colonial director, more precisely as chairman of our investment committee, Milt proved invaluable. He was an extremely conservative investor and would never consider lower—quality, high-yielding or longer-term bonds. He kept our investment portfolio very sound.

He also kept the wolf from our door with the help he gave us on that American City Bank loan, which was heading toward a big loss. About a year after he came on board, matters got so bad that Allen Stults summoned him downtown and asked if "these guys know what they're doing. Are they people of integrity?"

"Allen, these are talented, hardworking people of great integrity," said Milt. "It would be a grave mistake to call your loan with them. They will solve the American City Bank loan problem. They will also become one of American National's most important customers. Paul Johnson, Bill Duquaine, and their staff and directors are people I like and respect. I look forward to continuing to work with them."

That was enough for Allen Stults. "We're going to stay with these guys," he said.

Milt could have come back and told me this, but he didn't. He just said he had met with Allen, who was "pleased with our progress." It was Allen who told me the story years later, fortunately, while Milt was still alive, so that I was able to thank Milt, whose response was typical. "Paul, I was put on the board to evaluate your integrity and capabilities. In view of how successful you've been, it looks like I was right, right?"

Milt and I became close friends. He was Irish on his mother's side, English on his father's. The family names were Fairbanks and O'Connell, in addition to Hayes. There was also some Canadian ancestry. Milt never married, as far as I could determine.

The day of our monthly board meeting provided our main point of personal contact. I would pick Milt up at his Michigan Avenue apartment at seven o'clock sharp. We'd drive to Colonial Bank's neighborhood and stop for breakfast at the International House of Pancakes on Belmont Avenue near the bank. He often called this breakfast, when the talk ranged from the "Big Bang" origin of the universe to the expansion of the universe to other such matters, the highlight of his month. In his final months, in 1989 and 1990, our conversations, often also for Sunday brunch at the Hilton Hotel near his apartment, turned even more philosophical and religious.

From the beginning, we talked about how the universe was formed, where it was going, and how long it would keep expanding. We talked about his concept of God and my concept of the order of the universe. We discussed whether there was a purpose in life and, if so, what. I lent him several books, including *The First Three Minutes,* by the nuclear physicist

Steven Weinberg, because he wanted to learn more about the "Big Bang" and cosmological thinking. He collected articles for me on science, with a more religious bent.

Our discussions were animated. Sometimes we talked about religion. He told me about his upbringing as a Catholic—by an aunt after his father died when Milt was a kid—and how he had come to distrust many Catholic teachings as "impractical" and "unrealistic." But he had strong Catholic foundations and attended mass occasionally at Old St. Mary's in the Loop— more frequently in the last six months of his life. He was fundamentally a religious man.

I asked him once about his family. It was on one of our drives to the bank for the directors' meeting. He turned and looked and said very earnestly, "Paul, I don't have any family left. First Colonial is my family."

It was true. We were a family. For instance, we had wonderful birthday parties for employees. One I will never forget was a surprise party for me, at my Lake Point Tower apartment. My daughter Julie, in on the surprise, had managed to keep me in the apartment when I'd wanted to go downstairs for a newspaper. Then came a knock on the door. I opened it, and there was Milt—staid, serious, conservative Milt—standing at the head of a line of several dozen people strung along the hallway, wearing an Indian costume with feather headdress and tomahawk in his hand and a little impish smile creeping across his face.

Milt was shy and almost embarrassed by awards and recognition, but he still appreciated them. In his resignation letter to me, dated October 26, 1989, he wrote, "I have one important request. I want no party, no plaque—in fact, no recognition of any kind regarding what I have helped you build. I feel that my part has been minor and that you have been the force that has brought the organization where it is. My regret is that I will not see you as often."

I refused his resignation. He wrote back, conceding that "a sudden cut-off from all relationships with the First Colonial family would . . . cause [him] great distress." In any case, I convinced him we needed his advice and counsel. He agreed to stay with us on a consulting basis.

Milt shied from public recognition but was proud of his contributions to American National, First Colonial, and other businesses for which he worked. And like it or not, he did receive awards, particularly from First Colonial in his final years. And they meant a lot to him.

He was loyal to our organization and couldn't understand why, once a decision was made, everyone didn't line up enthusiastically, salute and carry it out even if they disagreed with it. He disagreed with some of my decisions and registered disagreement, but always privately, before or after a meeting about a decision or vote. I respected that side of him very much and valued his counsel.

He was also gracious. He never failed to say thank you, often in writing. In one of his last letters to me, a holiday card, he wrote, "May I express my deep and appreciative thanks for your kindness and help during my troubles in '89 [about which more below]. I treasure your friendship and help more than I can say."

Following a surprise birthday party for him at the Michigan Avenue National Bank—his last, as things turned out—he wrote: "What can I say? What words can describe my gratitude, my surprise, and my deep thanks for the birthday celebration? Your thoughtfulness and planning of this event was above and beyond what I deserved and expected. It will be forever the ultimate birthday party of my life. I reaffirm my complete dedication to you personally and to the 'First Colonial Family.'"

An earlier surprise party, in 1984, elicited similar gratitude: "I have had a number of [such] parties, but the one at the bank last Tuesday reached a new high, both as a surprise and as an outpouring of good will. I will treasure the beautiful attache case and use it proudly, but the most gratifying happening occurred at the end, when I caught you alone to offer my heartfelt thanks and you said, 'Well, after all, you are a member of the First Colonial Family and so you deserved this celebration.' I shall always remember this statement and will always be thankful that I am so included. The past seven years with you have been some of the most rewarding of my life."

Milt submitted his final resignation from the First Colonial board in October 1989, saying he couldn't keep up physically. I had already seen some deterioration, as in his unsteadiness at our Sunday brunches. He had Parkinson's disease, though we didn't know it yet. I talked him into staying on as a consultant, and we kept meeting and discussing the meaning of life. His philosophical and spiritual side expressed itself more strongly than ever in what were to be his last months.

Then in March of 1990, he was hospitalized after falling in his apartment and being unable to get up even to unlock his door. He had crawled around on hands and knees in the middle of the night, trying to attract someone's attention. He did not succeed until 4 p.m. the next day, when his longtime friend and neighbor, Muriel Lotzman, who had gone to check on him, had found his newspapers lying outside his door and heard him calling faintly for help. She got inside the apartment, found him, and called an ambulance.

I was in Africa at the time. When I returned, I called the hospital and said I wanted to see him. He said he wasn't "presentable." I said I didn't care how presentable he was, he should tell the nurse to make him presentable, because I was going to be there in a half hour. "Great!" he said. "Come on over."

His appearance was nothing a nurse could fix, however. It was shocking. Among other things was the condition of his knees, all marked up from the crawling. I had known he was sick and had wondered how long he had to live, particularly in the last few months. Now I knew it wouldn't be long.

I called his doctor, Dr. Charles F. Nadler, after my visit. He said Milt was weakened by Parkinson's disease and moreover was terribly depressed. He had even spoken of taking his own life. Dr. Nadler had seen cases like this. Milt, he said, could get much better or much worse, meaning he could slip away. Either was better than his present tortured state.

I visited Milt daily. There were ups and downs, but with net improvement in body and spirit, or so it seemed. I talked with Dr. Nadler and a neurologist about various drugs that would help him with his balance. A brain scan found a small blood clot on the right side of the brain. The surgeon said this was not a major issue: surgery was not necessary.

After Milt had been in the hospital not quite a week, the tests completed, some improvement noted, Dr. Nadler said he was going to discharge Milt to make room for "more needy patients." Milt didn't like that. He thought he deserved more time in the hospital and said so angrily. I said the doctor had kept him there as long as possible and it was time for him to start thinking about going home.

Dr. Nadler and I worked with Social Services at Northwestern Memorial Hospital, where he was staying. They helped us arrange twenty-four-hour nursing service for him. Milt objected to this at first, but soon acquiesced. He also agreed to use a walker that Colonial Bank President Bill Duquaine offered to buy for him. I was pleased at signs that Milt was willing, even anxious to get home.

The Polonia Agency lined up nurses to provide twenty-four-hour coverage. The doctor agreed to let him to stay in the hospital until we had his apartment ready. These conversations had begun on Thursday. By Tuesday the apartment was ready, cleaned by people from the agency. I asked one of our bank staff, Tony Prochenski, to help me pick Milt up at the hospital. Milt was worried about getting in and out of the car and suggested an ambulance. I said I thought we could manage.

At 9:30 that morning, I got clothes from his apartment, on the thirty-seventh floor. Then Tony and I drove off. At the hospital we got Milt dressed and into a wheelchair and, with a nurse's help, got him into the car. He was alert and seemed happy to be on his way home. He spoke directly and with humor. He gave no sign of despondency.

We arrived at the apartment at 10:30 or so. I gave him the walker that Bill had gotten for him. We met the Polish couple who had cleaned his apartment. Milt asked several times for the correct pronunciation of the name of the Polish man who was to remain as his nurse.

Milt and I talked for several minutes. I said there was a lot of mail on his desk and reminded him that I'd offered him a secretary to come over and help him sort through it. Milt looked at me and said, "Thanks, Paul. I appreciate your help very much." That's all he said. My last picture was of him sitting on the edge of his bed, calm and alert, clinging to his new walker.

Tony and I drove back to the office. I had a meeting in the board room and had just sat down, when my secretary, Lois, asked me to step outside. She took my hand and said, "We've got a problem with Milt. There's a doctor on the line who wants to talk to you." I picked up the telephone. It was a nurse. "We need Mr. Hayes's prescriptions," she said. "The doctor didn't sign them."

I said I'd get them back to her.

Then she added, incredibly, "I just talked to the nurse who's with him. He said something about Mr. Hayes crawling out the window."

I asked her if she was serious. She said she was. "Then we have a bigger problem than getting a prescription filled!" I told her and hung up.

I ran to Tom Maier's nearby office—he's First Colonial's CFO—and asked him to come with me, right away. We jumped into my car and drove the mile to Milt's building. There was a police car in front with flashing lights. We ran to the elevators, then ran down the hall to Milt's apartment. The door was ajar. We walked in. There were policemen, one of them a sergeant, and a yellow no-entrance tape in front of his bedroom. The nurse we had left less than an hour before stood, shocked.

"What happened?" I asked the sergeant. He gruffly asked me my name and what I was doing there. I asked him his name and what he was doing there. Someone had fallen out a window and they were investigating it, he said. I walked into the bedroom and saw the open window and Milt's walker next to it.

The sergeant came in and told me I was in a potential crime scene and had to leave. I was very distressed and told him I was part of Milt's family and that there had been no crime—that Milt had committed suicide.

Tom Maier came up, took my arm and guided me out of the apartment, down the elevator and to my car. Neither of us said a word on the way back to the office. But having Tom there for support at that time was incredibly important.

It seems clear now that Milt had decided very early in his hospital stay to take himself out but had kept it from his doctor and me. When I called Dr. Nadler to tell him what had happened, he was "absolutely shocked" and "couldn't believe it." He kept repeating it. Milt had been getting better and had seemed genuinely happy to get out of the hospital, he said. Milt had fooled us both.

As for myself, I was stunned. My mother wrote a euthanasia order for herself years ago that was eloquent in its simplicity. "I have lived my life with dignity," she wrote. "I want to die the same way." Milt apparently felt that way. He lived a life of dignity. And when he decided he couldn't live that way any longer, he ended it. I'm sorry he did it, but I understand the decision and sympathize with it.

On the night of his death, I achieved a certain catharsis by listening for a number of times to a recording of "Vincent" by Don McLean, the song about the artist Vincent Van Gogh. These lines touched me most: "Then, when no hope was left in sight, on that starry, starry night, you took your life as lovers often do."

Milt loved life and cherished his contributions to the lives of so many. But he decided his situation was hopeless. He wasn't going to get better but was going to be a burden to us. He was too proud to go on. It took courage for him to end his life the way he did. I respect him for that courage.

I wrote a eulogy about Milt that drew some wonderful responses. One of those I treasure most came from Hank Pearsall, chairman and CEO of Sanford Corporation and a First Colonial board member. "What impressed me most was your sensitivity and compassion in dealing with Milt's retirement, illness, and death," Hank wrote in a letter. "I'm proud to be associated with a company with such feelings, and I hope I will be able to do as well in similar situations."

Another response, addressed to Milt himself from Milt's friends Greg and Muriel Lotzman, shed light on Milt's suicide decision. "We frequently review our recent conversations with you," they wrote. "Were there clues as to what you were considering? One conversation centered on the Hemlock Society. You asked whether we were still members. A discussion took place about suicide and you said you felt it was justifiable when one felt that life had become intolerable. Were you then giving thought to what you would do when you felt your life was without dignity, that you were no longer in command?"

They closed with a comment that touched me deeply: "Your legacy to us, Milt, is Mr. Johnson, a rare jewel of a friend."

Another response, to me, was from another of Milt's friends, Bob Donovan: "The only reason I am writing is that I was so impressed that you took the time to write a eulogy for your friend in an age when everyone seems to be too busy to do such a thing, to praise the accomplishments of friends [on the contrary, they spend their time criticizing shortcomings]. Your eulogy was a breath of fresh air. Milton J. Hayes was fortunate to have such a good friend."

His former secretary at American National Bank before retiring in 1981, Mildred Simon, wrote to say how she came to realize "how much he appreciated you and the whole First Colonial Family. He enjoyed every meeting and frequently mentioned the birthday celebrations and retirement parties. All his friends would join me in saying thank you for your many kindnesses to a great man."

His friend Elaine Fielding wrote, "I am so happy Milton

had such good friends. I always felt he was alone, but now I know that isn't true."

Milton Hayes epitomized the First Colonial family. He was a gentleman, gracious and concerned for everyone in the family, a man of integrity and compassion, completely comfortable with us because he knew we would never compromise our principles, cut corners, or do anything illegal or immoral. He told me he would never have stayed with us if he had thought otherwise. He had no blood relatives but basked in the love, friendship, and camaraderie of his First Colonial family.

Chapter 3

Allen Stults:

Crucial Capitalizer

Not long ago, years after Allen Stults intervened in our bad-loan plight and sent Milt Hayes to us at First Colonial, I visited him in his lovely home in Tucson, Arizona, after too long a time of being out of touch with him.

One of the times I had been with him had been in 1976, when he led a group of bankers on a trip to Russia, Poland, Hungary, and Czechoslovakia. The trip was part of President Eisenhower's attempt to get affinity groups to meet their counterparts behind the Iron Curtain. It was called the "people-to-people" program. On this trip I got advice from Allen that I dangerously ignored, but it worked out all right. In Tucson, in March 2003, he reminded me of it, asking jokingly if I had taken any forbidden pictures lately.

We were outside the Kremlin, kept fifty yards from its entrance by a rope, apparently for reasons of security. We stood watching black limousines going through the gate and being saluted by two guards on either side. We were not to take photos of the limos, our guide and interpreter told us. Not good enough, I decided, wanting to push the envelope, as is my habit. I edged to the rope and shot one of the guards with my telephoto lens as he turned and looked at me. He was on me immediately, with outstretched hand demanding my camera. *"Davia,"* he said, meaning "Give me." "No," I said and quickly returned to the rear of our group.

He turned angrily to our guide and to Allen Stults. The guide said I'd have to give him my camera. I refused. Allen said so too: "Paul, I think it would be better if you did give him the camera." I told the guide to tell the guard I wanted to talk to his supervisor. She was aghast at this but told him. He got livid. But livid or not, he was stumped. He turned on his heel, marched back to his post, and stood fuming. My group could see it: I had faced down the Red Army!

Then an unsuspecting Scandinavian fellow, not part of our group, went up to where I had been standing, camera in hand as if to take a picture. His timing could not have been worse. The guard marched over, demanded and got his camera, marched back to the gate, opened the door to a small storage unit, and threw it in. Poor fellow, it was the price he paid for my photo of the guard, which I later sent to everyone in our group, and for a very good story.

Allen is remarkable. Approaching his ninetieth birthday, he was as thoughtful and intelligent as the day I met him in 1971 when I came to him for a loan. During this March 2003 visit, I was able to tell him how much I appreciated his faith in me that led him to stretch usual lending rules and give me $4.5 million to buy a bank that became a $2 billion organization, First Colonial Bankshares. He took my hand and said, "No, Paul, it's I who have to thank you for giving us the opportunity to lend to a successful person like yourself."

Allen had an interesting career. His year of birth, 1913, serves as a sort of omen or at least a good conversation piece. He was born on a Friday, the thirteenth. Lucky for him, he says, because he's "the luckiest man in the world." The Federal Reserve System was born that year too, the Panama Canal was opened, the Federal Income Tax Law was passed. So his birth year, 1913, was a landmark year in many ways, he says with a smile. And the year we visited in Arizona was the seventieth anniversary of his entry into banking and the twenty-fifth anniversary of his retirement from American National Bank.

Lucky sounds about right. He went to work ten days after President Roosevelt closed the banks, hired by the Chicago Federal Reserve at $58 a month and a six-day work week. He was a temporary help at first and then became a permanent employee because he was "very fast on [his] feet running between banks" gathering material to bring back to the Federal Reserve.

Times were very hard. Unemployment was at 28 percent. But nine months into his Federal Reserve job, he was sent to American National Bank to get a reference from a Mr. Wright. Mr. Wright was impressed and offered him a job at American National—at the same $58 he was getting at the Federal Reserve. Young Allen did not say yes immediately but took a chance and said, "Mr. Wright, Congress is discussing right now a minimum wage of $62 a month, and I'd like to receive that." Mr. Wright laughed at that and agreed. Allen had his new job.

He moved up the ladder slowly. His first job was watering flowers, he reported with a twinkle in his eye. He ultimately worked in every department and eventually became executive vice president, then president.

I asked him what he thought successful CEOs had in common. "Paul," he said, "The first thing is curiosity and the ability to ask the right questions. The second is to concentrate on a job, not looking for recognition, which will come if you do it well." The third is not to worry, which does nothing but "lessen your thinking capacity. There's a difference between being concerned and worrying," he said. "Being concerned is legitimate because it leads you to asking the proper questions to make a proper decision. But worrying is debilitating."

I asked him if he thought most successful CEOs have integrity. His immediate answer was "yes," but he went on to say that it is "very difficult to define integrity." He explained that he was a person who believed in shades of gray and not black and white. He asked rhetorically, "Are we all completely honest?" He answered, "That really is a matter of degree." There is a "breaking end point." Most successful people, he said interestingly, are "acceptably honest."

I told him I had heard that he had given Ray Kroc of McDonald's his first seed money. He said yes, he had done that. Ray Kroc had great talents, he said. He was someone "who knew what he didn't know." Kroc had tried to get his initial loan at Harris and Continental banks in Chicago and been turned down.

Kroc was "a tremendous guy," he said. Allen elected not to join the McDonald's board but sat in on most of the early board meetings and laughed at Kroc's enormous curiosity and his penchant for trying new things. Kroc was absolutely convinced, for instance, that french-fried zucchini would replace french-fried potatoes and spent $50,000 to find out if it would. He ultimately found out it would not but was brave to try it, Allen said.

As for himself in general, Allen said, "I can't be insulted. I have so much confidence that insults just roll off my back."

I asked what made American National Bank such a success, a bank that became known as "the bank for business." He said early in his own presidency, he had called his staff together and pointed out the window down to La Salle Street, where American National and Chicago's four other biggest banks were located—Northern Trust, Continental, La Salle, and First National Bank of Chicago.

"Why would anybody pass up any of those banks to get to us?" he asked. "The prices and products are the same. Why come to us?" He was making the point that they were in "a very personal business." The problem was that banks were "depersonalizing" it. Instead, he said, "every customer has to enjoy the transaction. The teller has to leave the customer with a smile. The key is that you treat everybody, including your coworker, as if he or she were your boss."

He believed that he created an esprit de corps that would

emanate to customers, who would say, "This is a nice place to do business." The individual has to enjoy the job and be proud of the organization. "My four Cs of corporate management were customer, coworker, capital, community. One of the problems of some recent mergers has been that all they looked at was the capital component, at the expense of the other three."

Hearing Allen speak of recent mergers, I was reminded of his strong support in the past for unit banking and strong opposition to branch banking in Illinois. This is where he and I had some disagreement. I did not believe that unit banking would serve the banking industry well in the long run and worked hard for multibank holding company legislation in Illinois. He was with the Independent Bankers of America and other groups that stalled such legislation. In my opinion, this did not help banking in Illinois, surrounded as it was by states allowing multibank holding companies—Wisconsin, Michigan, Indiana, and Ohio. This made Illinois, and particularly Chicago, a bank-selling region, in which others could buy up and build themselves into substantially larger organizations than any in Illinois.

In any case, Allen was a stickler for doing things right, which led to the question why he "bent the rules" and lent me the money to buy Colonial Bank and Trust when I had none of my own. He explained. He embraced "the old three Cs of lending"—character, capacity, and collateral or the borrower's own money which went into the deal. Character was by far most important, "at least 51 percent of the equation." Capacity— meaning "capability," a broader concept than most of us have in mind—is a strong second. Collateral, he said, is a poor third.

So lending me the whole amount needed to buy the bank went against the rules in one sense but not in his sense, in which character and capability overshadow everything else. "Paul," he said, "it was your character, your reputation, your business plan, how organized you were, how confidently you presented yourself that convinced me."

This was from a man who, as a tough manager in the '70s,

took American National Bank to high levels and prepared it for its sale in 1984 to First National Bank of Chicago at a very good price, taking good care of his shareholders and his staff. He's a man of integrity and talent—one of the key individuals in the success of First Colonial Bankshares.

As I left Allen's house, I thanked him. "If it hadn't been for your confidence in me, First Colonial might not have been," I said.

"No," he said, "as I told you before, Paul, thanks to you for passing up several banks and coming to me at American National."

Chapter 4

Buying All American Bank:

Ron Aronberg's Integrity

We bought All American Bank, in Chicago, in 1981 and in the process discovered a lawyer-director who became an integral part of our overall team. All American, which had $30 million in assets, was in the heart of the huge Northwest Side. Its neighborhood was Italian and Polish blue-collar, like Colonial Bank's a few miles south and west of it. We at Colonial wanted more banks like this one, in neighborhoods full of ethnic groups frequently with their own neighborhood organizations and even newspapers.

All American's chairman and founder (in 1970) George Paulik was president of Armanetti liquor stores and had played football at Notre Dame in the early '50s. He picked one of his directors, Ron Aronberg, a lawyer, to negotiate for him. The bank's president was not in on the negotiations. Aronberg and I met several times. He was a senior partner with Aronberg Goldgehn Davis and Garmisa, headquartered in the IBM Building on Wabash Avenue in downtown Chicago.

We established rapport early, deciding on a formula for the price, 110 percent of book value, which had to be determined. Book value was the only issue. The loan portfolio—loans less an appropriate loan reserve for "substandard" and "doubtful" loans—was easily valued. The investment portfolio was another matter. Some investments were easy. Government securities, for instance, whose pricing was set daily, required no reserves held against them. Municipal bonds needed somewhat more examination.

There were some other types of investments in the portfolio, however, some fairly high-yield, esoteric paper that was new to us. The All American president thought highly of them and had persuaded the bank's directors to buy them. Once he priced them for the purposes of our sale, we had our purchase price.

Or so we thought. Our chief financial officer, who headed our investment committee, wasn't so sure. He did some consultation about the somewhat mysterious investment inventory and came up with a disturbing opinion—the All American president had valued them too generously. This was from a specialist at a large investment firm who told us the bank president had used one of several available pricing methods. The specialist repriced the portfolio to market standards, explaining his methodology to my CFO and me. The difference was significant. I called Ron Aronberg and said we should have a meeting. It was a few days before we were to close the deal.

I told him we had a problem. Apologizing for my timing, days before closing, I said it looked like his president had inflated the price of some investments, thus hiking the purchase price.

Ron didn't believe it. "Show me your figures," he said. I did. He understood immediately. "I'm going to get our president on the phone," he said. "Don't leave." I could hear only his end of the conversation. He went immediately to questioning the discrepancy. He said something to the effect, "But why didn't you use the usual way to price the instruments?" Then he said, "Then you agree Colonial has a legitimate challenge to your pricing?" Finally: "Thanks, I'll talk to you later."

He hung up, looked at me and said, "You're right!" The portfolio's bonds were overpriced and our calculation of book value was right. "I apologize," he said. "I knew nothing about it." He paused, obviously upset. "Do you still want to buy the bank?" he asked. I said I did. He reached across the desk, shook my hand and said, "We've got a deal—at the lower price."

A lesser man might have gotten defensive. But here was an honest man, a major shareholder, and the lawyer picked to negotiate the sale, putting his own president on the spot once he understood an error in pricing.

I was so impressed with Ron Aronberg's integrity in this matter that after the purchase I asked him to stay on as a director at All American. When we formed our holding company, First Colonial Bankshares, in 1984, I asked him to be a director of that too and picked him and two other directors for its executive committee.

Ron was also First Colonial's lawyer in most matters. Unlike many lawyers who are trained to look almost exclusively at legal risks, he had a good business sense. He still cautioned us if he thought the risk was too high. He was a voice of moderation. But what I remember most about him is the class and integrity that drew me to him in the first place. We remain close friends.

Chapter 5

Pat O'Malley and Michigan Avenue
National Bank

In the summer of 1984, on behalf of First Colonial, I negotiated acquisition of Michigan Avenue National Bank (MANB). The purchase would take us to the $300 million asset level and give us a key downtown location, at Michigan Avenue and Washington Street.

MANB had run into problems in the '80s with its loans and earnings. It was for sale. I told our executive committee I wanted to buy it. A friend of one of our executive committee members, Bob Leander, introduced me to the bank's chairman, Pat O'Malley. O'Malley had been its chairman since 1964, almost from its founding in the early '60s by Chicago Bears owner George Halas.

Pat had come to the bank as Canteen Corporation chairman. He had led Canteen to sharply increased sales and revenues as its president and CEO from 1961 to its quite profitable sale to IT&T in 1969. He had come to Canteen from Coca-Cola, where he had started his career in 1932 as a route salesman's helper in Dorchester, Massachusetts. After working his way up the ladder, he became Coca-Cola's vice president of marketing and sales in its Atlanta headquarters. While in this position, he narrowly lost out for the job as president.

By 1984 he was in his fifteenth year as chairman of MANB. We met to discuss our deal and hit it off beautifully. He was smart and I sensed he had integrity. Smarts and integrity I considered the most important things in someone I had to negotiate with.

First Colonial was not the only potential buyer. I sensed that Pat would be straight with us, negotiating what was best for his shareholders. But we were at an obvious disadvantage because of our lack of capital. We would have to do a public stock offering to raise the $9 million it would take to buy the MANB stock. That was no sure thing and would take some time. Pat decided the wait would be worth it, so completely did we fit the profile of the buyer they wanted.

Several key issues had to be resolved, however, and I was off to the Southwest for ten days of archaeological study with the Crow Canyon Archeological Center in Colorado. I left with Pat our ideas on how to resolve the issues.

Our trip took us through the Hopi Indian Reservation, in New Mexico. I had given Pat our itinerary, and when we checked into the Hopi tribal office several days into the trip, I was told a Mr. O'Malley wanted me to call him. I couldn't use the office phone because I needed privacy, so the staff directed me to a public phone, the only one on that part of the reservation.

Six Hopis were in front of me, waiting to use the phone. I waited with them. In a half hour, I was on the phone with Pat in his office in Chicago. After we discussed several final issues, the deal fell in place for me. "Pat," I said, "here's our offer. It's a compromise for us on several points. I hope you have authority to make the deal."

He did have the authority, and what I said sounded good to him. "It's a deal," he said. In fact, it was the only deal of its kind sealed that week from a public phone on a Hopi Indian reservation, we were sure.

Our public offering followed. It was a big success, bringing in $9 million with the help of investment bankers Dean Witter and Chicago Corporation. We had enough to complete the deal. The Federal Reserve approved the acquisition.

Our practice was for me to become chairman of a bank we acquired until we found a board member to take over, but in this case we departed from that practice. I asked Pat O'Malley to stay on as chairman of MANB, with me as vice chairman. It was a sign of the respect we had for Pat. It was also one of the wisest moves I ever made at First Colonial. We promptly elected Pat to the First Colonial board.

As a board member, he was a pleasure to have around. One day, early in his time as a board member, he did a small thing that etched him in our memory as a keen listener and equally keen respondent. One of our long-time board members, Alan Schwartz, regularly said "Good morning" by name to each member when he arrived. As he walked past Pat O'Malley, he inadvertently said, "Good morning, Mr. O'Brien." To which Pat answered without a blink, "Good morning, Mr. Shapiro."

There were laughs all around at this, and from that point he was "Mr. O'Brien" and Alan Schwartz was "Mr. Shapiro" at various moments during meetings, whenever the spirit moved a board member to recall the exchange.

Pat had a very quick wit. We all wore the First Colonial logo pin on our lapels at bank and holding company board meetings. We wore it with pride. Pat arrived at one meeting without his pin. With a wink and a smile, I asked him where it was. "Oh, my goodness, I must have left it on my pajamas," he said.

I found out months later that my secretary, Lois, had promptly put in a store of pins in her desk for any director who had "left his pin on his pajamas."

Pat was the kind of man you met "with the awareness of a special man, genuinely interested in helping and never too busy or preoccupied to give time and personal attention," said the Reverend Gilbert Graham, OP, in his foreword to Pat's 1996 biography, *Patrick L. O'Malley: A Journey with Family and Friends*. He exemplified "humaneness" and was full of "devotion to people and deep concern for them, even for strangers," wrote Father Graham.

We saw that in Pat at First Colonial. He came early for meetings, so he could visit with people, for instance. He liked people. It was obvious. Consider his work with a key officer of our organization, Mike Clawson, MANB president.

Mike was a U.S. Naval Academy graduate, class of 1972. He spent six years in the navy after that, holding a command position aboard a destroyer, the USS *Cole.* Leaving the navy in 1978, he joined American National Bank, eventually heading its commercial loan department and then becoming president of its community bank in Libertyville, a Chicago suburb.

We needed a new MANB president. Bob Sherman, president of First Colonial Bankshares, knew Mike Clawson from American National and recommended him. Mike and I met. We liked each other right away. I made him a handsome offer. He accepted and came to us as the bank's president.

Mike fit our criteria. He had high grades at the Naval Academy and passed our psychological testing with flying colors. There was just one question: Was he "uptight" by our standards? Navy regimentation had left him reserved, of serious demeanor, not entirely amenable to the loose teasing camaraderie of the First Colonial family. Bob Sherman and I discussed the problem, and we knew we had the answer—Pat O'Malley.

Pat and I were meeting often for lunch, usually at his club. We would bring each other up to date and discuss company business. I would pick his fertile brain.

At one of these lunches, not long after we hired Mike Clawson, I asked Pat a favor. Would he mentor Mike? I told him we felt Mike was very talented and had the makings of an outstanding executive. But there was the demeanor challenge. I asked Pat to work with him, so that some of Pat's charm, sense of humor, and speaking ability would brush off.

He said he would love to do it. He went ahead and met with Mike. They lunched together almost monthly, and Mike developed phenomenally well. He became a very effective bank president and one of the top officers of First Colonial. At present he is the Chicago market president for U.S. Bancorp. Mike and Pat continued their friendship and monthly luncheons, which went on for thirteen years.

Mike says of Pat: "Probably the most significant impact Pat had on others was how he lives his life. I could pile on adjectives. He is gregarious, energetic, smiling, curious, etc., but most importantly, he's involved. All of our associates who had contact with Pat came away with the same thought. He was an inspiration and model for how to live your life, especially as one gets older. His schedule kept him perpetually in motion. The simple fact of his having lunch with me, forty years his junior, almost every month for thirteen years is an example of how he stayed current and involved."

Pat ran a meeting with the precision of a drill sergeant. The bank board meeting started at precisely 9:00 a.m. (and ended at precisely 11:00). Directors quickly learned to be in their seats when Chairman O'Malley's gavel came down. At one of the first meetings, shortly after the bank was bought by First Colonial, Alan Schwartz was unfortunate enough to arrive several minutes after Pat had called the meeting to order. As Alan entered the boardroom, Pat glanced up and said dryly, "Good afternoon, Mr. Schwartz." I don't believe Alan (or anyone else) was ever late for a board meeting after that admonition!

Pat also had no tolerance for long-winded oratory at our meetings and was quick to cut off any lengthy speeches. But he always did it politely. As Mike Clawson observed, "In a similar manner, he would bring to a close a meeting he was attending, but not presiding over. More than once I saw him start a round of applause when he thought the speaker should be done. The audience would join in and the speaker had no choice but to stop."

At the end of a meeting, which was always well organized and expeditious, Pat would turn to me, on his left, and ask,

"Any words of wisdom, Paul?" And I would give a brief summary of holding company activities. He would then turn to board member Ed McCaskey and ask, "Ed, would you give us a benediction?" McCaskey would recite a poem or sing a song or give a soliloquy, all with a serious face. It would crack everybody up.

Pat had a brilliant career in Chicago, both business and civic. Moving to Chicago in 1961, he became a friend and ally of Mayor Richard J. Daley and was appointed to numerous important positions, including chairmanships of the Chicago Planning Commission, the Convention and Tourism Bureau, and the Regional Transportation Authority.

He gave his time to numerous charitable organizations, including United Cerebral Palsy Foundation of Chicago, and received numerous awards from luminaries such as the Reverend Norman Vincent Peale and Illinois Governor James R. Thompson. But being proud of his Irish heritage, he was particularly pleased to be grand marshal for the 1985 St. Patrick's Day parade, on the day when the Chicago River was dyed green.

Pat didn't care for golf and was not much for athletics. But I managed to introduce him to horseback riding. It was in 1988 at my cattle ranch in Lander, Wyoming. I had invited the First Colonial board for a meeting. We would use the board room of a local bank, one of two banks in Lander. The president, a friend of mine, loaned us the room and agreed to tell us about running an agriculture-and-livestock bank such as his own. It would be an interesting comparison to our Chicago community-bank operation.

A number of our board members and some wives were horseback riders. Tom Wigdahl was a superior polo player, Bob Leander rode frequently in Arizona, and Bob Sherman, Wally Zook, and I had ridden for years. Pat O'Malley had never ridden a horse in his life.

I told Pat about a horse I wanted him to try to break and ride. He was named "Killer," I told him, because he was a retired bareback bronc that no cowboy in the rodeos had ever been able to ride. So we had a perfect combination, a horse that had never been ridden, and a rider who had never ridden!

When it came time for our intrepid rider Pat to ride "Killer," he was ready. But somehow there was no "Killer." Pat managed to look disappointed. Instead, we gave him "Goldie," another horse. He got on Goldie and, after a few circles around the arena, took off with a number of other riders on a trail ride into the beautiful sage brush hills—with an enormous smile on his face. He was a rider, at seventy-seven years of age!

Pat was one of the most active, well-known, and revered business and civic leaders to grace Chicago. Asked many times over the years why he never ran for public office, he would smilingly relate a pledge he made to his beloved wife, Helen, who during their engagement heard he might run for the city council. "You have to make a choice," she told him. "It's me or politics. I'm not marrying a politician."

Helen backs him up on the story and adds happily, "He kept his promise. He's been involved in public life, but he never ran for office!"

Lucky for First Colonial, because Pat became one of its most respected and loved members, our own Saint Patrick! His integrity, his class, and his compassion fit into the organization perfectly. He helped elevate First Colonial to the position of respect it held and for which it will be remembered.

Pat and I always enjoyed our luncheons at his Mid-America Club atop the Standard Oil Building looking out on Meigs (air) Field and McCormick Place. In July 2002, I was coming to Chicago and asked Pat if we could have lunch. I had not seen him since his beloved Helen had passed away in the previous February.

"Of course," he said. "We'll meet at my club at the Standard Oil Building."

I was startled at how frail he was, but we had a wonderful luncheon. He talked fondly of Helen, and we reminisced about our "great trip" with First Colonial.

It was the last time I saw Pat. He passed away a few months later, on November 28, 2002. We were all deeply saddened. He was a fine and valued friend and a man of great integrity and loyalty. I'll miss him very much.

Chapter 6

The First Colonial Bankshares

Corporation Board:

Working Leadership

The board of our holding company, First Colonial Bankshares, was strong, responsible, and active, as it was supposed to be. Many had been with me from the start. Bob Leander and Bill White, for instance, had chosen me as buyer of Colonial Bank in 1972, acting as that board's search committee. I kept them on the Colonial Bank board and put them on the First Colonial board when it was formed in 1984. Bill Duquaine, whom I had brought down from Milwaukee to be executive vice president of Colonial Bank, was a director of Colonial and of First Colonial.

John Burns had been a Colonial Bank director under previous ownership. Elaine Mason, who owned a local tax service, became one not long after I bought it. Ron Aronberg handled the All American Bank purchase so well that I kept him on that board and in 1984 put him on the First Colonial board.

Alan Schwartz, then president, now chairman, of Tennis Corporation of America, operator of forty-plus tennis clubs in the United States and Canada, and now also chairman and president of the United States Tennis Association for 2003-2004, was a tremendous help in gaining control of Northwest Commerce Bank. I knew he would make a key player and put him on the board of All American, near his place of business, and on the First Colonial board too.

Another key executive was the Northwest Commerce president, Wally Zook. He was a big help and displayed complete loyalty and integrity in our gaining control of Northwest Commerce. I also asked him to serve as a First Colonial director.

From the board of Avenue Bank of Oak Park came Hank Pearsall, who remained an Avenue Bank director after we bought it and also joined the First Colonial board.

From Michigan Avenue National Bank came its chairman, Pat O'Malley, to serve on the First Colonial board.

These were people I could count on. I knew it and they knew it. It had to be that way, because I needed their counsel. I took everything important to them for their advice. They served on committees that had to deliberate and decide and report to the full board for more deliberation and approval. This was clear to me from the start.

These were the key committees:

☐ Audit: The bank's auditor reported directly to this committee, as required by regulators and as essential to the well-being of the organization.
☐ Marketing: Alan Schwartz, a master marketer, headed this committee, which proved fundamental to First Colonial's success.
☐ Compensation: Bob Leander and later Pat O'Malley headed this committee, which helped start our aggressive bonus plan and generous stock option program for staff and directors.

There also had to be a strong executive committee, to discuss and recommend issues to the board. For it I picked

Alan Schwartz, whom I named as chairman, Bob Leander, Ron Aronberg, First Colonial President Bob Sherman, and myself. Our chief financial officer, Tom Maier, and later his successor, Tom Cox, attended meetings *ex officio*. Wally Zook joined the committee later.

Our Tuesday-night dinner meetings at the Standard Club, before the Wednesday board meetings, went three or four hours. Alan Schwartz ran them with care and deliberation, smoothly and with attention to detail. He was so well prepared that substance was always at the forefront, even as we, frankly, enjoyed ourselves. We got down to cases, freely disagreeing with each other if necessary, all the while becoming fast friends.

Chapter 7

Mike Singletary:

First Colonial Bankshares Corporation's

Linebacker

In the fall of 1992, our advertising agency suggested we find a "celebrity" or at least a well-known person to represent First Colonial as a public relations figure. Many banks had sports figures speaking at special events and financial gurus for shareholder meetings. We had never done much in that area, and there was some skepticism about it, because it seemed to go against the grain of our community-oriented customer base, which was predominantly blue-collar and conservative—people not prone to celebrity watching.

However, we decided to try to find someone who was well known enough to draw a crowd to our banks for personal appearances. We wanted someone sincere and classy who would represent our company appropriately—someone who shared our values of community and family. A tall order!

We looked first at the sports world. We knew no one with the Chicago Blackhawks or Chicago Bulls organizations, but we did have Pat McCaskey, son of Ed McCaskey, chairman of the Chicago Bears, on the board of Michigan Avenue National

Bank. Ed had married the Bears's founder and coach George Halas's daughter, Virginia, and Halas, recognizing his business savvy and winning personality, had put him in charge of the Bears organization.

We had bought the Michigan Avenue National Bank in 1984 after it had encountered some serious problems through purported mismanagement by its president and staff. The directors determined to sell the bank to someone who could solve the bank's problems and put vitality back into it. Among them were Ed McCaskey and the bank's chairman, Pat O'Malley. First Colonial was their choice for its acquirer.

The bank's board was an interesting amalgam of old cronies of the McCaskey and Halas families. Its two jewels were O'Malley, former chairman of Canteen Corporation, and Ed McCaskey. When Ed McCaskey had to leave the board several years later because of health problems, he recommended as his replacement his son, Pat, the Bears's director of public relations, who continued the tradition of the McCaskey benediction.

At the end of a meeting, as he had asked Pat's father before him, O'Malley would ask Pat to "please close with a benediction or final thought for the day." Pat would comply, as his father did, providing a fitting end to a board meeting.

After one of those meetings, I asked Pat McCaskey for a moment of his time. We sat down in the board room, and I told him of our wanting a sports figure to participate in some public relations activities for First Colonial. He asked what the person would do, for what audience, in what setting, giving what message. I said I envisioned his visiting each of our banks for an evening with our best customers, following a practice used successfully by other banks. We wanted a class individual, I said, not one of the many cocky, profane athletes we both knew about—someone who would embody the First Colonial spirit and attitude.

He said, "Paul, I have the man for you. It's Mike Singletary.

He'd be perfect, if he'll do it." I thanked Pat and told Bob Sherman, our president, and Debra Pawlik, our marketing director, that I thought we should approach Singletary.

Mike was the Bears's middle linebacker. At Baylor University, he was known for his fierce competitiveness, devastating tackles, and big glaring eyes as he looked across the scrimmage line at opponents. His nickname was "Samurai"—he was the ultimate warrior. At Baylor he cracked or shattered sixteen of his own helmets in his four-year career, because of his ferocious tackling.

I wrote to Mike asking for a meeting, telling him Pat McCaskey had recommended him. Would he have lunch with Debra and me to discuss a business proposition? He said he'd be glad to.

Debra and I were not optimistic. Mike was a star, All Pro, and an expected shoo-in for the college and pro-football halls of fame—he was inducted into the first in 1995, the second in 1998. We also knew he had other sponsors, maybe even a bank.

We met for lunch at the University Club. We liked him instantly. He was well mannered and looked you right in the eye. Our impression was that he was a man of integrity and class. He asked about our company—its values, its personality, its customer profile. I told him we were a group of seventeen independent community banks, involved with our communities and our customers. I told him each of the seventeen had its own president and local board of directors that Debra had put together two clubs, one for senior citizens and another for kids, the "Su-ee the Saver Club," with a little piglet as a mascot.

His eyes lit up. Debbie said she could see Mike coming to a bank for a family get-together, with soft drinks and coffee, with Mike giving a talk and signing autographs—something casual and child-oriented.

He was intrigued, but there was a problem. He already had a banking client, Citicorp, who was paying him a staggering amount, far more than we could pay. We might be able to offer a tax—deferred compensation, I said, trying to solve the money problem. That appealed to him. We left the meeting knowing he would fit beautifully into our First Colonial family but admitting to each other that our chances were slim of getting him to leave Citicorp.

A week passed. Mike called. "Mr. Johnson," he said, "my wife and I would like to meet with you and Ms. Pawlik." I was thrilled. This time we had dinner—the four of us—at the Rosewood Restaurant in Rosemont. The first part of the meeting was getting to know each other better.

Mike and his wife, Kim, had met at Baylor, where she had tutored him in math. She was an enthusiastic woman, speaking warmly of their family of four (eventually six) children and how devoted she and Mike were to the children and their church. Mike was very religious and had even considered becoming a minister. We established early rapport with Mike and Kim Singletary.

Then Mike got down to business. "Mr. Johnson," he said, "Kim and I have been talking about it, and we really like you and your bank and the opportunity I would have to choose my speaking topics and talk to kids. It sounds great." Citicorp's meetings were downtown luncheons. No kids were present. And he was asked to bring some of his football trappings with him. He said he didn't enjoy that much, as it seemed contrived and too much bent on exploiting the football aspect.

I said we'd love to have him represent us, but the amount we could pay was much less than what he was getting from Citicorp. I had an idea, however, that could solve that problem. I told Mike and Kim how we could pay him in tax-deferred stock options that someday, after his high-income, high-tax days were over, could be worth more than what he would have if we paid him in cash. Mike stopped me. "Mr. Johnson," he asked, "what's a stock option?"

I explained that it was a contract to purchase stock sometime in the future at a specified price and said I thought the stock would be worth much more then than that price. Even so, I said, we could pay in options only half what Citicorp was paying him. But if the stock went up appreciably he could sell it and pay the lower capital gains taxes on the appreciation instead of the ordinary income tax he was now paying, I added. This holding onto the stock for a longer time and not having to pay taxes on it would be a great way to provide for their kids' college education, I suggested.

"If the stock goes up, right?" Mike astutely observed.

"Right," I said.

They were skeptical. I didn't blame them. "Mr. Johnson," Mike said. "We've got to talk to our financial advisor about this option idea. Could you give us something showing him what you're thinking of?"

"Of course," I said. "And take your time. We know this payment system is unconventional. At the same time, I really believe it will be more rewarding financially in the long run. And it will be a lot of fun. But you need to be totally comfortable with the option concept."

Mike got back a week later and asked to have lunch. He came alone and got right to the point. "Mr. Johnson," he said, "my financial advisor says option payments are much too risky. What if the stock doesn't go up? The options would be worthless. Right?"

"That's absolutely right, Mike," I said. "And I don't blame you for turning us down. It's a risk."

He smiled. "I'm not turning you down. I'll do it for you because Kim and I like your style, your interest and concern about your customers." He paused. "And I love to talk to and inspire kids and we believe in your option program. So we're going against our advisor and accepting your offer."

I was stunned and very pleased and said so. But I had a confession to make to Mike that I said might make him change his mind. "I started my business career in Milwaukee," I told him. "I saw every Green Bay Packer game played in Milwaukee during the Vince Lombardi years and watched them win two Super Bowls. Mike," I said, "I'll always be a Packer fan, and when the Pack plays the Bears, I'll be rooting for Green Bay.

I'll make you a deal, though. I'll always be rooting for you individually too."

He thought a few moments, smiled, and said, "Mr. Johnson, if there was one coach I would have loved to play for, it was Vince Lombardi. I understand."

The decision turned out a very smart one for Mike and Kim. The stock they acquired through options quadrupled in price, and they profited handsomely. And for us Mike did a superb job. Every month he'd go to one of our banks for an evening event which we would publicize to our customers in that community. The local bank president would introduce Mike after everyone had a chance at the hors d'oeuvres and beverages. Mike would stride up to the stage and begin.

Our deal was that he could talk about anything he wished. It would always be an inspirational, motivating talk. He told us that sometimes he wouldn't know what he was going to talk about until he was driving to the event. But it was always good and inspiring. The kids would sit on the floor in front of Mike looking up at him. He was their idol. He'd frequently talk to them directly and always with passion. The crowd loved it!

After about thirty minutes, to enthusiastic applause, Mike would go to a table set up for him. People would line up to shake his hand. He would autograph a picture of himself or a Bears memento someone had brought for an autograph—a football or a pennant.

He'd do this for up to an hour, shaking hands and signing for everyone. Then Debbie would whisk him away. He never left early.

He made it to every bank for these evenings and to several special functions. On one appearance we did the talking and signing at the Brookfield Zoo after the families had a chance to take their kids around to see the animals.

Independently of this, I invited Mike to bring Kim and his kids to my cattle ranch in Wyoming for hiking, horseback riding, and fishing. One day, Mike called and said he'd like to come to the ranch and bring his son, Matt. He asked if we could arrange it. We said, of course, we could, and we had a wonderful time with Mike and Matt.

My daughter, Deborah, and her six-year-old daughter Emily were there at the same time. Mike's boy Matt and my daughter's Emily became buddies. We picnicked at the beautiful Louis Lake in the mountains and flew kites and swam. As we drove past our llama pens one afternoon, I pointed out a large tree that had fallen on the fence and said I'd have to get a chainsaw and cut it in two. "Mr. Johnson," Mike said, "if you have an ax I'd like to cut it for you."

"Mike," I said, "that tree is a good three feet in diameter. Yes, we have an ax you can use. But please, we're away from Chicago, you're my guest out here. Would you please call me Paul?"

He paused and said, "Of course, Mr. Johnson."

I gave him a big double-bladed ax and stayed to watch. It was amazing. Chips flying everywhere, he cut that tree in two within minutes. I was impressed!

Next to the river is a good-sized hill that Mike announced one day he'd use to exercise on. We watched him run up on legs that looked like tree trunks. Then he came back down and ran up again, backwards. I asked why on earth he did that. He said he had developed his own exercise regimen and believed he had to develop the *counter* muscles in his body, to prevent injuries. It worked. He never had a serious injury.

During his three years with First Colonial, Mike became part of the First Colonial family. We respected him as a person, a dedicated family man and a wonderful motivational and inspirational speaker. We still feel that way about him.

Mike announced at the beginning of the '92 season that he'd be retiring at the end of it. He had helped the Bears win Super Bowl XX in 1986. He said he wanted to go out "on top." I watched several Bears games in that last season and saw opposing players come up to him after the game to shake his hand or give him a hug, such was the respect they had for him. It was touching, and highly unusual in pro sports.

By 1998 he was in two football halls of fame. We had inducted him into our hall of fame well before that. We kept in touch, and several years after he ended his career, he called and thanked me for suggesting the options, which had worked so well for him and his family.

Pat McCaskey had been right about Mike and Kim fitting in with the First Colonial family. I consider him one of the classiest guys ever to wear the First Colonial uniform!

Chapter 8

Bill Duquaine:

The Human Side of Banking

In 1959 I left my first job after the air force, with the Milwaukee-based investment firm, Robert W. Baird and Company, to become president and CEO of Wisconsin Capital Corporation, a small business investment company (SBIC) that I had started.

An SBIC was a government-subsidized financier for small businesses to help them start and grow. The government would lend the SBIC two dollars at low rates for every dollar the SBIC raised for itself. I raised $600,000 from friends, family, and Baird customers to start my company, the second SBIC formed in Wisconsin since the program started in 1958.

One day in 1969, I took a call from a man I did not know, J. Russell Duncan, of Sterling Precision in New York City. He wanted to buy a bank in Milwaukee, where he had once lived, had seen that I was with an SBIC, and wondered if I could put a deal together for him. We met; he set out his parameters. I told him that on a fee basis I would find a bank, negotiate the purchase, and obtain financing. We agreed and I went to work.

Through a friend at First Wisconsin Bank, I heard that the Milwaukee Western Bank might be for sale. Milwaukee Western was a $60 million asset bank near one of the city's largest shopping centers and its oldest, Capitol Court. A half million potential customers lived within five miles of it.

The owner, Harold Emch, was interested. We struck a deal. Then I went to the head of correspondent banking for First Wisconsin, Ray Callen, and put together a good loan package. We closed the deal for Russ Duncan in mid-1970.

On the way to the closing, Russ turned to me and said, "Paul, you've impressed me the way you've put together this deal. And I trust you. I want you to join my organization. I'd like you to have a senior position with the bank and be my representative on the board. I can't make you president, because you don't have any banking experience. But I don't have a lot of confidence in Dick Sachs [the president]. I want you to learn the business and watch the bank for me."

I was surprised and flattered. "But I know nothing about commercial banking!" I said. "You're a quick study," he said. "You can do it."

I asked what position I should take. He suggested "something with authority, like a senior vice president. How does that sound?" he asked. I said it sounded fine, and that's how I started my commercial banking career, as senior vice president and a director of the Milwaukee Western Bank. It was June of 1970.

I looked around me and decided we needed some new loan officers—a commercial lender and an installment lender. Sidestepping the president, Dick Sachs, whom I took for a smart investment type but poor judge of talent, I went to Russ Duncan, who told me to go ahead and hire people.

I got our commercial loan officer, Art Kramer, from First Wisconsin Bank. He put me on to a young installment loan officer at First Wisconsin, Bill Duquaine. Bill had gone through a good training course at First Wisconsin and had experience in lending at the downtown branch. Art Kramer thought I'd like him.

I did. We hired Bill as our installment loan officer. An ex-footballer at the University of Wisconsin-Milwaukee, he had a blond crew cut, boyish face, good sense of humor, but more importantly, was honest and a hard worker. He became a very effective loan officer. We related well. He was to become perhaps my best friend and most trusted executive at First Colonial Bankshares.

After I moved to Chicago in 1970 with Jim Howard and Growth Capital, I stayed in touch with Bill and his wife Dawn, who named their first child after me. Then we bought Colonial Bank in 1972, and I needed an executive vice president. I turned to Bill Duquaine. He was intrigued but felt intimidated by the big city, had heard about the Mafia in Chicago, and thought he could never convince his wife to move from Milwaukee.

But when I showed him around the city, especially the Colonial Bank neighborhood, he had second thoughts. He liked Colonial's neighborhood, as I knew he would. Of German stock, with a wife of Polish descent, and having grown up in a blue-collar environment in Milwaukee, he and I saw that he would fit well into the ethnic neighborhood of Colonial Bank.

He joined us as executive vice president. His wife Dawn and their two children, Paul and Lourdene, moved down from Milwaukee to Palatine, a northwest suburb of Chicago. He became my indispensable right-hand man at Colonial Bank and later at First Colonial. At the bank he became one of our two senior lenders, with Tom Szar, our installment lending officer.

Bill fit in well with the neighborhood and with our customers. He and I spent long hours in the bank, building its loan portfolio.

Both of us were athletic and very competitive. He'd come over for racquetball at Lake Point Tower, where I lived. He was strong as an ox and hit the ball hard. But I was more agile and maybe a little more cunning. I beat him regularly. He couldn't stand it. The game calls for getting to center court for best position. Bill would crush the serve right into my kidney to get me to move. It almost brought tears to my eyes. But I'd never admit it hurt, and I stayed in the middle.

One day we played doubles, with Bill and me as teammates against a friend, Russell Lee, and Mike Pyle, the all-pro Chicago Bears center. On the first play, Bill hit his trademark blast into Pyle's kidney. Mike blanched and, for the next point, retreated to back court.

It was well before graphite racquets, and we used wooden ones. I'd played tennis in high school and college and used a sweeping tennis swing. They served, I went back, took a huge swing with my heavy wooden racquet, and hit Mike, who was coming up on my left, flush on his eyebrow. He slumped to the floor, blood gushing from the cut. As we got an ice pack, he said, "Damn, this is tougher than playing the Minnesota Vikings!"

In 1973 we moved from our grocery store location to our new home on Belmont Avenue, next door to St. Patrick's High School. Bill was in charge of the move, which went flawlessly, including the deployment of police we had hired to guard the vault with shotguns as it was moved.

Our new facility was lovely. It had a huge, landscaped parking lot edged with sapling trees along the lot and the street. The trees were attractive to people other than us. One night Bill, our foreman on the job, Joe Nasca, and our architect, an old friend from Milwaukee, saw something unusual as they returned to the bank in their pickup after dinner down the street. Three guys were loading one of our not-yet-planted trees into their car trunk.

Our men screeched to a stop. Joe Nasca, a very tough guy who had grown up in the streets, was out in a flash. He cold—cocked two of them, one after the other, and took off after the third as Bill screamed, "Joe, don't kill those guys. I'm calling the cops!"

Joe was clearly a good man to have around. He and Bill became good friends. A year later, Bill came to me and said, "Paul, Joe Nasca is one of the hardest-working, most-loyal, and honest guys I've ever met. We should hire him for our maintenance manager. He'll save us a lot of money and will be a great employee." Bill was right. We hired Joe, who stayed with us until our sale to Firstar in 1995, by which time he had become a vice president. Bill always had a good instinct with people.

Bill's and my offices were side by side at Colonial Bank. We were in constant communication and developed complete trust in each other, business-wise and personally.

Bill was a proud man. He was not well educated, but had one of those special intelligences—common sense, with a great sense of people—that made him invaluable as a lending officer. I made him president of the bank in 1974. The staff loved him. He was tough and demanding, but fair.

There were a few rough edges, however. Growing up on Milwaukee's South Side in a modest, blue-collar area, Bill had picked up Milwaukee idioms and ways of speaking. He also dressed in the fashion of his old neighborhood. When I suggested changes in his speech and vocabulary and dress habits, being a proud guy, he took offense. But if his two-pant suits were all right in our bank's Belmont-Central neighborhood, they weren't in downtown Chicago, which, as bank president, he visited frequently.

I hit on an idea. I wrote up a little evaluation form, which included speech and dress, and invited the six-member senior staff to grade each other. Bill was rated very low in dress and speech. He was shocked.

But he had a strong desire to improve himself, so he came into my office the next morning and asked, "What's wrong with my suits and ties?"

I said, "You shop at Irv's [our neighborhood store], instead of Marshall Field's. It doesn't cost much more to shop downtown."

He didn't say a word but went to his wife, Dawn, for her opinion. She said I was right and told him, "Take his advice and help your career."

She and Bill went downtown to Field's and helped him

into a whole new wardrobe. From that day on, he was well dressed.

Bill Duquaine wasn't the only one in the bank with questionable grammar and speech patterns. So I went to a nearby college and hired an English teacher for testing and counseling. She devised a test on twenty-five of the most common mistakes in English. I invited our office staff to participate. One of our young lending officers, Thom Caravello, was upset. "What good can this do?" he asked. I said he should just try it. We took the test one evening—each scoring his or her own—and nobody, including me, got them all right. Many missed as many as half the questions.

Thom Caravello was contrite and grateful. "Holy smokes, Mr. Johnson. I've got some work to do."

Bill Duquaine, who had welcomed the test as another way to self-improvement, said, "Paul, I'd like you to help me improve my language skills."

I told him to try out new words and phrases. He worked at it. The first time, he told the staff they had just passed mustard. "Muster," I told him later.

He once bragged that his wife Dawn was a great storm trooper! I suggested he drop the storm part.

It was typical of Bill to go at things so energetically. He had a keen desire to improve himself and was brutally honest about what ought to be improved. This was one reason he rose to the top three in an organization of eight hundred people.

He was also active in the community—in the local chamber of commerce and on the board of nearby St. Patrick's High School.

He and I were in constant contact, traveling together to conventions, for instance. I saw he was somewhat uncomfortable with the downtown crowd of Ivy Leaguers and sophisticates but very comfortable with the average Joe. He was a friend of several aldermen.

But when we were about to expand the organization

substantially and raise money through stock offerings and private placements in 1982, I knew I needed someone else on our team at its top level—someone with the management skills, big-bank experience, and operational expertise that would complement Bill's talents and mine.

Bob Sherman was the man. Bob headed the correspondent division of the Chicago's American National Bank, a large, very successful bank and our main correspondent. He was smart, had a good education, was articulate, and had good operational experience. He was ideal for us.

But as a rising star at American National Bank who would someday have a shot at the presidency, he would not be an easy catch. I convinced him by offering him a block of options that gave him a better chance of increasing his net worth than American National would offer. He signed on, and to help him learn community banking, I made him president of one of our banks.

There was, of course, instant competition between Bill and Bob—Bill, my best friend and right-hand man for ten years, and Bob, the smart newcomer who had graduated with honors from a top school and had been a key officer at a sophisticated Loop bank.

But it worked out. Bill, Bob, and I enjoyed and respected each other and attended banking functions and conventions as a trio. Bill ran our biggest bank, the Colonial Bank, and was our chief credit officer. Bob and I worked together on acquisitions and set up our electronic data processing subsidiary, run by EDS of Houston.

By 1988 it was time for Bob Sherman to become president of our holding company, First Colonial Bankshares, so as to work with me in expanding it. I consulted with Alan Schwartz on the appointment. I always went to Alan when I had a big decision to make for First Colonial. He confirmed my decision and a few days later, at a seminar for our ninety officers and directors at the Westin Hotel, in Rosemont, I announced Bob's new position. I had told Bill about it two days earlier. He had been disappointed, though not surprised, but after my announcement was the first to come up and congratulate Bob. It was a gracious and important gesture.

Bill knew I had done the right thing for First Colonial, but he never quite forgave me. Bob moved to our headquarters at the Michigan Avenue National Bank downtown, where the holding company staff was based. He and I worked closely. Our Saturday morning meetings were critical times for the company. Bill stayed at Colonial Bank, and I saw less of him than I had before.

In these years, we lost three of our original Colonial Bank officers to cancer, each having worked in our original facility. They were, in succession, a vice president, Della Labattaglia; a thirty-nine-year-old chief lending officer, Rod Miller; and our long-time chief financial officer, Wally Krolski. We had cause to wonder about that coincidence.

Bill handled our lending policy and practices brilliantly. Our loan portfolio grew substantially, and yet our losses stayed low. Charge-offs, and therefore loan reserves, also stayed low. This contributed to our high profitability.

Bill's family prospered too. I watched his children, Paul and Lourdene, grow and develop into polite, well-mannered, delightful teenagers and adults. He was proud of them, as well he should have been. Things were going well.

But trouble loomed. One day in the summer of 1991, Bill told me he had been feeling lethargic and was having blood tests to see what was wrong. I told him to keep me posted. He had the tests and said they showed a very low iron count, for which he was taking iron pills. They helped and he felt somewhat better but still felt very run-down.

He went to Presbyterian St. Luke's Hospital for more tests. They showed he had some sort of blood disease, as he put it. I asked what. Myeloma, he said. I asked what that was, but he couldn't describe it well. But he said, "I can handle it. It's not that bad." I accepted that and was relieved.

But that evening he called an employee meeting. I didn't

attend it but learned later that he told the employees, rather emotionally, that he had a form of leukemia but was sure he could "lick it."

I was really surprised to hear this. He was sounding much more concerned than he had been with me. I asked him if I could talk to his doctor at Presbyterian St. Luke's. He said sure.

The doctor showed me in great detail Bill's iron-count swings. I asked him if it was serious. "Not very serious," he said. "He'll be somewhat more susceptible to other ailments, but *should live a rather normal life and won't die of this disease.*"

I was relieved but wondered why Bill had been so melodramatic with the staff. Knowing him to be somewhat dramatic sometimes, I brushed it off as a "Bill moment." And he was fine, for the better part of the year. He played some racquetball and golf. But he also began chemotherapy. Toward the end of the year he dropped racquetball. Then he broke his arm playing golf. He was losing weight.

His doctor had said Bill's disease was a "cousin to leukemia" and was not life threatening, but I was worried. I went to see Dr. Bob Eisenberg, one of our Oak Park directors, who headed the Physiology Department at Presbyterian St. Luke's.

"Bob," I said, "something is troubling me. Bill's doctor told me Bill had a blood disease, a kind of cousin to leukemia, but it was not life threatening. But Bill isn't looking good. What's up?"

"For God's sake, Paul, Bill has multiple myeloma and it's a fatal disease. Bill is dying," he said. "It's just a matter of time!"

I was stunned. I couldn't speak. I said, "That can't be. Bill's doctor—"

Bob broke in. "Bill's doctor lied to you."

He had lied to me, acting under the terribly mistaken impression that I'd fire Bill otherwise. I found myself almost as much stunned by that impression as by what I now knew, that my friend was dying.

Bill started to go down fast. He was losing lots of weight,

and the chemo and by now radiation treatments were taking a heavy toll. He was in and out of the hospital. I saw him almost every day. We reached out to each other with a closeness only impending death can bring. We laughed and told stories of our times together. We were good friends before, but now we formed a remarkable bond.

When he was in the hospital for good and fading fast before our eyes, he motioned me over once to say something. "Paul," he said, "you know I really like Florida. Why don't we sell First Colonial and go to Florida and start all over?" I told him there was nothing I'd rather do, to start again, with him.

I visited him almost every day in the hospital, on my way home from work. We'd talk about old times and old friends. One evening as I was about to leave, he said, "Let's walk down to the elevator." He had his hospital gown on, and I couldn't believe how he had wasted away. In good health he was a solid 250-pound, 5'11" man, with legs like telephone poles. Now he couldn't have been 130 pounds and had trouble walking.

We got to the elevator and said goodnight to each other. He paused, stepped forward, put his arms around me and said, "I love you, Paul."

I said, "I love you, too, Bill." It was the first time we had ever hugged and the first time we had ever said, "I love you." We were two macho guys who had never learned how to express ourselves to each other. I turned, got into the elevator, and lost it.

In his last week or so, Bill was seldom awake. I'd see him every evening. His wife Dawn, his daughter Lourdene, his son Bill, or all three were there. There wasn't much to say, as we watched Bill die.

The last time I saw Bill alive, Lourdene was there. Bill was asleep, as usual. Lourdene and I visited a little and then for some reason, as I left, I went over to Bill, leaned over, and kissed him on the forehead, then left in a hurry, overcome. Bill died the next day.

When I saw Lourdene several days later at Bill's wake, she said, "You know, Mr. Johnson, when you kissed my dad that night? Just as you left, his eyes opened. And he smiled."

Dawn told me that Bill had requested that I be one of his pallbearers. She asked me also if I would write his eulogy and deliver it at the funeral. I told her I had real trouble at funerals as it was, possibly because I attended my father's funeral when I was ten and my grandfather's when I was fifteen. It would be very difficult, I told her, but I agreed to be a pallbearer. And I would write the eulogy but couldn't deliver it. In an unbelievable act of love and courage, Bill's son Paul said he'd deliver it.

Knowing I would become very emotional, I took someone's advice and took a Valium before the funeral—the only Valium I have ever taken. It might have helped. But the walk down the church aisle was very difficult for me, bearing Bill's coffin.

As Bill's son Paul delivered my eulogy, my close friend Ron Aronberg sat next to me. He put his arm around me to give me comfort. And it did.

Bill's illness, death, and funeral were an ordeal. It was also a lesson not to take anyone's love or friendship for granted or assume it will go on forever—it won't—but to express your feelings to those you love sooner rather than later. A lesson too that it's okay for guys to express love and friendship for other guys.

I thank Bill for teaching me those lessons.

Here's an edited version of my eulogy to Bill delivered bravely by his son Paul at St. Ferdinand Catholic Church on September 21, 1993:

When Bill's family asked me to give his eulogy, I said I could write it but I couldn't deliver it. I was astonished at Bill's ability years ago to read a eulogy at his father's funeral in Milwaukee. I marveled at his courage, but I knew I could never do that for someone close to me.

Life moves too quickly, and we forget to give people we love the time and attention they deserve. It was that way with Bill and me. We had our misunderstandings from time to time, mainly because we didn't communicate as well as we should have. But I never questioned his devotion to me and First Colonial. He had an innate understanding of people that made him one of the best bank lenders I have ever known. I came to trust him completely when it came to judging people. I often told him I would take his common sense and understanding of people over that of any Harvard MBA.

When I hired him for the Milwaukee Western Bank in 1967, I loved his brashness and aggressiveness. I admired his honesty. He was never afraid to tell it the way it was, never failed to take a stand if had a contrary point of view. At the same time, he was a consummate team player and supported whatever decisions were made.

He was a gentleman. He was also ambitious. But his ambition was motivated not by a desire for wealth but by the will to succeed and make a contribution. He and I were both highly competitive. We talked about competition and appreciated the philosophy of Green Bay Packer Coach Vince Lombardi, who said, "I never lost a game. I won most games overwhelmingly. The others, I just ran out of time."

Bill, you didn't lose this game. You just ran out of time. Early in your final travail, Bill, I told you about Jack London's insight, "The proper function of man is to live, not exist. I will not waste my days trying to prolong them. I will use my time." You used your time. You used it throughout your life and never better than in your last years, when you reached out to comfort and encourage your friends.

Bill's sickness made a big change in him. Loving and compassionate, but sometimes brusque and tough looking, as a sick man he began reaching out to help others more than ever, and his brusqueness and toughness disappeared. He became the ultimate team player, performing his job as head of lending with great evenhandedness. More than that, he was a friend. His friendship was his best gift. He gave it generously.

My last time with him, a week previously, I found extraordinarily difficult. He lay unconscious, wearing an oxygen mask. I knew I probably would not see him alive again. His family was there. I marveled at their strength. Bill would raise his head slightly and open his eyes, and Dawn and Lourdene would comfort and soothe him. It was then that I began to realize what Dawn and the children had gone through, especially in this last year.

Bill's doctor misled me about Bill's disease. He told me it was not life threatening. Not until months later did another doctor tell me how sick Bill was and that he was lucky to have as many more or less healthy years as he did. I was stunned to hear it, and much more stunned to hear from the first doctor why he had not told me the truth, namely that he was not sure how I would react.

It was then that the gravity of the situation hit me. It was then that Bill and I began a new phase in our friendship that I can only say was incredible for me—the development of an affection and bond between us such as I think few people achieve. Thanks, Bill, I owe you so much for that rare opportunity.

About that time, I tried to encourage Bill with another of my favorite quotes, "I may not like the way life's cards are shuffled, but I like the game and I want to play." Bill played the game of life with dignity and enthusiasm. He was an inspiration to us.

Another quote was "It is better to light a candle than to curse the darkness." Bill never cursed the darkness closing in on him, his illness, but accepted it with dignity. His body was ravaged at the end, but his spirit stayed strong. He lit up our lives with his love of life and of his friends.

Bill, you were a man who counted. You were a genuine, contributing human being, and you died too young. Few people in my life have counted more to me than you. You and I shared unique experiences over our twenty-six years of friendship. You will be surely missed, and we will always love you.

William Cullen Bryant wrote in *Thanatopsis*:

So live, that when thy summons comes to join
The innumerable caravan which moves
To that mysterious realm, where each shall take
His chamber in the silent halls of death,
Thou go not, like the quarry-slave at night,
Scourged to his dungeon, but, sustained and
soothed
By an unfaltering trust, approach thy grave,
Like one who wraps the drapery of his couch
About him, and lies down to pleasant dreams.

Goodbye, Bill. Pleasant dreams.

PART I-B

THE COLONIAL STORY:

FINISHING FIRST

Chapter 9

Oak Park:

Community Spirit and Minority Lending

We wanted very much to acquire more banks in choice new locations. We found that package with our purchase of the Oak Park group in 1986. The largest of the group was Oak Park's $100 million Avenue Bank of Oak Park, on Oak Park Avenue in the center of town. The owner and chairman was a lawyer whose wife's family held its controlling block of stock.

At the same time, we picked up four other smaller banks in other suburbs—Northlake, Elk Grove Village, Downers Grove, and Glendale Heights. Each had a president, several of whom we kept, and some good directors, whom we also kept. Even these good directors had been mostly figureheads, but we were going to change that.

The Oak Park bank stood out for its several strong directors who wanted to be more than figureheads. One was Hank Pearsall, an Oak Park resident who was chairman and CEO of Sanford Corporation, a very successful local company.

Oak Park has a sharply defined identity among Chicago suburbs. Once the home of Frank Lloyd Wright, whose architecture is found in a number of homes and public buildings, the village has a very popular tourist attraction in his "home and studio" on Chicago Avenue. It is an affluent community with pronounced racial and, to a lesser extent, socioeconomic mix while serving as a higher-end suburb, twenty-five minutes or less to Chicago's downtown on public transportation or expressway. It is home to a large number of professionals who like the composition of the community and its convenience to Chicago.

The Avenue Bank president left for Arizona shortly after we took over. His successor was hardworking and diligent. But as we were soon to find out, he had ways of speaking often reflecting prejudices that would get us into some serious trouble.

Next to Oak Park, a mile east of the bank, is, surprisingly, a mostly low-income area, Chicago's Austin neighborhood. Its western boundary, Austin Boulevard, was also a socioeconomic demarcation line.

Many commercial banks in the '80s, including Avenue Bank, had done a poor job of offering loan and deposit services to Chicago's low-income areas, including Austin. ATMs were not available in these areas, and people had to use high-cost, check-cashing services offered by currency exchanges. Lending was not readily available either. Most banks were reluctant to lend in these neighborhoods, and many "redlined" them, making lending approval very difficult for residents.

In 1977, Congress wisely passed the Community Reinvestment Act (CRA) to encourage banks to lend in low— and moderate-income neighborhoods in their communities, consistent with safe and sound banking operations. Banks could borrow low-cost government funds for lending in these neighborhoods. That was the carrot offered by Federal Reserve governors. The stick was penalties for banks found in noncompliance with CRA rules.

It was up to neighborhood activist groups to keep banks' feet to the fire in this matter. One of the methods they used was to send low-income "loan applicants" into banks to test their CRA resolve.

We were tested in Oak Park by a couple who applied for a mortgage loan on a very run-down Austin property. We turned them down, legitimately because neither the appraisal nor the applicants' income supported the request. But our real estate loan officer committed an egregious error by using a racial remark on the written rejection of application. The couple sued the bank for racial discrimination on the basis of the remark.

It was a major lapse in supervision by our president, who was also failing to solicit Austin area businesses for business loans. Nor was he working with groups working to improve conditions in Austin, including Bethel New Life and the Garfield Austin Interfaith Network (GAIN), Garfield Park being the community just east of Austin, farther into the city, as he was expected to. In other words, he was a no-show in matters of CRA involvement. It was a lapse that was to cost us dearly.

We were sued, for one thing, by the couple who didn't get their loan. Worse than that, we ran into big trouble in our next acquisition effort. We wanted to buy two north suburban banks, the Highwood (Illinois) Bank and the New Century Bank in Mundelein, both owned by the Highwood Group, and applied to the Federal Reserve for approval. This put us directly in the line of observation, if not fire, of activist community organizations.

Several of these, emboldened by the suit, opposed our application. They were successful. The Federal Reserve board of governors turned us down, citing CRA noncompliance: "The board . . . has reviewed comments from three individuals . . . alleging that . . . the Avenue Bank of Oak Park has engaged in and continues to engage in discriminatory lending practices and . . . is not adequately addressing the credit needs of its entire delineated community."

The record showed that Avenue Bank did not have "a satisfactory record" and "for some time" had been deficient in CRA performance. The denial was "without prejudice to further applications" when the bank had its CRA record "in place" and "its policies and programs [were] working well."

This bad news came to us in a notice dated May 18, 1993. It told us among other things that Federal Reserve Chairman Alan Greenspan was among those voting on the matter. We were impressed. In fact, we were astonished that the entire board of governors and he had deliberated over the matter at all, when from our admittedly limited viewpoint there had to be more important things for them to worry about!

It didn't matter.

Back in Chicago, the sellers could have called the deal off on the spot, because we had no chance of satisfying the Fed within our contracted time limit, even if we did make it on the second try. But the seller's chairman, Danny Greco, said they would wait. "A deal is a deal and we want to merge with First Colonial." A stand-up guy.

I got immediately involved in the whole business of meeting with the community groups and found them responsible and dedicated. These were real community leaders. We established rapport quickly, but our president unwittingly continued to do what he could to throw us off track. This time he turned to one of the group, a black woman, at an early meeting and said, "I don't think *you people* understand what we're trying to do."

Whatever he had in mind by that, he appeared to be making a racial characterization, and the group reacted predictably and, in my view, appropriately, as if he had used a racial slur. We were finally convinced of what we suspected: that he had at least a streak of racial intolerance.

He also revealed a serious lack of understanding of the CRA imperative. We realized we had to make a change. We didn't terminate him but moved him to another First Colonial Bank that did not present the race relations challenge that our Oak Park bank presented. He had other talents that would find an outlet at the new location.

In his place, we installed an experienced banker who we knew would be alert to the Oak Park challenge—Marty Noll, an Oak Park resident of many years. I had known Marty since 1971, when, as a senior officer of American National Bank in Chicago, he helped us put together the purchase of the Colonial Bank. I knew he took easily to cooperating with community groups. Hiring him, we told these groups we were serious about doing better in the community.

We set to work at bringing banking to Austin. Among other things, we opened a branch on Madison Street a mile into Austin. We worked hard for the better part of the year to improve our record. Then we applied again for approval to buy the two Highwood Group banks.

Our application submitted, we asked for a meeting in Washington, DC, with the Federal Reserve staff. We showed up in strength we thought appropriate: our Oak Park president Marty Noll, our First Colonial president Bob Sherman, our First Colonial CFO Barb Kilian, and I. The Federal Reserve had eight people, all CRA staff, including two lawyers. One of the lawyers was CRA division head for the Chicago Federal Reserve Bank.

There was a third contingent. From our Oak Park-Austin area had come a representative of Bethel New Life, Lawrence Grisham, and one from GAIN, George Lawson, an older gentleman with extensive civil rights movement experience. I had told them we were going to Washington. They had offered to join us to help convince the Federal Reserve that we were doing a good job in Austin.

I introduced our people to the Fed staff and said we were there for two reasons: to give them new information about us and to hear what they thought of our application. I said we had an important decision coming up. Our purchase of the banks had a fast-approaching, drop-dead date. We might be able to renegotiate our contract, I said, but we had already renegotiated it once, at some cost.

The Federal Reserve staffers were very critical. Then they announced there would be yet another individual in the meeting, an objector to our petition whom we knew nothing about, a minister at a South Side church in Chicago some ten miles away from Austin. This man could not make it to Washington for the meeting but would participate by speaker phone, they said. We objected. He did not represent Austin, we said; and two who did, Lawrence Grisham and George Lawson, had taken two days out of their busy week to be with us in person.

The Fed staff apparently thought they had an important witness here, however, and were unmoved by our protests. They put the South Side minister on the telephone. He accused us of doing a bad job in Austin, of being out of contact with the community and uncommitted to it. As he continued in this vein, George Lawson got up from his seat silently, walked around the table to the speaker phone, leaned into it while the Fed staff watched, interrupted the objector, identified himself, and told the man in no uncertain terms what he thought of him and his criticisms.

He knew nothing about Austin, he told him, and furthermore was completely out of line in jumping in at the last minute without so much as informing the GAIN people, who had been working on the problem for many months, of his concerns or even of his interest in the matter. He was being irresponsible. He was offensive. He had no business saying anything at this meeting. It was an impassioned statement that effectively shut the man up. He got off the phone.

Lawson turned to the staffers, agape at this display of conviction and plain speaking and at the virtual demolition of their star witness. Then he told them with equal passion and eloquence of the faith his people had in First Colonial and Avenue Bank leadership. He told of the tremendous progress we had made in our community reinvestment in Austin—far more than they had seen from any other bank in the entire Chicago community. We were the bank and bankers of the year in his opinion. We deserved their approval.

The staff, apparently eager to make their mark in a politically hot matter, had not seen this coming. Their eyes widened. They looked at each other uncertainly. At that moment we knew we had what we came for. George Lawson made his mark that day. I'll never forget it.

The meeting was on January 12, 1994. The Federal Reserve wrote us on February 17, saying they approved our application to buy the banks. Again, Chairman Alan Greenspan had cast his vote, as had three governors in this apparently weighty matter. After a long, hard year's work by our top executives, including me, we had our victory. We had instituted policies, installed mechanisms, and in general done things we should have done in the first place. The Community Reinvestment Act had brought us up short, we realized that. It's a good law, for the banking industry and everyone else.

One of our important helpers in all this was one of our Oak Park directors, Hank Pearsall, who with his wife, Jane, had been involved for years in civic and philanthropic activities in Oak Park and Chicago. After watching Hank at work in Oak Park, I asked him to join the board of First Colonial, where he operated with distinction—with a positive attitude, incisive mind, and grace. Hank is a real gentleman.

After the sale of First Colonial to Firstar in January 1995, our seventeen bank presidents were terminated, among them Marty Noll in Oak Park, and the boards were disbanded. This left him and Hank Pearsall in Oak Park loaded with their good reputations and their First Colonial experience. They seized the day and started a community bank, locating it a few blocks up Lake Street from the old Avenue Bank, in downtown Oak Park.

Hank was not going to do this halfway, so he did an extraordinary thing. At fifty-five or so, after a career in manufacturing, he enrolled in an executive banking course that met for a total of two weeks over two years in Madison, Wisconsin, where he joined other bankers thirty years his junior. Why so much effort? Because he wanted to be as qualified as he could in his new capacity as chairman of the new bank.

The bank he and Marty Noll started, Community Bank of Oak Park and River Forest, has done very well, growing in assets and becoming profitable in a short time, as told in another chapter. It has joined the long and growing list of community banks that competed well with big-bank branches. Hank and Marty took three other members of the Avenue Bank board with them as foundation of their own board. Avenue Bank customers flowed to their new bank. In my opinion, Hank and Marty stand for community banking at its best.

Chapter 10

Going Public:

The Business of Growth

By the spring of 1984, First Colonial Bankshares Corporation was a three-bank, $300 million organization that had grown by borrowing purchase money. We knew we couldn't keep that up. The growth we had in mind would call for new capital—privately invested, then publicly. We would have to attract both, in that order. We would have to go public eventually, offering shares of First Colonial. An initial public offering (IPO) was in the offing.

I had a broker in mind, Mike Sammon, head of the banking department at the well-established investment firm, Chicago Corporation. I knew we had a good story to tell, and I told it to Mike, at the same time picking his brain about what went into a public offering. Our three banks—Colonial and All American in Northwest Side neighborhoods and Northwest Commerce in Rosemont—were growing and profitable, and not by accident. We had a well—reasoned strategy and what we considered to be the recipe for a winning IPO.

The issue came to a head in the spring of 1984 when we began the process of buying Michigan Avenue National Bank (MANB), a $200 million asset bank that would give us the

Chicago Loop location we badly wanted and bring First Colonial to half a billion in assets.

We knew we shouldn't borrow the whole $16 million to buy MANB. We would have to raise money from investors. Studying our options, we decided on a combination of public and private—a public offering of about $11 million and placement of about $2.5 million of equity notes with American National Bank. Immediately after the purchase, we would dividend up about $2 million from MANB, which had a surplus of capital, to the holding company, First Colonial, to pay down debt.

The market for bank stocks was good, and our shares would sell at a good multiple of book and earnings, Mike Sammon assured us.

Our biggest challenge would be to get MANB Chairman Pat O'Malley and his board to wait while we went through SEC and Federal Reserve approvals for the offering. The problem, of course, was that no public offering is a sure thing. They would need a lot of faith in us to wait while someone else might be offering cash on the barrel head. We worked this out with them, agreeing on a time by which we would have raised our purchase money with a Class A stock offering.

Our chief financial officer, Tom Maier, and I set to work. We submitted the necessary papers to the SEC and the Federal Reserve and chose the Chicago Corporation—henceforth "Chicago Corp.," as it's almost universally referred to—as our head underwriter.

We needed only $9 million to make the purchase, so the $11 million stock sale would leave us $2 million for later use.

We structured ownership in an unusual manner. In 1984, when my handpicked group of ten—directors and senior staff—and I bought out my fifty-fifty First Colonial partner of twelve years, I said I'd never again put myself in a fifty-fifty position and would always have control of the organization.

So we immediately recapitalized the corporation, dividing

shares into Class A, paying a 15 percent higher dividend, but carrying only one vote per share, and Class B, with twenty votes per share. The price of each would be the same, but the coming IPO would offer only A shares. The B shares, with their much stronger voting power, would remain with the corporation.

Moreover, because of my original large stock ownership and the new B-share arrangement, I would control 70 percent of the company while owning just 10 percent of the stock, as agreed by my nine partners in the IPO.

I also was to have full say on board membership. In the words of our SEC filing, "the members of the private investor group [agreed] for . . . ten years to vote all the securities . . . held by them for nominees for directors designated by Mr. Johnson [who will thus] be able to elect all the members of the board of directors." I was gratified by this further vote of confidence in me by my partners and by the faith showed in me. I was eventually even more gratified when it paid off handsomely for them.

Now it was off to the IPO. Chicago Corp. had to get comfortable with the A and B stock concept. They did. We negotiated a selling price and commission. We approved the "selling group"—the other investment firms that would be selling shares. Tom Maier, our CFO, was extremely valuable to me during this process. I did the negotiating, as usual.

Federal Reserve and SEC approvals took somewhat longer than expected, but both finally came through on September 25. We set a day in December for the offering. Chicago Corp. filled out its selling group, which included firms in Cleveland, Detroit, and St. Louis. An investment firm in Milwaukee with which I had started in business, Robert W. Baird and Company, asked to be part of the group.

Tom Maier and I did "road shows" at each of these firms— for their sales departments—so they could get a look at us as key executives. Chicago Corp., as lead underwriter, took the largest batch of stock. This led to a big problem.

With the offering not long off, Mike Sammon came to me and said he didn't feel good about it. He felt they had taken on too much and asked if he could bring in "a national wire house," Dean Witter, to make sure that we could quickly sell the million shares.

I said that sounded all right. I preferred the stock stay in the Midwest and with smaller firms. I wanted to see it in "strong hands," I told him. But if he thought the move was important to our success, I was ready to go along with it.

Then trouble. The offering was set for a Tuesday. Over the weekend *Business Week* came out with a cover story about Chicago's much-troubled Continental Bank. The cover showed crumbing Ionic pillars. One of the country's biggest banks was to be taken over by the FDIC. And we had a bank's public offering on our schedule!

Tom Maier and I met on Monday with Mike Sammon and Chicago Corp. President Jack Wing, in Wing's office. Wing delivered the bad news. The Dean Witter sales manager in New York said they could not sell the shares at $11. The price would have to go to $9.

We were stunned. I said our agreement was for $11, what happened? He said he'd let the Dean Witter man tell us. It was the *Business Week* article, the man told us on the speaker phone. The whole bank stock market was hurting. It was $9 a share or no offering.

I said we had picked them as the co-underwriter because they were supposed to be able to sell stocks! Take it or leave it, he said in effect. We had to take it, and leave $2 million on the table.

It didn't matter. The offering was oversubscribed and rose several points in several weeks. In a year the stock was at $15, up 70 percent.

In typical wire-house fashion, Dean Witter "flipped" a number of accounts for short-term profits by favored clients. The more responsible houses, like Chicago Corp. and Baird, recommended long-term holds. Their customers would profit handsomely over the years. Many of the original buyers stayed with their holdings until our sale to Firstar ten years later or until one of its subsequent mergers, with Star Banc or U.S. Bancorp, realizing significant multiples on their investment.

I never again did business with a wire house. All our financings from then on were done with investment firms we could count on, like Robert W. Baird, Chicago Corp., and Stifel Nicolaus, of St. Louis. These small firms were like community banks. They almost always had their customers' best interests at heart and stayed close to them, providing good counsel, good products, and good service.

Chapter 11

Assimilation by Firstar:

How a Big Bank Blew It

Several studies I had read by consulting firms had concluded that most acquirers did a pretty poor job in assimilating purchased banks into their system. I was curious about these findings, in fact a little incredulous because we had acquired more than ten banks ourselves and had done a pretty good job of transitioning new personnel and operating systems into our own organization.

That's why I was unprepared for how poorly Firstar handled the assimilation of First Colonial Bankshares. In fact, it was inept.

Firstar had made two acquisitions before us, of several small Minneapolis banks and (a major acquisition in 1991) of banks held by Banks of Iowa, headquartered in Des Moines.

At the time of our sale to Firstar, its chairman and CEO, Roger Fitzsimonds, told me candidly that he had been disappointed in their assimilation of the Iowa bank group, but that his senior staff had learned from the experience and our merger would be relatively seamless and expeditious. I knew of the Iowa problems because the Chicago law firm that handled our sale to Firstar had represented Banks of Iowa. One of its partners filled us in on that.

But the basic failure of our merger with Firstar gave me an insight, graphically and firsthand, of flaws in big-bank management and philosophy. Subsequently, I have observed that flawed mergers by big banks are more common than successful ones, as consultants have pointed out.

There are several keys to a successful merger.

The acquirer must assume control at the time of contract and not wait until the date of takeover, a period usually of about six months. First Colonial signed the purchase agreement in June 1994, but the effective date of the merger wasn't until January 31, 1995. During that time, Firstar and First Colonial prepared for their mandatory shareholders' meetings for approval. Also, the Federal Reserve gives competing banks and other interested parties the opportunity to submit objections. SEC approval and Department of the Treasury antitrust approval also have to be obtained.

Assuming control right away is critical. Among the CEOs I know of, the one who understands this best is Jerry Grundhofer, now CEO of U.S. Bancorp. When his company, Star Banc Corporation, purchased Firstar in June 1998, he let Roger Fitzsimonds, chairman and CEO of Firstar, keep the title of chairman but took control right away, leaving little or no authority with Roger. There was no question that Jerry Grundhofer was in control and calling the shots. He evaluated key personnel for future disposition and assignment. He and his extremely competent staff studied Firstar programs and systems for change or elimination once approvals were given. Everyone at Firstar had direction and caught the excitement of the change. They understood from the start the direction that the newly merged company would take. Final approval and takeover was anticlimactic. Jerry's team had already taken over, and all were on board and were headed in the new direction. They hit the ground running.

Not so with Firstar's purchase of First Colonial Bankshares.

Shortly after the contract was signed and the acquisition was announced, I asked senior management at Firstar for some direction for the approximately six months we knew it would take for SEC, Federal Reserve, and shareholder approval.

I wanted to keep First Colonial personnel motivated and inspired and keep as many of them in the organization as possible, knowing that some would be riffed and that many would be approached by other banks during this time of uncertainty.

I met with our holding company staff first—our president, marketing director, CRA officer, chief financial officer, and auditor. I told them their jobs were in jeopardy, and so were those of their staffs. I told them that I was the most expendable in Firstar's book, but that most of them would, nonetheless, lose their jobs once Firstar consolidated the merged company. I also told them we had negotiated excellent severance packages for them with Firstar if they were terminated or chose to leave. We had used consultants to work these out and had made them deal-breakers for any prospective buyer who balked at them. While I expected our senior management team to be looking elsewhere for positions, I asked them to stay until we were taken over, as a matter of loyalty to the organization and in the interests of the merger. I told them one of the main reasons for staying was to help their Firstar counterparts learn our programs, meet our staffs, and understand our systems firsthand, so the merger would be efficient and as seamless as possible.

It never happened.

Every day our holding company staff reported for work at 8:30 or earlier prepared to help Firstar staff learn our Chicago marketing avenues and programs. Not once in the six months did a Firstar person contact them.

It was astonishing.

At a dinner we requested with Firstar senior management, we got a pretty good inkling of how they were looking at our organization and their lack of concern about the possibility of our key people leaving. Firstar was represented by their chairman and CEO, Roger Fitzsimonds, and their president, John Becker. Our executive committee of Alan Schwartz, Ron

Aronberg, and Bob Leander, our president Bob Sherman, and I were there for First Colonial. During dinner I turned to Roger and told him we were starting to have some difficulties with our staff in that headhunters and other banks were approaching our key personnel. I suggested that he or John Becker speak to our group and give them some motivation and inspiration, asking them to stay with the organization with comments on what they were expecting to do in the Chicago area, etc. In other words, a pep talk.

Roger turned to me and said in a somewhat cavalier tone, "There'll always be someone to take the places of the people who leave." We were stunned at that comment, but it gave us an idea of what we might expect during the transition.

Firstar had five banks in the Chicago region with approximately $300 million in assets, and with First Colonial's $1.8 billion, we would have over $2 billion in total assets.

My successor in running this $2 billion organization was announced at the press conference on the acquisition date. This was Firstar's Jay Williams, who was considered one of the country's top retail bankers. He had some experience with Firstar's community banks, though mostly in a staff capacity. He was very well thought of, appropriately, at Firstar headquarters and was a definite favorite of their CEO. A very bright, energetic man, he was also a gentleman and turned out to be compassionate and dedicated.

But from the start, he was hamstrung by Firstar senior management, which did not release him from his responsibilities in Milwaukee until very late in the transition, so that he could focus on Chicago. It was a huge mistake.

Meanwhile, I urged Roger Fitzsimonds and John Becker to give us some direction. We were willing to make modifications in our loan policies, our deposit gathering programs, our asset liability strategies, etc. to help position them for a smooth takeover.

As importantly, I continued to urge Firstar senior

management to meet with our staff to answer their questions about their "new bosses." I had told our staff at the time of acquisition that I had known a number of Firstar senior management for years and knew them to be honorable, compassionate and trustworthy—one of the main reasons we had sold to them.

An example of their lack of interest in or understanding of our programs was their treatment of the Doers Club. Over the years, our financial/social program for the age-fifty-five-and-over customers had grown to twenty thousand households in the Chicago metropolitan area, with half a billion dollars in core deposits. Half of our total retail deposits, in fact, were held by our Doers Club members, resulting in one of the lowest costs of deposits in Midwest banking. Because of these low-cost deposits, First Colonial consistently had a net interest margin exceeding 5 percent—well above the average of 4.5 percent.

During the six months between the contract signing and approval, I became increasingly concerned about Firstar's lack of comprehension of the value of this program and the necessity to reassure our Doers Club members and coordinators. It is understood that, after an acquisition is announced, headhunters swarm in to try to pick off the top people of the acquired company because of the uncertainty of who the acquirer will retain. Our top Doers Club personnel were especially vulnerable because most of the banks in Chicago, including the big ones, were trying to replicate our success in this area.

But Firstar inexplicably did nothing to encourage our coordinators to stay on or even indicate to them that they were going to continue the program. Without that encouragement and with concerns over working for a big bank, our key Doers Club coordinator was hired away by a competing community bank located close to the Colonial Bank. This individual started a new club and, because of her loyal following, took half of the Colonial Bank's Doers Club with her.

After the takeover Alan Schwartz and I, as directors of Firstar Illinois, pleaded with Firstar management to modify the club if they wanted to, but at least retain the Doers Club program and encourage its staff to stay.

In typical big-bank fashion, they instead hired a consulting firm—from Minneapolis, not even from Chicago—to study and report on the viability and importance of the program. Not only did the Firstar staff not interview any member of our marketing department or Doers coordinators, but the consultants didn't either!

This was dumbfounding to us.

The consultants' report, which finally arrived in my successor's hands *nine months after* the acquisition, said— definitely keep the program, but cut back on some of the expenses. But it was too late. The Doers Club staff, sensing that Firstar management was not going to support the program, eased themselves into the personal banking area and abandoned the program. First Colonial lost a huge portion of core deposits and, as we anticipated, the net interest margin of Firstar Illinois fell from over 5 percent to 4 percent within a year.

The marketing group from Minneapolis concluded in September 1995: "Doers is a good program." They went on to say, "We will retain the senior club program and general concept."

Another quote from the study was "Doers is a good program. First Colonial was wise to recognize the importance of this class of customer and to establish this program to retain them. Doers customers are only 21 percent of the total, but represent 53 percent of total balances." The problem for Firstar is that this report came out nine months after the takeover of the bank and fifteen months after the announcement of the purchase. This was much too late to stop the hemorrhaging of our key Doers Club personnel and the loss of customers to other banks. This was a graphic example of a big Milwaukee bank not comprehending the competition of the Chicago market. While Firstar and M&I controlled a majority of the deposits in

Wisconsin, not one bank in Chicago controlled over 9 percent of the assets of that city. Hundreds of banks shared the business in the Chicago area; therefore it was much more competitive than the Wisconsin market.

Senior management at Firstar should have understood that and didn't.

I realized that because of that experience alone, well-run community banks had little to fear from the big banks.

A number of our key staff were offered positions with Firstar, but fearing the big-bank mentality and seeing the ineptitude of our merger, some left for positions with other community banks. Several, having learned about entrepreneurship, started their own companies.

A fundamental error most big banks make is turning their community-bank acquisitions into cookie-cutter branches. So the Firstar management team had little understanding of Chicago banking and tried to model their new branches after their Wisconsin facilities. Initially, they even attempted to apply their Wisconsin-based compensation standards to Chicago compensation realities! Because of that initial miscalculation, a number of our best officers left for other organizations.

Many customers are disaffected with the big-bank mentality and lessened quality of service. This experience opens up an opportunity for a well-run community bank in that community.

Another crucial error at First Colonial was Firstar's insistence on overlooking the successful lending formula we had used for years, which was putting character and collateral before capacity. Firstar and many other big banks developed a "sophisticated" cash flow formula to evaluate loans. The problem with that formula is that cash flow frequently varies from season to season. First Colonial customers of fifteen to twenty years, people of integrity and reliability, suddenly were asked to leave the bank because their credit standards didn't fit Firstar's new formula. Even though this new policy was reversed several years later, it was impossible to make up for the loss of those good customers.

In addition, Firstar and the big banks were not interested in smaller commercial loans because they are not "profitable"—so those customers received little or no service, and many left. We at First Colonial knew that smaller customers grow to be larger customers—and loyal ones at that.

First Colonial also had many commercial loans where we had taken additional collateral—mortgages on properties. This extra collateral threw them into Firstar's definition of real estate loans category and there were strict guidelines set by Milwaukee as to how many asset dollars could be allocated to a particular loan area. So to cut back on excessive "real estate" loans, many of our good customers were asked to leave—just so that category could fit into Firstar's modified model.

Their arrogance was shocking. One of the reasons Firstar bought First Colonial and paid such a handsome premium was because of our financial results, which was a reflection of our products and services as well as their delivery to our customers. We had accomplished this while competing in the Chicago banking world. One day shortly after the merger, several key Firstar staff members were meeting in the board room and one of First Colonial's executive secretaries that they had retained overheard one of the officers commenting somewhat snidely, "Well, now we'll bring First Colonial into the twenty-first century." And there's no question in my mind that he meant that. They were soon to learn that our community-banking formula worked extremely well in Chicago and their Wisconsin-oriented big-bank formula was not a good substitution.

This mind-set is prevalent during many big-bank purchases of community banks. A variance of this was Bank One's John McCoy's "uncommon partnership" philosophy which built Bank One of Columbus, Ohio, into one of the country's most formidable banks. John told me once how, in buying a small bank in Indiana, they had discovered a unique consumer loan product that that bank had used successfully. He gave that new bank president the job to replicate that program throughout the Bank One system. When they acquired the Marine Bank in

Milwaukee, he told me that they had a better municipal bond department than Bank One did, so they shifted that whole department to Milwaukee. John understood, better than most large-bank CEOs, how to assimilate purchases into a system, encouraging the founders and staff of the community banks to continue in that spirit.

Then Bank One got too big.

First Colonial had seventeen banks in the Chicago area with seventeen presidents, each with its own board of directors, all from communities that the bank served. We had a bank as far north as the Wisconsin border, the Fox Lake State Bank, and as far south as Burbank and as far west as Naperville. Each of those banks could price their deposits according to local competition, in which each had a substantial loan authority. Each bank had its own advertising budget, to be spent as the president determined. The president was rarely transferred and frequently lived near the bank. He participated in local organizations that represented a cross-section of the community.

Customer loyalty to these community banks was superb and each bank grew in loans and deposits at the expense of the branches of the big banks, including First Chicago, Northern Trust, Continental, LaSalle Bank, and Harris Bank. Those banks simply couldn't compete for retail business with us.

The Firstar purchase changed that success pattern significantly.

First the presidents of our seventeen banks were let go, replaced with branch managers at salaries half of the presidents'. The boards were disbanded, saving Firstar all of about $1,000 a month per bank! And products and pricing were standardized regardless of the competitive pressures of the different communities. Many of our customers moved their deposits and loans to other community banks. In addition, many of our staff, put off by the big-bank philosophies, went to competing community banks. With the reputation enjoyed by First Colonial Bankshares, they had little trouble finding good positions.

That shifting of personnel had nothing to do with the way

Firstar treated our staff. Firstar staff was equitable, fair, and generous—they were genuinely good people who did what they could to keep our staff motivated. Many of our top officers stayed on—frequently with different assignments. But having come from a culture of flexibility and autonomy that was First Colonial, the Firstar structure—including a "regional CEO" in Chicago that had to report on everything to Milwaukee—made many of our staff long for the environment that top community banks engendered.

Firstar did not understand the Chicago market as well as I imagined and were very slow in adjusting to it. This is a common failing of big, slow-moving, highly organized reporting structures. The first several years of the transition were very difficult for Firstar, which lost millions of dollars in loans and deposits and a large number of key personnel. I was astonished at the ineptitude of this otherwise "well run" regional bank in transitioning First Colonial into their organization.

I was asked to identify four of the best directors of First Colonial to serve on an advisory board of Firstar Illinois—the combination of First Colonial and the Firstar Banks. I recommended Alan Schwartz, Ron Aronberg, and Bob Leander. Firstar's CEO approved this selection. I went to my successor, Jay Williams, whom I didn't know very well, and told him I would also serve as an advisory director if he wanted, but that it probably wouldn't be a good idea to keep the old CEO around. He considered that and asked me to stay on. I did so, spending the first several months introducing him to key people, bankers, regulators, investment bankers, media people, and large customers in the Chicago area.

Three directors from Firstar's group of banks were also asked to serve on the advisory board, Robert Elliott, Dennis Flynn, and Craig Stern. This board still meets quarterly under Jay Williams's successor since 1998, Mike Clawson.

During the first year, seeing the appalling lack of understanding of the distinct differences between the Chicago and Milwaukee markets, all of the directors urged the Firstar team to modify many of their cookie-cutter policies. Firstar President John Becker frequently came to our meetings. This was a very good idea. It gave us the opportunity to speak directly to Firstar senior management. But John responded very slowly to the challenges of the Chicago market, which we directors knew so well. They started to modify their approach after about a year, but it was too late to maintain the vitality of the organization they had purchased.

This experience opened my eyes to the vulnerability of the big banks. It didn't take long to corroborate my instincts that well-run community banks with their presidents and local boards could easily outperform big-bank branches. I could see that many top qualified and motivated bankers would frequently prefer to operate in the quick-acting community-bank environment than in the big bank, heavily structured, frequently ponderous structure.

Shortly after I moved to Napa, Wells Fargo bought out one of the two remaining community banks in Napa in 1999, the Napa National Bank. While not as well run as most of the community banks in Chicago, a much faster track, it was still a community bank with many loyal customers who relished banking with a locally owned bank.

Wells Fargo proceeded to assimilate Napa National more ineptly than Firstar did First Colonial, demoralizing staff and driving away long-term customers who were used to the personal services of the local management team. Accustomed to being able to talk to the bank president or another person of authority, they were now transferred from one computer phone voice to another, eventually ending with someone in a far away city. In short, the new owner was dismantling the community-bank structure.

In the midst of it all, I got a call from a friend, Congressman Mike Thompson, who lived in nearby St. Helena. He asked if I would assist a group of investors who were convinced that a de novo community bank in the Napa Valley could compete against Bank of America and Wells Fargo. The more I talked to people in the area, the more I saw frustration, even anger from former customers of Napa National about their treatment at the hands of Wells Fargo.

Wells Fargo, like Firstar, is a well-run big bank, one of the top big banks recommended by analysts. They have a fine ROE and a very low expense ratio, the latter the mantra of banking today. Cut expenses! Downsize! Get rid of the costly small accounts! Beat the other big banks efficiency ratios. Get it below 45 percent—please the analysts—and don't think too much about several years down the road.

There is no question that our de novo bank, Napa Community Bank, will compete very successfully against the big-bank branches. We understand the formula for success.

Big banks have abandoned the smaller customer, retail and commercial, and they will find it more and more difficult to keep top personnel, many of whom will be drawn to the flexibility and fun of the community bank, not to mention the opportunity for options, a piece of the action, that most big banks can't replicate.

Community banking is the wave of the future.

PART II-A

COMMUNITY BANKING'S GOLDEN
FUTURE: THE ARGUMENT

Chapter 12

Community Bank Versus Big Bank

Two major elements of big-bank strategy show why a well-run big bank cannot compete with a well-run community bank. One is big-bank zeal to drive down its efficiency ratio, basically an indicator of how much money is spent to generate a dollar of revenues. The other is the centralizing of decision making at the expense of local managers.

Big banks compete with each other in the first, seeking analysts' approval. The efficiency ratio is closely tied to cost-cutting, which rests almost entirely on payroll. All big banks in the last ten years have implemented cost-cutting, which they developed or hired outside consultants to develop at cost of millions. The goal was always to consolidate or eliminate positions. But it is impossible to maintain a given level of service with significantly fewer staff.

So they give up trying to serve "small customers," whom

they classify as "unprofitable." They are unwilling to devote time and resources to developing these customers into "profitable" ones.

Customer loyalty is sacrificed for efficiency. Service is exchanged for a "best cost" strategy.

I learned this in the aftermath of selling First Colonial Bankshares to Firstar, most dramatically from a Firstar board meeting I attended in Milwaukee eighteen months after the sale. As one of Firstar's larger shareholders as a result of the sale, I had been asked to be a director. The meeting on July 18, 1996, was a dreadful eye-opener.

At the meeting, Firstar Chairman Roger Fitzsimonds announced "two massive initiatives." The first was a huge cost-cutting called "Firstar Forward." The second was a form of "functional realignment."

The cost-cutting, explained in board material called "Planning for 1997," would be directed by a consultant picked by the executive committee. The "Planning" preamble emphasized cost—cutting, with barely a nod towards improved service. The goal was to lower the efficiency ratio from the low sixties to the low fifties in a year, Fitzsimonds told us.

The planning document called competitors' efficiency ratios "important benchmarks," to which would be pegged "the vast majority of our businesses and products." We would follow a "best cost" strategy in our search for "superior profitability." We would have to have "lower total costs" than the competition. Firstar Forward would "streamline our structure."

Our value to customers would lie in "operational excellence," as in "streamlined processing" of small business lending. Everything would pay its own way, as we would "review profitability of all distribution centers [bank offices, ATMs, phone centers, kiosks, the Internet] and eliminate, modify and reposition resources as appropriate."

There was no mention of customer service. There was nothing about keeping customers, serving them better, or improving services. Everything was cost-cutting. Customers were not king. Efficiency ratio was king.

Weeks later, the consultants—from the East Coast—in their presentation stressed that we could eliminate many staff without loss in revenue growth.

I didn't believe it and said so at the directors' meeting, much to Fitzsimonds's consternation. I knew we could not drastically reduce staff without loss of revenue growth. And I knew it would be folly to budget for the next year based on that mistaken notion. In fact, neither happened. The projected efficiency ratio was not realized, and revenue growth did not rise but declined. Probably worst of all, it was not the efficiency ratio that plummeted, but staff morale.

The only winner was the consulting firm, who pocketed well in excess of $10 million for their services.

Cost-cutting is something any business does. Many banks, large and small, have done it. If it's done wisely, fine. But if poorly, as by Firstar, it causes irreparable harm to customer service, the heart of a successful bank.

So much for the first "massive initiative" announced at the 1996 meeting. The second big-bank strategy, the planned "functional realignment from geographical responsibility," as Fitzsimonds put it, was even more illustrative of a big bank's inability to compete against community banks.

He meant getting rid of community-based line organization, with Chicago-area presidents and branch managers reporting to a Chicago executive, for instance, and each bank or branch staff reporting to the branch manager, but having all report to big—bank headquarters, in this case in Milwaukee. The big bank's regionals and super-regionals would refer there for decisions about branches' commercial, consumer, and real estate lending, deposit generation, and the rest, all in the name of efficiency.

Close contact with each market would be abandoned for efficiency's sake. This is vintage big-bank thinking. It's cost effective, after all. But it flies in the face of community-bank experience, which calls for decisions on a local basis, without concern for what's happening elsewhere in the system.

This is how community banks stay in touch with their customers, by deciding locally about local requirements. With this so-called functional realignment—dysfunctional, for my money—Firstar was taking big-bank thinking to its logical conclusion, at the expense of knowing what customers wanted and working towards getting it for them. It was condemning itself to being just another "efficient" big bank, squandering First Colonial's rapport with customers and customers' loyalty to First Colonial.

What's more, this "functional realignment" marked the beginning of the end for Firstar as an independent, respected regional bank. The original First Wisconsin National Bank, and then its successor, Firstar, had been well run and community bank-oriented. But senior management's falling for the siren song of efficiency ratios led to Firstar's falling behind its peer group and becoming "marginalized." This is what other consultants told Firstar directors at a 1997 meeting. Taking this to heart, the directors decided they had to protect slipping stockholder value, and Firstar was sold to superbly run Starbanc, of Cincinnati, led by Jerry Grundhofer. From this sale Firstar stockholders came out big winners.

The Firstar efficiency initiative was another example of how big banks create openings for community banks who supply what big banks ignore. It's happening. In 2002 alone, ninety-one new community banks were established in the United States, for a year-end total of 7,887, according to the FDIC. In 2001, 129 had been started, in 2000, 192.

These new banks have relied on senior executives' "rainmaking" ability, to be sure. These executives often enough have come from bigger banks, bringing with them customers and prospects they have persuaded to follow them to "the more friendly confines" of a new community bank.

Which is just the point. The customers know a good thing.

There's more to community banking's success than rainmaking. The Bank Administration Institute's Peter Soraparu said it this way in a 1999 paper, and he might as well have been speaking for this banker: "Many a career community banker might [say] the ex-mega-bankers are simply returning to the basics of the business," including delivery of "effective, personal service." Right!

PART II-B

COMMUNITY BANKING'S GOLDEN

FUTURE: THE EVIDENCE

Chapter 13

Wintrust Financial Corporation,

Lake Forest, Illinois: Ed Wehmer

All but one of the banking organizations discussed in this book have grown mostly or entirely by acquisition of existing banks. The one that has grown almost entirely by starting new banks is Lake Forest, Illinois-based Wintrust Financial Corporation, with $4.7 billion in assets and net income for 2003 of $38.1 million.

First quarter 2004 results were impressive. Net income was $11.6 million, up 40 percent over first quarter 2003. Net income per share was $0.54, up 20 percent. Book value per share was $18.26, up 33 percent. Market price per share was $48.63, up 70 percent. Total assets were $4.962 billion, up 27 percent.

Wintrust has until recently done nothing but start new banks—seven in suburban Chicago—and facilities—thirty-one—in twelve years. Not until 2003 did it buy a bank, and the two that it did buy that year had been started de novo during the twelve years of its own existence.

The Wintrust plan has been to enter a town without a community bank and start a new one. The towns are affluent. In some cases they are recently bereft of their community bank because a big bank has just bought it. Wintrust puts together a board of high-profile local businesspeople and finds an experienced local community-bank executive for president. Board and president are given authority and autonomy and aim for top market share in that community.

It's been a winning strategy. Stifel Nicolaus's (Midwest) Regional Banking Review, which covers sixty-eight institutions in twenty-two states, for the second quarter of 2003 has Wintrust as tops among banks in long-term shareholder gains, with a five-year annual compound growth in year-end stock price of 22.6 percent vs. 2.9 percent for the median bank.

In 2003 Wintrust stock had risen in value from $31.32 to $45.10 a share, an increase of $13.78, or approximately 44 percent. In 2002 it rose 54 percent. In 2001 it rose 91.8 percent. At year-end 2003 it was selling at approximately 245 percent of book and twenty-two times earnings.

Other figures document Wintrust success:

- ☐ Its five-year 32 percent annual compound growth in earnings per share, second highest of sixty-eight banks covered, the median of which had 12.2 percent growth.
- ☐ Its five-year 18.5 percent book value growth, eighth highest. The median had 9.9 percent growth.
- ☐ Its more than tripling of total assets in five years, from $1.3 billion in 1998 to $4.7 billion at year-end 2003.
- ☐ Its total equity of $350 million, up from $227 million, an extraordinary 54 percent for the year. (The major components of this increase were its $38 million net

income, $46 million common stock sales proceeds,
$38.6 million in stock purchase of two banks, and
$6.4 million by exercise of stock options.)

☐ Its return on average equity of 14.4 percent.
☐ Its near quadrupling of earnings per share, from $0.50
in 1998 to $1.98 in 2003.
☐ Its more than sextupling of net income, from $6
million in 1998 to $38.1 million in 2003.
☐ Its more than tripling of net revenue, from $45 million
in 1998 to $193 million in 2003.

Wintrust had nine banks on December 31, 2003, and all
but two started de novo. Here they are, with age, asset size,
and (for seven) market share in their respective communities:

Market		Assets	Share
Lake Forest Bank & Trust	13 yrs.	$1.030 billion	#1 of 7
Hinsdale Bank & Trust	11 yrs.	$741 million	#2 of 14
North Shore Community Bank & Trust	10 yrs.	$834 million	#1 of 9
Libertyville Bank & Trust	9 yrs.	$586 million	#1 of 8
Barrington Bank & Trust	8 yrs.	$553 million	#2 of 8
Crystal Lake Bank & Trust	7 yrs.	$428 million	#2 of 13
Northbrook Bank & Trust	4 yrs.	$255 million	#2 of 11
Advantage National Bank	2 yrs.	$107 million	
Village Bank & Trust	9 yrs.	$79 million	

The nine are growing in dollar size at rates of $60 million
to $90 million a year.

REASONS FOR GROWTH

"Big banks still don't get this customer service thing," said
Wintrust's 2002 annual report. "That may be one reason we
keep taking market share from them."

A Wintrust bank is expected to open a new branch every
one or two years. Four or five branches are planned for the
next twelve months—ending in December 2004.

The holding company would like to start a new bank every two years.

It's buying banks too, using its highly valued stock as currency, announcing in late 2003 the acquisition of the $74 million Village Bank and Trust, of Arlington Heights, and the $107 million Advantage National Bank, of Elk Grove and Roselle, Illinois. Both are "accretive," said Edward J. Wehmer, Wintrust CEO, meaning they immediately increase the buyer's earnings per share, in this case Wintrust's. They are "non-dilutive" of earnings per share.

A tenth bank was being organized de novo in the Beverly neighborhood of Chicago.

It's all expected to add up to growth of $1 billion a year, said Wehmer.

He is Wintrust's principal architect. He devised its exemplary philosophy and strategy, a model for all who aim at developing a multiple de novo bank organization.

He came to the founding of Wintrust, of which he is president, chief executive officer, and a director, in 1991 after seven years as chief financial officer of River Forest Bancorp, Inc., now Corus Bankshares, Inc., Chicago, and president of Lincoln National Bank, River Forest's largest bank subsidiary.

He had spent seven years before that with Ernst and Young, the accounting firm, specializing in bank mergers and acquisitions. He was involved in over one hundred acquisitions in that time. He is a 1976 Georgetown University graduate and has lived in Lake Forest since the mid-eighties. He and his wife Dorothy have six children. The six kids and living in Lake Forest were to motivate him in starting Wintrust.

I met Ed at our interview on October 30, 2003, having heard of him for years from investment bankers Mike Sammon of Friedman Billings and Joe Stieven of Stifel Nicolaus and from fellow bankers.

We got along quickly. He's a likable guy, gregarious, affable, direct. You pick up immediately his smarts, his enthusiasm, his warmth, and his candor. He's a people guy, long on charm and earnestness, the kind you like to be in business with.

Stifel Nicolaus's Joe Stieven says he has "a positive, infectious personality" and that "if he were a football coach, he'd be the kind you would run through a brick wall for. He's charismatic."

We talked about his background and his main reason for starting Wintrust, namely because he wanted to work close to home. He had six kids and had been commuting to downtown Chicago for years, working for Bob Glickman at River Forest Bancorp. "It was tough to leave that job, because we were building something great, but I wanted to do something close to home," he said, adding "for myself."

His Ernst and Ernst (later Ernest and Young) years had put him in the middle of one hundred acquisitions—by others, needless to say. He got tired of it and in 1984 joined River Forest Bancorp, where they bought "broken banks," including Lincoln National, which he headed, and "fixed them." River Forest was at about $180 million in assets when he left, ready for something new.

"The idea of starting Lake Forest Bank? Not mine," he said. It was banking executive Howard Adams's idea. Bryan Baker, who worked for Adams, told him they wanted to open a de novo bank in Lake Forest. Would he be interested? He went to meet Howard, "a compelling person" who sold him on the idea.

He went to work, getting two River Forest colleagues, David Dykstra and Randy Hibben, to help him write a business plan. He would supply the beer and cigars, and they could spend an evening putting together a plan. It took two hours, from which came a plan they "haven't strayed far from since."

Hibben came with him from River Forest. (Dykstra came later.) They raised $6 million locally for bank capital and opened Lake Forest Bank and Trust on December 27, 1991. They had decided there would be more, if this one was a success.

It was. In 1993 they started Hinsdale Bank and Trust. Rich Murphy left River Forest Bank (part of River Forest Bancorp) and joined them at the new bank, where he is now president. Dennis Jones was its CEO. Then they found some bankers and directors who lived in Wilmette who were fed up with Bank One and wanted to start their own bank. With them they started North Shore Community Bank and Trust in Wilmette in October 1994. They were greeted by "a groundswell of interest," and off they went "to a great start."

Dykstra joined them from River Forest Bancorp in June 1995 and helped them put together a "sound" capital plan for expansion, beginning his "important" work for them as chief operating officer.

They started Libertyville Bank and Trust in October 1995. In 1996 they organized their multibank holding company, Wintrust Financial Corporation, and went public with it. Wintrust was formed by merging their four de novo banks, all established in 1991 and since, with Howard Adams's Crabtree Capital Corporation, a finance company.

Adams also had a premium insurance company–FIRST Insurance–which was losing money but "had potential." So when they went public, FIRST went into the merger too. Everen Corporation took them public, and the offering sold out, much of it through their banks into the local communities. "We wanted as much local ownership as we could get."

In 1998 smooth sailing gave way to stormy waters. Wintrust, "about $1 billion in size and not making much money," went through a "fairly traumatic time" when governance problems arose with Howard Adams, and the Wintrust board removed him.

HOW WINTRUST IS RUN

It's a company run in "very decentralized" fashion. The holding company does most of the asset/liability work. Data processing is outsourced to Metavante in Milwaukee. A marketing staff of eleven helps each bank. The bank boards are responsible for bank staff salaries and all basic bank decisions. "We rely on the boards. The recipe is local decision making—for starting each bank, for running each bank."

Ed quoted John Lillard, chairman since 1998, about Wintrust's competition and how it competes. The competition comes in "two forms—cost-conscious large, impersonal banks and smaller banks which lack what we're developing organizationally, namely strong oversight by the holding company, policy-setting cross-fertilization, cross-selling of brokerage services, and niche lending. We've got a team and a structure which keeps us winning on both fronts."

Wehmer continued. Wintrust's incentive-compensation plan for senior management "ties us all together," he said. "One guy falls, we all fall." It has to be that way: "Egos can ruin a business. You can't have politics in a business."

What does he look for in a president? "Integrity and experience, for starters. A lending background. At the same time, familiarity with all departments. You want a generalist. It's hard to find it all in one individual. Sometimes you need two who complement each other. You have to know them personally. Our best have been people we have known personally. As far as making a big-bank executive a community-bank president, it's very hard. It usually doesn't work."

On the contrary, their good people come from "successful community bank molds like yours, Paul, First Colonial Bankshares."

I was gratified to learn that two of my top First Colonial staff people, Barb Kilian and Rich Pasminski, are with Wintrust, along with one of our bank presidents, Ed Werdell.

The pitfalls of community banking? "You can't screw up operationally. The banks that falter usually have operations problems from the start. A good operations person is critical."

Other pitfalls? "On the asset side. Some bankers get themselves into a position where they don't have enough capital and they feel they have to stretch their lending standards by getting into high-risk areas like indirect auto paper, SBA pools, and other bad asset categories."

Wintrust is "asset-driven," he said. They generate more loans than they need, preferring to stay in the 85 percent loan—to-deposit range. In 2002, for instance, they sold off $311 million in excess premium finance receivables.

I found it interesting that Wintrust's premium finance division made up 23 percent of its loan portfolio, while commercial and commercial real estate accounted for only 44 percent.

Wintrust's control of nonperforming loans and charge-offs is excellent. According to the Stifel Nicolaus report, its nonperforming assets in September 2003 were 0.34 percent, while their peers had it, a relatively few months earlier, in December 2002, at 0.71 percent. Net charge-offs in three quarters of 2003 were 0.19 percent; for peers in the full year 2002, they were 0.4 percent.

In the Stifel Nicolaus third-quarter update, Wintrust's asset quality remained "sound." Reserves were covering 160 percent of nonperforming loans. Net charge-offs remained "low" at 0.19 percent.

Wintrust's growth depends heavily on its investments. "To make a bank grow," said Wehmer, "you need capital, which means you have to invest money. When you grow to a certain size, you have to invest some more, because you have to reinvent yourself every two years, and that means investing more to get to the next level."

Does he prefer cash or stock deals in acquisitions? "Cash. We do not like to dilute stock. But this year [2003], when we made our first ever purchases, our stock was so high, we used it in buying our two banks. And since then, we've been hearing from a number of banks that want to sell."

Some Wintrust charters are national, while others are state; so they deal with different regulators. Why not stay with one regulator? "Frankly, I like getting different points of view, from the OCC and the state banking commission. But all our banks are Fed members, and we maintain a good working relationship with the Fed."

And the regulators? "We like the regulators. I have all my net worth tied up in this organization, so they're watching my net worth! That's comforting. No complaints."

I asked how the holding company allocates expenses, noting that the banks are not allowed to pay dividends, "upstream" them, to the holding company for the first three years. "We strictly observe the relevant Fed regulations," he said. These are 23A and 23B, which prohibit upstreaming dividends to a holding company. "As for determining banks' share of expenses, we work out something fair and equitable." Costs are kept low in part by the small size of the holding company staff, only twenty-two people, including himself.

And no lawyers. "Why would you need lawyers on staff?" he expostulated. "We have none. Zero." Not for putting together applications for de novos? "You don't need lawyers for that. Our senior vice president finance, Barb Kilian, who used to work for you, can put one together in her sleep. It's easy."

So what do the banks pay? I told him the bank I had just founded in Napa was paying its holding company in the first year $16,000 a month for so-called services. He laughed at that. "Our largest bank, Lake Forest Bank and Trust, $1 billion in size, pays only $26,000 a month!"

I was impressed with how reasonably they allocated expenses, especially in the case of their newest de novo bank, Northbrook Bank and Trust. In 2001, Northbrook Bank's first year, Wintrust allocated expenses for marketing, investment counsel, asset/liability counsel, human resources, holding company salaries, and compliance of $6,500 a month.

For EDP and item processing—contracted to the highly regarded, Milwaukee-based Metavante Corporation, as they had been for all Wintrust banks—they allocated the cost of processing, an average $5,325 a month.

The $5,325 average developed from a low $3,300 for the

first month to $6,300 for the twelfth, reflecting common holding company practice of passing on only actual EDP and item-processing costs. Not all do so, by the way. Some allocate a fixed yearly amount. In any case, the Northbrook Bank average of $5,325 in its first year is very reasonable, considering its growth in that time to $90 million in assets! So for EDP, item processing, and all other outsourcing, the year's cost to Northbrook was a cost-effective and reasonable $141,900.

Your bank boards? "Having strong local boards is one of our biggest strengths. The more eyes the better! A board costs about what a loan officer costs. But a good one produces three times the business that a loan officer will. It also gives the bank tremendous credibility in the community. I can't estimate what that's worth.

"I'm not concerned about 'controlling' the boards." Boards and officers of all the banks meet monthly for planning.

"Our goals are $50 million to $75 million growth a year, an increase of ten to twenty basis points in return on assets and a new branch every two years. We believe every bank will eventually become a billion-dollar bank."

At over $4 billion in size, what about listing on the New York Stock Exchange? "Nope. NYSE listing is more an ego trip than anything else. We're comfortable with NASDAQ. We trade about 120,000 shares a day, and it's a good regulated market."

They have recently begun airplane financing. Two pilots at the Crystal Lake Bank wanted to do it, he said okay. They're doing well at it. "Airplanes don't go down in value. I expect our banks to come up with new, good ideas like this."

Your real estate: own or lease? "We own almost all of it. We're in the business of creating value, and good real estate does that."

How do you keep your capital in line with your growth? "We sell stock. In June 2002, we sold 1,363,000 shares of common stock at $28.70. We raised $36.5 million that way. In

September 2003, we sold 1,377,108 common shares at $35.80, raising $46.1 million.

"We also issue trust preferred stock. We started in 1998 with a $31 million sale. Now we have $76 million on our books. Meanwhile, our equity capital has increased from $75 million in 1998 to $300 million as of this past September 30."

What about preopening expenses? "They shouldn't be more than $200,000 if your chartering procedure is efficient. The bank staff should be in place for about two months before the bank opens. Then it's nine to fourteen months to break even. We lose about $300,000 during that time. So with preopening expenses, which we charge off, we are down $500,000 in capital before our de novo becomes profitable."

Facilities, interior decorating? How important? "Very. We spend a lot on the building and the interior. We feel we have to look good, so that customers are comfortable in our setting."

Some other principles of success? "What I call 'waveability' is one. When a customer comes in, I want our staff to wave, say, 'Hello, how are you?' By name, we hope. Make it a really friendly atmosphere.

"Another is to keep those egos in check. We're here to make money for shareholders, not massage our egos."

Your background, experience, and characteristics that may have led to your success? "My background in public accounting has been a big plus. And I lead by example. I don't ask others to do what I won't do. I believe in treating people like I would like to be treated.

"We've attracted some really good people to our organization. When you create something like this, it's a real rush. Two of our guys just exercised their options, and each made $1 million. Wow! I really enjoy helping my people make money!

"And you need to have fun while you're doing it. And I have no tolerance for bull— or excuses. I can be demanding.

"A lot of our people have been with good community banks, organizations like yours, First Colonial Bankshares, then have the experience of getting sold to a big bank. They quickly see that they don't likc the big banks, and when they land here, they don't want to lose it. They know how much better it is to be with a community bank.

"For planning purposes we have a retreat each June. The night before, we get our few key managers together for dinner with a glass of beer, and sit down. It starts with "Hey, guys, what's on your minds? What problems do you have?"

Last year, "four people in a row got up unsolicited and said basically the same thing: 'You young people who don't know what it's like to work for a big bank, cherish what you have here. Fight for it. You've got something great.'"

Holding company board compensation? "A director gets $1,200 per meeting and generally $500 for committee meetings. The chairman of the board gets a $65,000 retainer. The chairman of the risk management committee gets a $45,000 retainer. The audit committee chairman receives a $30,000 retainer. Chairmen of the compensation and corporate governance committees each get a $20,000 retainer. They can take it in stock or cash and may defer it."

The compensation committee is a responsible one, and Ed Wehmer is not a greedy CEO. His 2002 salary was $498,000. His stock options in 2001 amounted to 19,050 restricted shares valued at $358,000. In 2002 he was awarded restricted stock awards worth $55,000.

WINTRUST GOING FORWARD

Ed discussed specifics.

"The efficiency ratio is sometimes misleading. We manage off Net Overhead Ratio. The three major expense areas are salary, occupancy, and other expense. We use benchmarks to compare our banks' expenses. Our company and subsidiaries have only 822 full-time employees.

"As for interest rate management, or asset-liability control, we know that if rates go up two hundred basis points, our earning should go up about $1 a share.

"As for our wealth-management services, the Wayne Hummer purchases—Wayne Hummer Investments and Wayne Hummer Asset Management Company—have been very good for us and have excellent potential. We've already paid for the acquisition. We can make money on the liquidity balances, which are sizable. We can make loans on those balances. It's something an investment company cannot do."

Indeed, this Wayne Hummer acquisition was a shrewd move. It shows in Wintrust's high percentage of noninterest income of total revenues, 39.6 percent, contrasting with the median peer bank's 29 percent, as contained in the Stifel Nicolaus Second Quarter Report. It's an unusual figure, quite impressive for a bank of this age and size.

Wintrust's wealth management services are trust services, asset management, brokerage, and mutual funds.

Fee-based income was driven not only by wealth management fees (up 15 percent to $7.7 million), according to the Stifel Nicolaus Third Quarter update on Wintrust. It was also driven by fees on mortgage loans sold (up 20 percent to $4.6 million) and sale of premium finance receivables (up 83 percent to $1.2 million).

Other fee-income areas include mortgage banking, administrative services, and covered call premiums.

The future is bright. Wintrust "remains one of the true high-growth banks in our coverage and in the country, for that matter," says Stifel Nicolaus. "Historically, such high-growth banks have traded at a premium to peer of 25 percent or more."

"I couldn't do that? Could you do that? How can they do that? Who are those guys?"—the famous line from the 1969 movie classic, *Butch Cassidy and the Sundance Kid*—is used in Wintrust's 2002 annual report to praise Wintrust employees.

It's praise for a team, of course. Like any good CEO, Ed Wehmer, a self-effacing man, knows the value of a good team. But he as CEO puts that team together and leads. He is prime motivator, cheerleader, the one who leads. He's smart, experienced and driven and leads by example, with integrity and compassion.

Who are those guys? It's Ed Wehmer, with John S. Lillard, Wintrust's chairman, David A. Dykstra, the chief operating officer, and an outstanding staff.

It's an extraordinary team. But as Ed Wehmer says, "Heck, we're young, Paul, we're only one-third up that mountain."

Chapter 14

Bridge Bank NA, Santa Clara, California:

Dan Myers

The founders of Bridge Bank, NA, of California's Silicon Valley, are proud of their bank, and with reason. It makes an extraordinary story. Embracing ambitious goals, they boldly embraced a business plan that forecast a nineteen-month loss to shareholder equity of $6.2 million, including $1.1 million in preopening expenses, and lived to tell a tale of record-setting profitability and growth.

Bridge Bank, based in Santa Clara, was the first nationally chartered de novo startup in Silicon Valley in sixteen years. It became the fastest growing in California banking history.

Its initial public offering raised $19 million in April 2001, apparently the most ever (by $5 million!) for a new bank in Silicon Valley, after aiming at $15 million to $17 million.

Its second, a mere fourteen months later, raised $14.4 million after aiming at $12 million. It had commitments of $19 million but had to forego the difference because of Controller of Currency rules limiting the amount by which the offering bank may exceed its stated goal.

For 2003, its second full year, it had net income of $1.5 million, an improvement of $4.2 million over the 2002 net loss of $2.7 million. Its return on average assets and return on average equity were 0.68 percent and 5.56 percent, respectively. First quarter 2004 earnings were $466,000, and total assets were up $69 million or 25 percent from year-end 2003.

This bank had gone from its IPO to $350 million of assets in thirty-four months. It had turned profitable in its sixth quarter, its second full year.

At the year-end 2003, it had 1,500 satisfied customers, business customers all, with an average deposit of more than $100,000, all but forty or so rarely visiting the bank, but instead using courier services and the Internet.

How does all this happen? Who makes it happen? Its organizers, of course, seizing the moment when the market was ready, devising a plan and staying with it, predicting the outcome with airtight analysis, and not losing confidence as early losses piled up. These are people who told each other not that they would raise $8 million capital and work towards $100 million, but that they would raise $15 million and work towards a billion dollars.

The initial public offering of stock at $5 a share had 549 subscribers. Its $19 million-plus was the largest initial capitalization yet achieved by a preopening de novo commercial bank in California, the fifth largest ever in the United States. The second offering, in June 2002, at $6.50 a share, 30 percent more than the first, had 303 subscribers.

The bank started with seven executive vice presidents and a senior vice president, of a total staff of sixteen, obviously with an eye on big things to come. Eighteen months later, the staff was sixty.

Preopening expenses had been substantial, $1,100,000. So were operating losses—$5,119,000!—for the eighteen months that passed before they broke even. For three quarters ending September 30, 2002, for instance, net loss was $2,708,000.

But losses declined sharply. For the quarter ending September 30, 2002, the loss was only $485,000, compared to the previous quarter's loss of $928,000.

It was according to plan. But such a nervy plan, that looked ahead to an almost $6.2 million loss to shareholders equity nineteen months from opening!

Big things were happening, of course, to put minds at rest. By year-end 2001, seven months after opening, assets reached $96.3 million, more than any California bank had ever reached at the end of its first year.

By May 14, 2002, the end of the first full year of operation, the bank had $122 million in assets and $107 million in deposits.

In October 2002, it was awarded the Preferred Lender Accreditation (PLP) by the U.S. Small Business Association, which qualified it to approve its own loans and confirm SBA loans within twenty-four hours of application. (At year-end 2003 it had SBA loan offices in Sacramento, Santa Clara, and San Diego and stood in the top ten percent of lenders in California, producing more than $90 million in lucrative SBA loans in eighteen months.)

Bang! came the first quarterly profit, at year-end 2002, after nineteen months. Assets were $181 million. A month later, Bridge Bank stock was trading on NASDAQ.

Eight months after that, at the end of the third quarter in 2003, noninterest income of $1,859,000 was primarily from SBA loan sales of $1,497,000, which had averaged about $600,000 per quarter in earnings for the previous six quarters. Assets were $245 million, ROAA 0.82 percent, ROAE 6.96 percent, and profit year to date was $880,000.

Three months later, fourth-quarter 2003 net income had been $625,000. It was Bridge Bank's fifth consecutive profitable quarter. Return on average assets and return on average equity were 0.91 percent and 9.06 percent respectively. For the year net income was $1.5 million, half of that from the last quarter, as we see. ROAA and ROAE for the year were 0.68 percent and 5.56 percent, respectively. Total assets were $276.5 million, up from $181.2 million a year earlier, for a $95.3 million gain, 53 percent.

The two offerings of stock to the public—$19 million at $5 a share and $14.4 million at $6.50 a share—was selling at $12.90 a share on the NASDAQ exchange.

WHO HAS BEEN IN CHARGE HERE WHILE ALL THIS WAS GOING ON?

The founders have been running things. Daniel P. Myers, the CEO, a ripe young forty-three, worked in independent Silicon Valley commercial banks for twenty-one years before leaving his last position, as chief operating officer of Heritage Bank of Commerce, the $400 million lead bank of Heritage Commerce Corporation of San Jose, to join in organizing Bridge Bank in early 2000.

Hired by Phil Boyce, an acknowledged astute Silicon Valley investor and one of the valley's most influential bankers, at Pacific Valley Bank of San Jose, right out of college—DePauw University, Indiana, zoology major, minor in economics—Myers began a round of banks after Pacific Valley, where he had been little more than a go-for: Cupertino National Bank for eight-plus years, Burlingame Bank and Trust, where he became chief credit officer and then a senior vice president of the Pacific Bank when it acquired Burlingame.

It was "time in grade," as Boyce told *Silicon Valley-San Jose Business Journal*, and as such good training for a banker. Back then, he said, Myers was a "very persistent" fellow, eager and willing. "He's a self-driver. He motivates himself," said Boyce, who the *Business Journal* said is "known as one of Silicon Valley's most astute investors," in the same article. "He is very bright and confident. When you put those things together, you have a winner."

He's "an old-fashioned banker," the sort who "loves to visit his clients," said another former employer, John Rossell, who hired him at Heritage Bank. What's more, "he's a good administrator, witty and smart, a very creative commercial lender, and a strong advocate for his clients."

He's "ideal," says the Bridge Bank chairman, Allan C. Kramer, MD. "He's innovative but cautious and knows where he wants to go."

Kramer has been this route before. He was a founder of National Inter-City Bank in 1984 and helped merge it into another de novo bank, Silicon Valley Bank, for which he became a director. When he left the merged bank in 1995, its assets had reached nearly $2 billion. His role in founding Bridge Bank, which he called "the culmination of [his] twenty years in banking," was crucial, in that it was he who, on a tip from Bank of America veteran Dave Campbell, another director, contacted Dan Myers and recruited him as CEO.

Equally crucial was the role of Richard Brenner, a Silicon Valley pioneer and leader for over twenty-five years, who approached Kramer with the Bridge Bank concept in the first place. Brenner, founder and CEO of the Brenner Group, the largest provider of interim professional financial services to the early-stage technology industry, is ironically one of only two (of eight) Bridge Bank directors without direct banking experience.

The other is Francis J. Harvey, former top-level Westinghouse Electric executive who at year-end 2003 was awaiting Senate confirmation of his nomination by the president as chief information officer for the Department of Defense.

The other directors have experience that with Kramer's and Myers's adds up to over 150 years. David Chui was an original member of the Cupertino National Bank board. Barry Turkus was a founder of Silicon Valley Bank. Tom Quigg was with Bank of America for thirty-seven years, David Campbell for twenty-five years. Campbell was also a director for several community banks.

WHAT HAS BEEN THE SECRET
OF THEIR SUCCESS?

The CEO is at the heart of it, says Director Fran Harvey. "Dan brought not only wide experience in community banking but also high energy and enthusiasm. He has been unusually persistent about strategy. Early in 2002, three quarters or so into our existence, we kept losing money. Dan had said it was 'part of the plan,' but I can remember wondering if we were on the right track. There we were in a local economy that was in a rather deep recession, and he insisted on expanding—into SBA lending, factoring, asset-based lending, and so on.

"This meant adding staff and losing more money. But Dan always gave us a detailed break-even analysis showing when the new line of business would break even on a stand-alone basis. He also communicated a strong commitment to make it happen.

"I decided his persistence was based on his vision for the bank and that his was exceptional leadership ability. And I supported him. And as Dan had said would happen, the losses disappeared in the second half of 2002, in the last quarter.

"Our basic concept was to take advantage of a unique window of opportunity. At one time Silicon Valley had fifteen community banks. Most were absorbed [most recently Cupertino National Bank, purchased by Greater Bay, and Plaza Bank of Commerce, purchased by Comerica]. Now Bridge Bank is the only independent business bank under $1 billion serving the valley."

The quality of deposits is at the heart of things. Bridge Bank, "not asset-driven but funding-based . . . put a premium on core deposits." At year-end 2003, 35 percent of its deposits—$78 million—was noninterest bearing; and 33 percent—$74 million—was in money market accounts. Only a third—$34 million—were in time deposits over $100,000 and these only with customers of the bank. There were no brokered deposits. The total number of deposit accounts was 1,636 for a hefty average of $126,000 per account.

The bank's emphasis on core deposits is one explanation for its near 5 percent net interest margin (NIM)—compared to averages for California banks of 4.6 percent, for U.S. banks of 4.19 percent, and for its peer group of 4 percent—and this in a mere thirty-one months. In fact, Bridge has been above the California-bank average NIM since its fourth quarter.

The SBA lending has been mentioned. The bank also does a good deal of construction lending—for buying raw land for development, construction (commercial and residential, multifamily and single-family), home improvement, and speculation.

Its asset-based lending is secured primarily with accounts receivable and inventory. It also provides factoring of accounts receivable.

Loans at the close of the 2003 third quarter were $58.4 million commercial, $40.3 million SBA, $37.1 million construction, $19.5 million real estate, $10 million capital finance, and $4.5 million in other categories. Loan reserve was at a conservative 1.42 percent. There were no loans ninety days or more past due. There had been no charge-offs in the bank's two-plus years. The ratio of total capital to assets was a strong 15.37 percent, almost twice the OCC 8 percent minimum for a bank's first three years.

I wondered if there had been surprises. "The dramatic drop in short-term interest rates. With all the capital we had raised, we had an investment challenge!" Dan said.

"Another challenge was no surprise: Silicon Valley was in recession when we started. But I've been pleasantly surprised at how well we have done in spirit of that."

But the Bridge Bank organizers were at their best in anticipating challenges, in a sense eliminating the surprise factor. They did this in part by consulting with Ed Carpenter, founder and CEO of Carpenter and Company, the hugely successful investment banker in Irvine, California, whom I write about in another chapter. My first inkling of Bridge Bank came from him during our interview.

"This is a bank with an unusual plan adopted by an unusual group of organizers. They intended from the first to manage a very large amount of assets and started with a board and staff that could pull it off. The board was very experienced and of unusually high caliber. Some had even been bank presidents. In their CEO, Dan Myers, they got a rare combination of youth with great energy and solid experience."

It was Carpenter to whom six of the original prospective organizers came to talk about starting the bank (and to whom the board came later to sign him on as manager of their second public offering), and I can see Carpenter's hand throughout the formation and operation of Bridge Bank. Carpenter continues to remain close to the bank, Dan Myers told me.

As Myers told the *Silicon Valley-San Jose Business Journal*, the organizers wanted to "get the bank opened and moving." Many of them had started banks and knew the process. They used consultants for specific tasks, "to compress the time frame."

For instance, they had to be "armed with more than a gut-level feeling" as they entered their capital campaign; so they needed "specifics [such as] how the banking market is doing, what the investment returns have been."

Getting to operational specifics, I asked about the bank's compensation program. Myers and Chairman Kramer gave Fran Harvey much credit here. Harvey, who joined the board a few months into the bank's operations in July 2001, was chief operating officer of Westinghouse's $6 billion Industries and Technology Group when he left the company after twenty-eight years.

He heads the bank's compensation committee, which has a "generous" ten-year option program with three-to-five-year vesting, he said. Options account for 18 percent to 20 percent of total shares outstanding.

It's a matter of keeping top people, he said, noting the program's several components. Incentive payouts, for instance, are based on achieving quantifiable targets. "It's very sophisticated." In addition, the CEO has a "discretionary pot" from which to award other payouts as he chooses.

Compensation is one of five board committees. The others are (1) Loan, whose four members meet weekly, (2) Asset/Liability, (3) Audit, and (4) Marketing. The board meets monthly. CEO Myers and Chairman Kramer meet weekly. Directors are all depositors. A few have borrowed from the bank, in full compliance with bank regulations.

A management dynamic is "managed dissent," whereby no one is bashful about putting forth his own views but does so while respecting others' views.

I asked about the CEO's relationship with directors and which is more important to success, the CEO or the board?

"The CEO, or the board, or both," Myers said. "It depends on what the organization aspires to. If the bank wants to become just another community bank, then CEO or board can be dominant. But if the organization wants to deliver superior performance and rise above its competitors, then CEO and board work together to manage and govern the bank."

An operational note with special resonance for this book's treatment of de novo bank options: Bridge Bank is an industry leader in outsourcing. It contracts out everything but ALCO. This means what is required in or by credit review, compliance, CRA (Community Reinvestment Act), loan review, financial reporting (by Price Waterhouse), EDP, and item processing.

More specifically, its vendors provide systems and services for a virtual laundry list of functions: mainframe, statements and images, back-up site, ACH, item capture, wires, lockbox, bill-pay, and credit-and-debit cards. The suppliers are out there, qualified and inexpensive, says Myers. "It's much more cost effective."

BRIDGE BANK ON BALANCE

Bridge Bank scores very high in several achievement—calibration points that recur in this book.

☐ Its ratios are excellent: Earning assets to total assets are high, at almost 95 percent. Loans to deposits are low, at only 82 percent.

☐ It observes FASB 91, amortizing fee income over the term of a loan, not taking it up front.

☐ Its board and CEO are experienced and qualified. The board is small but effective. Allan Kramer commented: "We are creating shareholder value. It's what a board is expected to do." The CEO demonstrates drive and talent.

☐ Its business plan is simple, its organization "streamlined." Dan Myers observed: "We are very focused. We have a clear definition of ourselves as a business bank. We know where we want to go strategically. We execute with discipline."

Chapter 15

First Community Bancorp,

San Diego, California: John Eggemeyer

John M. Eggemeyer III is a good guy who's finishing first as one of the most successful and respected community bankers in the country—"one of the smartest bankers around, credible, candid, incisive," says Kathy Smythe, of the investment bankers Keefe Bruyette and Woods.

He is principal architect and chairman of First Community Bancorp, a San Diego-based bank holding company with $2.4 billion in assets at year-end 2003, and chairman and CEO of Indianapolis-based Union Acceptance Company, one of the nation's largest independent, indirect automobile finance companies.

His Castle Creek Financial and Castle Creek Capital, together comprising a merchant banking organization specializing in banking, thrift, and financial service which he founded in 2000, has invested in twenty-five companies and raised over $1.5 billion in capital for its portfolio companies.

First Community Bancorp, started in 1996, is the holding company for San Diego's First National Bank and the Los Angeles area's Pacific Western National Bank. The two together have thirty-two offices in Los Angeles, Orange, Riverside, San Bernardino, and San Diego Counties.

First Community's 2003 earnings were a record $32.1 million, $2.02 per share, compared to 2002's $16.9 million and $1.58. Its fourth-quarter 2003 net income was $8.4 million, 53¢ per share, compared to $6.4 million, 41¢, in fourth-quarter 2002.

First Community has been a bank-acquirer of the first order, acquiring eight between 2000 and mid-2003, including six in 2002, in the process tripling its assets. Many of these, "beset by bad loans or other problems," came "on the cheap," said the San Diego *Union-Tribune*, citing Los Angeles-based Professional Bancorp, bought for $8 a share, "a substantial discount" to its fifty-two-week high of $21.

Writing off the worst loans, Eggemeyer revived Professional Bancorp, which later merged with his other banks in the county under the name First National Bank of San Diego, which he acquired in September 2002.

The following seven banks, worth $1.6 billion, he acquired between January 2002 and April 2003:

Pacific Western National Bank	January '02	$259 mil. Assets
W.H.E.C. (Capital Bank)	March '02	148 mil. Assets
Upland Bank	August '02	112 mil. Assets
Marathon Bancorp	August '02	111 mil. Assets
First National Bank	September '02	688 mil. Assets
Bank of Coronado	January '03	80 mil. Assets
Verdugo Banking Company	April '03	179 mil. Assets

Eggemeyer is also a director of Minneapolis-based, $11 billion TCF Financial Corporation.

I know John well. We met in Chicago over ten years ago, related well to each other, and stayed in touch over the years. I consider him a friend.

He has a lovely family—his wife Martha and their three sons and twin daughters.

He's a Hoosier by birth, born and raised in Richmond, just east of Indianapolis. He went to Northwestern University on a football scholarship, proving in his words a "very average" offensive lineman. He intended to teach history and coach football, but a few weeks after graduation in 1968 wandered into First National Bank of Chicago one day, remembering a discussion he'd had with a campus recruiter.

"In my khaki pants I walked in and announced, 'Here I am!'" he recalled.

They gave him a part-time job, and he decided business was the life for him. In short order, he entered the University of Chicago MBA-finance program, remaining with the bank, where he eventually rose to a vice presidency, acquiring extensive experience in corporate lending, problem-loan collection, ALCO, and capital management.

In 1977 he joined Northwest Bancorp, in Minneapolis, where he stayed four years, serving successively as treasurer, senior vice president of finance, and controller, with involvement in acquisitions, venture finance, and consumer finance.

In 1981 he went to Chemical Bank in New York City as senior vice president of finance, leaving in 1982 to take over a "highly troubled bank," the old and revered First National Bank of Denver, one of fifteen banks held by First National Holding, Inc. "I was there a little over a month when the regulators came in to meet with our board about what they had found in their examination," he recalled. "'This bank is in terrible trouble,' they told us. They intended to place it under a cease-and-desist order, which is usually a death sentence. Not knowing any better, I said, 'Why don't you listen to our plan?' They looked confused. 'Okay,' they said. 'Come and present your plan.'"

They did. It was to increase loan reserves to 4 percent (they are usually 0.8 percent) and reduce staff from 2,400 to 1,250. It was a case of "telling the truth with the result that regardless of the problems, people roll up their sleeves," he recalled.

The bank was too dependent on brokered CDs, for one thing. John went to three big banks for help—his former employer Chemical Bank, Bankers Trust, and Security Pacific—asking $100 million from each in guarantees. Then he went to Bankwatch and said, "If you reduce the bank's rating, it will fail." They didn't.

"I told the regulators that if they allowed us to proceed with our plan, they'd be the first to know if things were not working. I had from Thursday to Tuesday to get all this done. Everything worked the way it was supposed to. The FDIC was amazed. Our board had First Interstate lined up to purchase the bank at a distressed price if the regulators didn't approve the plan. They did, and First Interstate moved away from the deal. As the plan was put into action and succeeded, our stock went up. Six months later, we had a buyer, at a very attractive price."

That was the saving of First National Denver. Once it was sold, a few years later, John returned to Minneapolis, joining First Bank System as executive vice president and president of its subsidiary, First Trust. He was there from November 1984 to April 1987, responsible for consolidating and managing its trust business.

"It was a terrible mistake. I did it for family reasons. First, the trust business is not nearly as exciting as banking. But from it I learned an important lesson, that once you've been a CEO in a stressful situation, it's hard to go to work for someone else. In this case my boss micromanaged my every decision. I couldn't put up with it. The outcome was inevitable. I was fired.

"I was mad at that and thought it would give me a black eye in banking. Now I know that was naive. I went to an investment banking company, Drexel Burnham Lambert, in Chicago, where I was manager of financial institution restructuring. I learned some important things there.

"One, that investment bankers are expected to sell what their traders want them to sell, not what's best for their clients. Two, how to close deals. Three, that I could create the job I wanted to do. So I went out to banks and thrifts and taught them how to restructure, how to get away from volatility.

"Drexel expected me to sell products they had. But the more I studied their junk bonds, the more I realized they were toxic wastes that were weighing companies down. So I decided to build a business around showing banks how to restructure around their core business.

"Drexel failed in January 1990. There were no jobs in the industry. I had been divorced two years earlier, and my new wife, Martha, convinced me to go out on my own. I had no money and no job, but a wealth of experience.

"I did one of those instinctive things you do in life. I printed up some business cards and went into business. It was one of my most rewarding years. I learned a lot about people during that time. Some who I thought were good friends never returned my phone calls, but some surprised me with their generosity. Who really are your friends? It was one of the most enlightening experiences of my life.

"Right off the bat, I got some very lucrative work. That was in February 1990. I've been buried in work ever since!"

His career has had "defining moments." One was his realizing, while at Northwest Bancorp in the late '70s, that in the non-dynamic though very stable Midwest, banking had to get into nonbank activities to increase earnings. One such activity was consumer finance. Indeed, one of the last things he did at Northwest was to put together the acquisition of Dial Finance.

Another defining moment was during his time at Chemical Bank, during a board meeting with Michael Blumenthal. "I was only thirty-five. He and I got into a lively debate about the future of interest rates and how best to structure an impending debt offering. Not until after the meeting did I remember that he had just retired as Secretary of the Treasury."

About his career in general: "I wish someone had given me a book on how to be successful, so I wouldn't have had to learn it the hard way. But I'm proud of what I've done, and I'm pretty good at knowing what I do well. I'm also pretty intuitive. A business acquaintance once called me intuitive. I was hurt.

I'd always thought I was intelligent, and now someone tells me I'm intuitive, which I equated with lucky.

"Fact is, I've been able to generate a lot of trust and confidence in people. That's been an important part of my success."

What else? "I have an organized and systematic approach to evaluating a situation. At Drexel I learned something at the famous 'predator's ball,' a gathering of some of the best entrepreneurs in the country. Many of them were what I call 'one-trick ponies.' They were successful once but found it hard to repeat that success. Others had multiple successes.

"What I observed about them was that each had a vision of what they were doing and where their success came from. And they pursued it. They were disciplined. They didn't hesitate to pass up deals that did not fit their formula. A key is to look for opportunities that fit *your* idea and systems.

"Over my fourteen years, I have tried to maintain a consistent vision of how to be successful. When I came to California in early 1994, a Chicago friend, John Rose, and I wanted to pull together three or four troubled community banks he had been meeting with. Our thought was through a holding company to get some economies of scale, put all the bad loans in a central point and inject some capital. It was a colossally dumb idea!

"To get four CEO bankers in the same room to agree on what assets to put in a pool would be a heroic undertaking, with no possibility of success. We decided we could recapitalize and fix banks one at a time, and merge them later. We persuaded three banks to go along with that model.

"We got the money from mutual funds and hedge funds who liked my background. We did not use conventional partnerships. What we did was buy stock on the same terms as they did with the same profit on a success. But we said, if they didn't like what we were doing, they could throw us out.

"This was very unconventional. We were telling them we would not ask them to do anything we wouldn't do. And with our dollars, which were much more precious because they represented a huge portion of *our* net worth.

"Paul, as you know, I'm not a self-promoter and keep a low profile. I don't give many speeches. I think what people say of me is 'John is a person you can reach an agreement with and the resultant contract will reflect what is said.' I've never tried to renegotiate a deal, partly because we figure out what a bank is worth before we go in.

"Another important way of doing business is to try always to do the right thing for the employees. I remember that my father got thrown out of a job at the worst possible time and I remember his pain and what it did to our family. When we make an acquisition, within forty-five days we get with the employees and give them in *writing* what to expect and what their compensation will be. We work out a generous severance package. I know how disruptive this is to families.

"I've never been sued. I've never sued anyone. The only time I've been in a courtroom was as a juror. A basic philosophy of mine is you never know when you have to walk over that bridge again, so don't be vengeful or bitter. I don't go into business situations when I feel uncomfortable with the people involved.

"In 1995 we got into a situation in a deal that would have been terrific for us, but I felt uneasy about it. We hadn't signed the agreement, but we paid money to get out of it. One way to avoid fights is to avoid fights. We've acquired nineteen banks in California since 1995 and have had only one unpleasant experience."

I asked if he knew my friend, Joe Stieven, of Stifel Nicolaus. "You bet I do!" he said. "I put together a deal to buy the $1.6 billion mutual thrift, United Postal Savings. I met Joe through that deal. We made six and one-half times on our money on the IPO price in eighteen months. Joe and his family made a lot of money on that deal!

"The company was a jewel, but there was a lot of noise; so we came up with a plan to get rid of the noise prior to the conversion. We did a subscription and had Keefe Managers and Franklin Mutual Shares standing by to purchase any unsold shares. The deal was a success from day one, and both have been significant investors since."

After United Postal came highly successful investments in Lafayette American Bank in Bridgeport, Connecticut, Western Bancorp in Newport Beach, California, Regency Bank in Fresno, California, and most recently, First Community Bancorp.

"We formed First Community Bancorp in 2000, having invested in its predecessor, Rancho Santa Fe National Bank, in 1995 at $3.60 a share. The shares are worth $34.50 today."

Rancho Santa Fe and another he bought in 1999, First Community Bank of the Desert, were described by the San Diego *Union-Tribune* as "small banks . . . struggling with deadbeat real estate loans." Eggemeyer "slashed costs and shifted focus from low-interest deposits to lucrative small-business loans," as he had done with other struggling banks, the *Union-Tribune* reported.

I asked about Castle Creek Capital. What is it, when did you start, how did you get the name? "From a town. The first left turn out of Aspen is Castle Creek. It's one of my favorite spots in the world," he said.

As for Castle Creek's origins, "In late 1994 my friend John Rose, whom I mentioned earlier in connection with an idea we had that did not work out, wanted to start a bank investment fund. He told me he had a friend, a college roommate, whose family would put in $10 million. Was I interested? Not at $10 million, I told him, but $25 million, I'd be interested; $25 million it was."

They started Castle Creek in 1995 at $73 million capitalization and eventually returned over twice the investors' money. When the fund is liquidated in 2005, the return will be a compounded 28 to 29 percent per year.

Because its biggest investment was a California holding company—Western Bancorp, which they sold in 1999 to U.S. Bancorp—the fund had to become a bank holding company.

The percentage of their investment varies. "We aim at being lead investor. So Western Bancorp was at first a 38 percent-ownership stock. But it was down to 11 percent ownership when we sold, due to our issuance of its stock in various acquisitions.

"Our goal is to produce a net return to investors which is at least two times the bank index over the comparable time span. We want to double the bank index. So we don't take credit risk, nor do we leverage our banks. There are two ways to do this. One is to buy underperforming banks and improve them. The other is to do roll-ups and get economies on scale."

I asked about Union Acceptance, the troubled auto-finance company in Indianapolis.

"We bought too early. We thought we understood the business, but we didn't. We didn't understand the company's problems well enough. Most important, we did not, we could not, anticipate the huge drop in used-car prices after September 11.

"The company went into bankruptcy. I've spent most of the last year trying to fix it, trying to wring out of the deal all that we could. We got it through bankruptcy quickly. The creditors appreciate our efforts very much. But it is too early to know what the company may be worth for the shareholders."

We got back to First Community and John's philosophy of how to run a community bank.

"Management is everything. Great management can be quite successful in poor times and can do great things in great times. Banking is a mature industry. As an industry it won't grow much more than the overall economy. There's not enough growth in it to excite investors. There will be more consolidations. It's inevitable."

At such a time, the key is aggressive management of expense—interest cost, operating expenses, loan losses. "Interest cost is the biggest expense. Our deposit structure has more to do with our success than anything else we do. The goal is to have the lowest-cost possible mix of deposits while at the same time servicing our customers.

"You have to go for 40 percent demand deposit accounts, not the 20 percent industry average. You want only 15 percent to 20 percent in CDs, against the industry's 40 percent to 50 percent.

"Our net interest spread is 5.5 percent, our net interest margin typically 6.25 percent, as opposed to under 4 percent for most banks. When we buy a bank, we move it towards a high percentage of demand deposits. Then we aggressively reduce rates on their CDs. Those customers will leave, but it helps our deposit mix.

"Everything runs off our deposit structure. We don't grow loans faster than our demand deposits, for instance. If your cost of money is low, you don't have to take risks on credit.

"Our net charge-offs since 1995 have been close to zero. We write off the bad loans of banks we acquire but still carry a large reserve of 1.65 to 1.75 percent. It gives a real comfort level.

"The second cost-control element is operating expense. You want to reduce operating costs, but not beat the company until it bleeds. California banks have several interesting characteristics. Their demand-deposit accounts cost more and therefore expenses are higher because real estate drives *everything*. Many banks pay, directly and indirectly, for title and escrow companies' big demand deposits. Not us. We don't do title company business and so are not saddled with these expensive accounts.

"We're not a retail bank either. As a business bank, our average account is $55,000. Retail banks' average account is $2,000. So our cost per dollar is a lot lower.

"The third cost element is branch size. The average deposit per branch is important. When we buy a bank, we want it in our market area. That way, we get *real* economies of scale because we can consolidate deposits in fewer offices. The average California branch has $44 million in deposits. Ours has $65 million, and that's rising quickly.

"The fourth element is, be careful how you spend your money. Our efficiency ratio, now at 52 percent, is continuing to improve as we consolidate. But management of operating expenses is not the only reason our efficiency ratio will improve. Another is interest rates, a big factor. As rates rise, our net interest margin should increase considerably. This too boosts our efficiency ratio.

"Noninterest income is for the most part not important for us. We make loans and accept deposits, but we have low fee income. We don't observe the old truisms. We are truly a 'monoline bank.'"

What about your relatively low loan-to-deposit ratio?

"If you get to 100 percent loan-to-deposit ratio, you spend too much time worrying about funding your balance sheet or not enough time managing deposit costs. I prefer to have a loan-to—deposit ratio around 85 percent with high liquidity and enough yield on loans to get a 6.25 percent net interest margin and 15 percent liquidity. If you get above that, you begin to lose your deposit pricing discipline."

Start-ups? "We don't do start-ups. I don't like the idea of losing money starting out. It doesn't feel good. We want to grow and have profits now. I would never make a deal that isn't accretive.

"Furthermore, we fight to take volatility out of earnings. We've always had premium valuation because we've increased earnings without volatility."

Subchapter S banks? Industrial banks? "I haven't given them much thought. But for the S corporation and its requirement to limit the number of investors, the advantages are greatly reduced by the new tax laws. As for industrial banks, they don't facilitate my way of doing business but force you to own higher-risk assets because you fund them with higher-cost CDs. That's 180 degrees from what I do. I dismissed that idea long ago."

How important are your boards? "A good banker puts together good people in the community who are willing to invest capital. Our boards are helpful in our smaller banks. On our corporate [First Community Bancorp] board, we have good people, usually all of them successful in larger corporations. They all have interesting points of view. I don't believe in compromising the cohesion and efficiency of a board by using board seats as part of the 'currency' in an acquisition."

How do you treat FASB 91? "We amortize fees over the life of the loan. We're really a business bank. We don't make home mortgage loans. We have our own home-mortgage broker [which packages home mortgages and sells them in the secondary market], in a separate division, across the street."

I asked about location. "If you want to grow and the area isn't growing, you have to steal business. It's hard work! I'd rather be in markets that grow faster than the national average over a longer period of time."

What's the future of de novo banking? "There will always be de novos. The last five years, there were a bunch of them, fifteen in San Diego County alone! But the pace will slow. There will be fewer."

How do you use options as officer incentives? How do you report them? "Our plan is shareholder-friendly. Options are expensed on a current basis. We're in the process of converting to a performance-based restricted stock grant, which I really like. We've essentially copied TCF's plan, which has been well received by investors since it was introduced three years ago.

"The CEO and his direct-reports [those who report to him] are given performance grants with a seven-year life that do not fully vest until earnings per share double and don't vest at all until EPS hits 75 percent. This plan clearly links key officers to shareholders, as opposed to the usual ten-year plan that requires only that the officer stays around that long!

"The next tier [of options] is not performance-related, but

vests over time. This seems appropriate, since nonexecutive officers, important as they are, have little control over strategy."

How do you report your purchases, and how do you pay for them? "Purchase accounting has its advantages, but for a company growing as rapidly as ours, it interferes with building real-time data for purposes of analysis.

"In our purchases we usually use a combination of stock— which trades at a very nice premium, seventeen and a half times this year's earnings, for instance—and cash. We trade at premium partly because analysts and investors know our model is simple and nothing will blow up. Our ROA is 1.6 percent but will be going up, because we've doubled in size in the last two years. That model puts a lot of goodwill on our books."

"John," I said, getting to one of this book's central issues, "tell me the difference between big-bank and community-bank strategies. You've been with several big, successful banks, and now you're a successful community banker. What are the differences?"

"Big banks are in a fundamentally different business. Because of the acute need to improve productivity, there was intense focus on production definition and distribution. Walter Wriston came to this understanding when he hired John Reed at Citibank. As part of banking's slow evolution, retail [consumer] banking became a classic product, for instance.

"First, there were acquisitions, then a need to standardize. It was very hard on customers, but big banks had no choice. They had to do it.

"Then there was an evolution of corporate business—a wholly different matter—in which the balance sheet is no longer a repository of loans but a warehouse for ultimate distribution.

"Now capital markets are highly standardized. The trick is taking those loans, putting them into a format, being sure those loans conform to standards.

"Left in the middle of all this is what small banks can do, fitting a lot of square pegs into round holes. The big banks don't know how to do that.

"A community bank rises or falls with how its staff interfaces with customers. That's easy if you're working in a small radius. On a national level it's much more difficult.

"On the other hand, in community banking you can't achieve scalability, which is not economies of scale but a driving of volume into a fixed base for an ever-decreasing cost of doing business."

John summed it up: "Paul, whatever the bank, the challenge is to work hard to understand the problem facing you, then put together a plan that aggressively addresses the major challenges, then execute.

"I was president of a large bank holding company and president of its largest bank, which was horribly troubled, at thirty-six, and luckily didn't know how dumb I was! Much of my thinking was naive. We had a simple but clear vision of what had to be done. We attacked the problem with a vengeance and never stopped to worry about failure. Maybe that is why our improbable plan to save the bank worked.

"Out here in California, it's been a very interesting time and I'm enjoying it. Banking is not the staid business it was in Minneapolis in the '80s. Opportunities are unlimited for those who dare to be different and who can execute. One thing that has never changed is that good execution *always* beats even great strategy. High-price consultants don't tell you that."

This book is *Good Guys Finish First*. John Eggemeyer is one of our good guys. As Kathy Smythe said, he is a man of his word. He has integrity and compassion. He's also one of the smarter bankers around. There are a few bankers around with whom you would not want to be in business. John Eggemeyer is one with whom you would *always* want to be in business.

Chapter 16

Vintage Bank, Napa, California:

Terry Robinson

When bank consultant-watcher Gary Findley named high-performing California banks for me, one of them turned up in my own backyard. This was the $366 million Vintage Bank, of Napa, chief competitor to the bank I founded, Napa Community. I wasn't too surprised at Gary's pick. We had studied Vintage in the process of organizing our bank, and we liked what we saw.

Napa exemplifies the process that deprives a community of community banking and at the same time presents opportunity for new banks. Vintage, around since 1985, once had two community-bank competitors, Napa Valley and Napa National. Napa Valley was easily the strongest in the area, with 40 percent of the market. The other two community banks and several branches of larger banks, including Bank of America, had the rest.

Then Napa Valley was bought by WestAmerica in 1993, and the two remaining community banks, Vintage and Napa National, made hay. How so? From poorly handled assimilation of its new property by WestAmerica that like big banks everywhere, did not know the territory. What happened?

Customers fled Napa Valley, now a WestAmerica branch, because it was no longer the bank they knew, and no longer offered the level of service they had become accustomed to.

Then Napa National went, bought by Wells Fargo in 2002, and again the community-bank advantage was dissipated. And again the remaining community bank picked up windfall customers, a bonanza, in fact, of disaffected people.

This was Vintage, which in 1989 had $30 million in assets but by year-end 2003 had over $366 million—largely because of the two big-bank acquisitions and subsequent loss of community—bank-style personal service. So Vintage grew rapidly and along the way became a perennial Findley Reports "super premier performing bank," in other words top of the line, and for good reason.

By 2003 its return on average assets was 1.55 percent for the year. Return on average equity was 18.56 percent. In the five and a half years ending year-end 2003, it had only one sizable loan loss—$150,000, with a recovery of $50,000—for a ratio of net loan losses to beginning gross loans of zero!

The architect of this striking success is Terry Robinson, who joined Vintage Bank at forty-one in 1988 as president and CEO. The bank was three and a half years old and had $26 million in assets. It also was operating, thanks to loan problems, under a memorandum of understanding from the Federal Reserve. "Fortunately, the bank's directors already had their arms around the problems," he recalled. Because of his experience, he fit perfectly the Ed Carpenter model of a community-bank CEO.

Now fifty-six and CEO of its holding company, North Bay Bancorp, since May of 1999, he is well groomed and articulate, possessed of a great smile that contributes to his being a natural salesman. He is known as a great motivator of people and is very involved in the community, open and sincere and a man who clearly loves what he's doing.

He joined Idaho-based Boise Cascade Corporation right

out of college—the University of Idaho, where his undergraduate degree in 1969 was in accounting. He had been born and raised in Idaho. After two and a half years, he took a leave to get his MBA in finance at the University of California, Berkeley, from which he joined Arthur Andersen in administrative services. In this capacity he helped audit the then two-year-old Napa Valley Bank. This is how he got to know Napa.

After three years at Andersen, he moved back to Boise to help start a de novo bank, the American Bank of Commerce, where he worked eleven years, rising to executive vice president and director. It was about $50 million in assets when it was sold in 1996 to First Security Bank, which lost him to Vintage Bank in September 1988. He heard of the opening through friends at Andersen.

The bank was in its original small facility on Soscol Avenue. It reminded me of First Colonial starting one of its banks in a trailer in Chicago. I thought Vintage Bank's start was similar.

The Vintage directors had begun conversations with the Department of Financial Institutions and the Federal Reserve about acquiring property down Soscol Avenue on which to build their bank. They broke ground in November 1988 and moved in ten months later. The first-floor area was 7,200 square feet, the upstairs three thousand square feet. It's where they are now.

"It was a lot of property for a small bank," said Robinson, especially regulators wanted fixed assets to be no more than half a bank's capital, which initially for Vintage was only $3.1 million.

Once the new building was in use and once new customers began to arrive because of the Napa Valley Bank sale, Vintage Bank began to open branches—on Browns Valley Road in 1990 and in the Bel Aire Shopping Center in 1996, on the site of a closed First Interstate office, both in Napa. The expansion was financed with a $2 million secondary offering in 1994.

SOLANO BANK

Mostly because they wanted to expand into neighboring Solano County, where they envisioned faster growth in May 1999, they formed a holding company, North Bay Bancorp, by a simple exchange of Vintage Bank stock. North Bay did a $5 million secondary offering in Solano County and raised $4 million in a private placement from existing Vintage shareholders, capitalizing the new bank at $9 million. It opened in July 2000, with a two-hundred-shareholder net increase, from nine hundred to eleven hundred. Three years later, North Bay did a $10 million trust-preferred issue.

While starting the Solano Bank, they made an important addition to their ranks in the person of Glen Terry, who came as founding CEO of the new bank in August 1999, after four years, 1993-97, as CEO of Napa Valley Bank following its acquisition by WestAmerica Bank. Glen Terry became president and CEO of Vintage Bank early in 2002, when Terry Robinson moved up to CEO of the holding company.

By mid-2003 Solano Bank had three branches in three communities—Benicia, Vallejo, Fairfield, where there was also a loan production office. The bank has its headquarters in Vacaville. John Nerland was its president and CEO.

Meanwhile, Vintage opened another branch on Main Street in St. Helena, in January 2000. For it Terry Robinson found the ideal manager, the recently resigned manager of the St. Helena Napa National (now Wells Fargo) branch, Jim Wright. He hired Wright as soon as the latter's noncompete period had elapsed. He "knows everyone in town," he said, and "has a huge following." By mid-2003 the branch was at $20 million in assets. The branch picked up four other St. Helena people from the WestAmerica Bank branch. The branch had a staff of seven by year-end 2003.

Yet another branch was opened mid-2003, the New Gateway branch in southern Napa County.

The two banks have room and capacity for growth, says

Robinson, who is not resting on laurels of their current 18.56 percent return on equity (ROE). Other branches are planned— one in the fast-growing Napa Valley communities of American Canyon (early 2004), Calistoga, and (maybe) Yountville, where Vintage Bank already has an ATM and after-hours depository service.

As markets, the two counties, Napa and Solano, differ considerably. Napa has "name value" but won't grow as much. Solano is well heeled, "less staid," and more open to change. Both have a strong sense of community, especially Solano County's Vacaville and Benicia.

Napa County's Fairfield, with its Travis Air Force Base, on the other hand, is more transient. Vallejo is appealing in some respects but has "challenging" demographics. "It's hard to get things moving there."

The boards are quite active. Like all boards, they have "phases," Robinson said. Early in a bank's life, directors bring business. "You rely on them for that," he said. "Equally important," they establish a bank's ethical standards, as in its credit culture, operating philosophy, and treatment of employees.

It has helped to have Conrad Hewitt, for instance, retired commissioner of California's Department of Financial Institutions and a director of the holding company, and Vintage Bank's chairman and holding company director, local CPA Jim Tidgewell.

The two banks have $450 million in assets between them and 156 full-time employees, which makes for a weak 70 percent efficiency ratio. But it's temporary, says Robinson, citing recent startup of the new bank (Solano) and branches.

Net interest margin is above average, at 5.15 percent. But their cost of funds is low, and at year-end 2003 demand deposits were at a healthy 25 percent of total deposits.

LOANS

Asset quality is crucial. Bad loans make banks fail. Robinson's advice is not to "overreach." It's what new banks commonly do, "but they are very vulnerable at that stage." Vintage and Solano banks have "very conservative" loan-deposit ratios, less than 70 percent at Vintage, 75 percent at Solano.

The DFI [California's Department of Financial Institutions] imposes loan limits of roughly $5 million on Vintage and $2 million on Solano, but bank policy imposes on officers a relatively low limit of $1 million, usually requiring anything higher than $1 million to go to directors, depending on collateral. The two banks participate in each other's loans, as would be expected.

They spread a loan's cost over its duration, as mandated by FASB 91. They do not do "aggressive accounting." They limit holding company charges to the Solano Bank as mandated by Federal Reserve statutes 23A and 23B.

With all this, the loan "pipeline," or ongoing supply, is "strong." Real estate loans loom big, 75 percent of total, as is common for California community banks. There's "a lot of comfort" there, as Robinson put it.

REGULATORS

The banks get along well with regulators, routinely consulting with them before major changes. Now and then the banks "go to the mat" with regulators, as Robinson put it, but not often. The Holding company director Hewitt, the former state commissioner, helps considerably in this regard.

The bank examination process is better these days. Examiners are "less process-oriented and more results-oriented, because more of them are bankers and fewer are bureaucrats."

Indeed, the choice of Federal Reserve membership was motivated by the nature of the examiners' oversight. Though a state bank, Vintage Bank joined the Federal Reserve Bank because the Fed is more flexible than the FDIC, in the view of its directors.

ADVICE FOR STARTING A BANK

Looking back, Terry Robinson is happy for the organizers he got for his bank, who became its directors. He is glad they were not just "a bunch of buddies" but a variety of people from various walks of life. He is convinced a community bank is "doomed" without such directors, people who are in it not "for the quick buck or preferential rates" but for a bank's overall success.

He is also all for the "fundamentals" of community banking. The banker has to know what he's doing. People want to deal with people who can handle a problem. They want someone they know in the driver's seat, someone who assumes a high profile in the community. A CEO has to put in a "horrendous" amount of time. It takes a terrific commitment. He doesn't have to be a world-beater. "He just has to keep from doing dumb things." And he has to take good care of his employees or they won't stick around.

One of the specific challenges is outsourcing. Vintage at first did its own electronic data processing. It was a mistake. A de novo bank should outsource everything, Robinson said. Fiserv, "a huge player" in EDP and item processing, or a concern like it would do fine. Fiserv uses the widely used ITI software, which is a plus.

Some outsourcing has to be delayed, such as the recent arrangement with MoneyLine, an Internet-based mortgage service. They had been reluctant to connect too soon to nonbankers, with their different approach to things. Once the two banks "got their legs," it was time to do so.

THE GOOD-GUY FACTOR

Do good guys finish first? Robinson thinks so, while admitting to "a segment" who cut corners, use aggressive accounting, and worry more about themselves than shareholders and employees. He avoids these people. It's not hard, he said, mainly because most community bankers are "extremely good people."

He enjoys his work, he enjoys life, whether helicopter—skiing in Canada, "shushing" through deep powder, or riding his Harley Davidson. Not the latter anymore, however. He is selling it, maybe for a '50s hot rod.

Skier, biker, or hot rodder, he remains the architect of a top-performing bank in yet another community where big banks bought little banks and thus created an opening for yet another little bank.

Chapter 16a

Dave Gaw, Organizer

This chapter could be "How Not to Start a De Novo Community Bank," and the founders of Vintage Bank would not object. They wouldn't object because after their poor start they got their arms around their situation and turned the bank into a Gary Findley super premier performing bank. But it wasn't easy.

Early on there were too many nonperforming loans, recalled David B. Gaw, a Napa Valley attorney, one of Vintage's principal organizers, who headed the bank's loan committee for more than eight years, learning on the job how to be a banker.

There was no profit for three-plus years. There were problems with regulators, who urged management changes. This occurred when they were "pretty close" to making a profit and the stock had bumped up (temporarily) from $10 to $18 a share.

It was too late. The management could not realize their vision for the bank. The founding president left, and so did several directors, including the chairman and largest shareholder, Dr. Houghton Gifford, and a valued CPA, Don Livingston. They made do with an interim president while searching for a permanent CEO. There were morale problems with staff.

It wasn't what Dave Gaw had in mind when he had suggested over lunch in 1983 to Wyman Smith, a partner in the firm Gaw had cofounded eight years earlier, that they start a savings and loan. Napa had no locally owned financial institution but the recently opened Napa National Bank. Several others bought into the idea, but for a bank, not an S&L; and Vintage Bank, well named for Napa Valley, was on its way.

They hired a consultant and worked for a year raising money and recruiting people. The consultant didn't work out: one of his bad ideas was to open in a tiny five-hundred-square-foot space on Soscol Avenue, rather than in a free-standing building. Luckily, they also brought in Arthur Andersen people from San Francisco, who were "wonderful," Gaw recalled.

For directors they got "a good cross section" of valley people. The problem was that none had any banking experience.

Selling stock was not a problem. Napa Valley Bank had done so well, and shareholders were enthusiastic about investing in another community bank. They raised $3 million.

So it went in the preliminaries. Faced with loan and other problems, they had to do something. They got a new credit administrator in Kathi Metro, who joined Vintage from Napa Valley Bank. She helped their loan underwriting "enormously."

They brought in some "great" directors. Gaw named James E. Tidgewell, Harlan R. Kurtz, Thomas H. Lowenstein, and Carolyn Sherwood.

Then came their big break in the CEO search. They had been interviewing potential CEOs and had narrowed the choice to two, "a sixty-year-old with great credentials" and Terry Robinson, "forty or so and hungry," who had been "up in Idaho for a number of years in banking," said Gaw. "We picked Terry."

"In he walked, and everything changed. Morale went up in weeks, as he developed a mission statement which he advocated strongly" and implemented his open-door policy. Some who had left the bank came back. Earnings started to go up.

"His philosophy is, be consistent, you don't have to be a

star. As Jim Collins says in his book *Good to Great*, citing the ancient proverb, there's the hedgehog and the fox. The fox jumps around while the hedgehog plods along. Terry is a hedgehog. He has purpose."

On the Vintage Bank board are what Gaw calls "different mind-sets." The chairman's position rotates every two or three years. There have been six chairmen. Gaw considers this "healthy." He has just stepped down as bank chairman and director but has stayed on as a director of the holding company, North Bay Bancorp.

The bank entered Solano County; why? It's one of the fastest-growing counties in California; Napa County is one of the slowest. Solano had no independent bank in its southern half when Vintage Bank opened there in 2000. Gaw knew the area, having started a law office there fifteen years previously; it had become the county's largest law firm. Terry Robinson looked the area over and liked what he saw. "It's how you decide things like that. We knew what we were doing."

They told the state's Department of Financial Institutions they wanted to blanket the area for their own protection from competitors and wanted to start three branches. The department did not like that at first, "but we convinced them."

Banks succeed or fail based on four considerations, as Gaw sees it. They get or hire: (1) a good consultant, (2) a good CPA firm, (3) a good board, and (4) excellent management.

Directors have to know it's hard work they are signing on for. "Bank board work is different. It's not like a regular business. But it's a great experience, and you can learn from it and apply it to your own business."

Most important is management, because management runs the bank, not directors.

Regulators? "They're wonderful. It was a good thing they were there during our crisis. You get frustrated with them sometimes, but they're very important partners."

Community banks ten years from now? Twenty years? "I can't believe they won't continue to do well. There will always be people who want to be involved with them. The industry may evolve—and that will happen—but community banks will still be there."

Are you glad you did it, start and stay with Vintage Bank? "There were days—there still are days, when I wonder about the time commitment. But I'm glad I did it, yes. It's been wonderful."

So picking the wrong consultant, hiring the wrong management, recruiting directors with no banking experience was no way to start a community bank. But founders can learn. Vintage Bank founders did. And now they have a top-performing bank.

Chapter 17

Modesto Commerce Bank,

Modesto, California: Jeff Burda

Modesto (California) Commerce Bank has the usual ingredients for de novo community-bank success, and then some. Its president and CEO, Jeff Burda, is experienced and competent. Its board is experienced, drawn from the community, and hardworking. Its focus is clear and profitable. It is entirely community-oriented. Its employees are imbued with enthusiasm that helps the bank achieve top-level efficiency.

In addition, Modesto Commerce's capitalization went according to an extraordinary plan by which ninety community leaders were recruited as "founders" who not only invested amply but also took responsibility for attracting a set volume of loans and deposits, achieving for themselves a handsome profit.

In fact, Modesto Commerce, a $330 million bank, was bought in November 2003, by Bank of Stockton, paying a big price—eighteen times trailing twelve months earnings and double book. Stockton had targeted the Modesto area for expansion, had even bought land for a new bank and was planning to file for a charter when Modesto Commerce became available. It was just what Stockton wanted.

For one thing, its president, Jeffrey Burda, was the ideal

community-bank CEO as Stockton's Tom Shaffer understood it and as described by veteran California bank consultants Ed Carpenter and Gary Findley. He was the right age, mid-forties, with the right experience, community banking; and he was committed to entrepreneurship. Hoefer and Arnett's Steve Didion, who midwifed the sale to Bank of Stockton at that excellent price, felt the same way.

Burda's experience: he had entered banking (inauspiciously, as it happened) after several years in accounting with Peat Marwick Mitchell. This had come after college (University of Notre Dame), a short but sweet six-month golfing career, and an MBA in accounting (Santa Clara University). This was in 1980. The bank was in Turlock, fifteen miles south of Modesto, eighty—some miles east of San Francisco. It was not a good bank. He said so and was fired—a few years before it went under, messily and with years of litigation.

It was Burda's lesson in how not to do community banking. His second try was more of the same, until he became part of the solution to a bad situation, at then four-year-old Modesto Banking Company. He joined Modesto in 1982, at thirty, as chief financial officer. Eight years later, this bank, twelve years old and with assets of $175 million, got a very bad headache.

A devastating array of problems—"inadequate capital . . . a large volume of poor quality loans . . . hazardous lending and lax collection practices . . . inadequate provisions for liquidity and funds management . . . inadequate routine and controls policies, operating [so] as to produce low earnings . . . operating in violation of applicable laws or regulations," to quote the FDIC cease-and-desist order—had generated a memorandum of understanding from California's Department of Financial Institutions and a "formal agreement" with the Federal Reserve. The president quit abruptly. It was not a happy moment.

Burda, thirty-eight years old, had greatness thrust upon him. The board named him president, and he saved the bank, drawing on what he had learned in twelve years of banking and on a nicely timed uptick in interest rates. The bank's mortgage department produced excellent earnings that paid for the bad loans. The crisis passed, the bank was sold—in 1993, to California Bankshares, which was later sold to U.S. Bancorp, Portland, Oregon, which was later sold to U.S. Bancorp, Minneapolis.

He stayed with U.S. Bank-Portland for a year as a regional vice president in Sacramento, learning how a big bank works and not particularly liking it. Then came a fateful New Year's Eve telephone conversation with a friend, Modesto businessman Jeff Grover, about starting a bank. The conversation developed into a sort of New Year's resolution. By spring, 1997, wheels were turning. Burda left U.S. Bancorp in June.

Modesto was the focus. Bereft of community banks after its two were sold, the city was ripe.

The two Jeffs readied a plan, taking their cue from how Sterling Bancshares, in Texas, was founded in 1974. They would raise $7.5 million, of which $3 million would come from thirty "founders," each putting up $100,000. The founders would be "a broad spectrum" of business and civic leaders who pledged to bring in at least a million dollars each in business loans or deposits.

The response was excellent. The Founders Club, recruited by ten directors picked by Burda and Grover, grew to ninety. The public offering in December sold $9 million of stock in a few weeks. But an even broader base of community support was in order; so there was a secondary offering in March 1998, that, oversubscribed by $2 million, raised $4.5 million. Two hundred other investors had come in with the minimum $5,000 each. The bank had $13.5 million to start with.

Burda and Grover had wanted as few directors as possible. Nine of them became founders. Four directors had already been community-bank directors.

Having a plan was half the battle, said Burda. Getting the right people was the other half. You have won or lost "before you open the door," he said. The goal was to be dominant in the community as a business bank concentrating on businesses of $500,000 to "several hundred million" ("high net-worth") customers. "We don't say 'small businesses.' We say 'owner-operated businesses.'"

BRANCHES

Branches have figured tactically, two in Modesto and one in nearby Turlock. But no more are planned, regardless of what Burda calls "a big push" to open branches. A "herd mentality" is at work, he says. "I don't understand it."

The Turlock branch, opened in March 2002, is called Turlock Commerce Bank, a division of Modesto Commerce Bank, which gives Turlock a sense of it being their own. Preparing for it, the founders were encouraged in the fall of 2001 to invest in a convertible preferred issue, the conversion tied to the new branch's deposit level for the fourth quarter of 2004.

It would be a stair-step conversion, with maximum conversion of two for one if the branch reached $57 million in average deposits—$1 million for each founder who bought the stock at $25 a share. The stairs did not matter, as it turned out, because the $57 million was reached, and it was two-for-one for the founders. Another good day for them.

THE RATIOS

And typical for the bank as a whole, whose ratios at year-end 2003 were quite good:

Return on Assets	1.55 percent
Return on Equity	17.55 percent
Net Interest Margin	4.33 percent
Efficiency Ratio	36.65 percent

The efficiency ratio, very low and very significant for a smaller community bank, results from Modesto Commerce's business-customer focus. From fifteen employees when it started in 1998, the bank had forty-seven in 2003, one for every $6 million or so in deposits.

The bank has a very high 30 percent ratio of demand deposits to total deposits—all business-related, of course.

The bank's net interest margin (NIM) has slipped, to about 4 percent, as it slipped for most banks because of interest-rate compression.

The bank raises money as needed by means of an Internet-based service, "CD Express." One-year money would cost more if they got it locally. The bank's loan-to-deposit ratio is a conservative 75 to 80 percent.

The bank had a good deal of liquidity in mid-2003—$25 million in capital and $50 million in federal funds. Its investment policy was also conservative: its portfolio was in government agencies.

LOAN LOSSES

Loan loss has been negligible. In five years, the bank had written off a grand total of two loans—$560,000 gross—out of 174,000. Loan reserve was 1.3 percent. "It's the kind of loan customer we have," he said. "The founders [as loan customers] represent gold-plated credit."

Commercial or working-capital loans were $85 million. Real estate loans, all of it secured, were $135 million. Consumer loans were $5 million. Very little construction lending is done, all of it in mortgages presold in the secondary market. By year-end 2003, total loans were $220 million.

The bank does no mortgage lending, annuities, or insurance. They would be "distractions." Besides, some of the founders are in these businesses.

The bank outsources everything:

- ☐ Electronic data processing is done with Jack Henry & Associates through a service bureau out of Denver.
- ☐ Item processing is with Fiserv, which sends items to San Leandro, from which they are sent to Denver.
- ☐ Asset liability reports they generate with Profit Star software.
- ☐ Loan review is handled through Steve Schendel, in the East Bay.
- ☐ Auditing is done with Moss Adams, formerly Grant Thornton, with its Stockton office, at a yearly charge of $40,000.
- ☐ Marketing is through a local company. They use little advertising. Focus is on one-to-one selling and direct mail.
- ☐ Legal work is done with a local firm.

Burda believes in outsourcing. "If you don't, you get distracted. One staffer oversees all of it, which puts us way ahead. Our time is entirely for client issues."

A major factor in Modesto Commerce success is that "almost all" its personnel returned to community banking from community banks that had been purchased by bigger banks, because they prefer community banking. "They are very productive," he said. "It's the main reason for our good efficiency ratio."

"A de novo bank relies on excellence inside and outside the bank. The one you can control," he said. "The other is the environment in which you operate. It's a big help that Modesto Commerce is the only community bank in town. There were two community banks. U.S. Bancorp bought one; WestAmerica bought the other. Our competition is U.S. Bancorp, WestAmerica, Union Safe Deposit, and Wells Fargo. It's from these banks we have gotten most of our business. Having no community-bank competition helps greatly. Timing meant a lot to us."

Burda is a CEO who has done all there is to do in banking including marketing. He feels he has developed "an environment that makes people successful." He knows "what gets you in trouble." At Modesto Commerce he has "established a good credit culture," firmly believing that a de novo bank cannot afford to make bad loans. His board does not approve loans. That would be "scary," he said. Loans are for bankers to make, not bank directors.

Loan fees are mostly amortized (spread over the length of the loan), but "you're allowed to cover costs immediately, and some go into earnings. But the costs you cover have to be justified."

He's active in the community. He's been chairman of the Chamber of Commerce, chairman of the community hospital, president of the country club; he has headed up United Way.

Banking organizations are another story. They are expensive, for one thing. Modesto Commerce people belong neither to ABA nor California Bankers. "We believe in talking to our [community-banking] peers," he said. "That's a better use of time."

The founders remain important. "They're special. We do a lot with them." There's a founders golf day, "which they all enjoy," holiday open houses and the like. "We stay very close to our founders." Not all of them brought in a million in business, as was intended, but "all but a handful did. The founders' base did very well. There's no question about it."

If he had it to do again, he'd consider one change, making Modesto Commerce a subchapter S bank, thus eliminating double taxation. This is very important for Modesto Commerce, whose corporate tax is a high 41 percent. On the other hand, a subchapter S bank is limited to seventy-five shareholders. This works well in a family-owned bank, but not for a broad-based community startup.

His startup pay, $100,000 for the first three years, rose to $175,000 in 2003. Senior staff, officers, and directors all received options. Senior staff received incentive options. He received ninety thousand options, 4 percent or so of outstanding shares. With the fifteen thousand shares he bought as his $100,000 investment as a founder, he had 105,000 shares and was thus the bank's largest shareholder. For him it meant a $2,730,000 profit in five years.

The founders each got $390,000 in five years, four times their $100,000. "Not bad," he said. The multiples were eighteen times earnings and about 2.05 times book value.

Between him and new-owner Bank of Stockton is a noncompete agreement for a one-hundred-mile radius. He has "a rolling" (automatically renewed) two-year contract and happily anticipates life with Tom Shafer and the new parent. Theirs is a long-term horizon, he said. It is not a public company, but family-owned, with the "different viewpoint" that goes with that.

There will be no name change, no terminations, no reductions in staff.

Like other bankers here quoted, Burda has had good relationships with state and federal agencies and is bullish on regulators and always gives them "a heads-up" when a problem arises. Not all CEOs feel that way.

He started off at Modesto Commerce on good terms with them because he had saved the previous bank he was with, which was headed for an FDIC loss. Regulators are more particular these days about whom they will approve as a CEO, he noted. They require more experience. When he went to them to start Modesto Commerce, they said, "Great!"

Chapter 18

Valley Commerce Bank, Phoenix, Arizona:

Bob Homco

Valley Commerce Bank was opened in Phoenix, Arizona, in 1995. By 2003 its assets had grown to $155.5 million, and it was an unqualified success. But it might have been a bigger success if it hadn't been for the controversies and law suit involving Joe Reid, of Capitol Bancorp, who was an early investor in Valley Commerce and its first chairman and CEO.

Reid lasted 15 months at those positions, before being asked by the board to resign. He did resign but only after "the independent directors of the board voted by a majority of 70 percent to seek termination of [his] employment as chairman and CEO," according to a letter from Valley Commerce director Jay Fishman to shareholders, September 30, 1996. Once Reid had resigned, the board installed Homco as CEO. Fishman, a member of the Capitol Bancorp board since 1991, resigned from that board at this time.

Two shareholders, James Dykstra and Jerry D. Collins, on July 7, 1997 sued the bank[1] and 13 bank-related individuals,

---

[1] Superior Court of Arizona, Maricopa County, case #CV1997-012425, "James Dykstra, Jerry D. Collins, Michael Kasten, and Michael J. Devine, plaintiffs vs. Jay Fishman et al."

including Fishman and Homco, on five counts, which read in part as follows:

Count 1: "Alleges that the defendants committed state securities fraud by misrepresenting things in their prospectus . . ."

Count 2: "Charges defendants with state securities fraud . . . and scheming to sell bank shares below their fair value."

Count 3: "Seeks an injunction against the bank's future sale of shares . . ."

Count 4: "Seeks a mandatory injunction because the defendants (specifically Fishman) did not get approval and register the bank holding company Fishman formed."

Count 5: "Seeks dissolution of the bank because it is being operated fraudulently by Fishman, others, and the bank holding company."

About 10 months later, on April 30, 1998, Judge William J. Schafer III, of Maricopa County (Arizona) Superior Court, rendered summary judgment in favor of the bank and all other defendants. More arguments ensued. Two Capitol Bancorp directors, Michael L. Kasten and Michael J. Devine, joined the suit as plaintiffs. About 10 months after that, on March 4, 1999, Judge Schafer again granted summary judgment for the defendants, "dismissing the plaintiffs' complaint and awarding the defendants their costs of the suit."

Once the suit was settled, Homco, who hadn't counted on all that trouble, moved into high gear for the bank, of which by now he was CEO as well as president. He drew on his own history—13 years with Norwest Bank of Minneapolis and 10 with Biltmore Investors Bank of Phoenix. He was a Hoosier by birth, in South Bend, Indiana, an Illinoisan by upbringing from fifth grade, after his family moved to Chicago-suburban Lansing, Illinois, where he lived for 18 years.

The family was strapped financially. He picked beans and took on other jobs to help out. College was not an option. He joined the Air Force during the Vietnam war, spending four years at Eglin AFB, Florida, and in Thailand working as a mechanic on F-4 jets.

Back in civilian life in 1969, he worked briefly in Florida, then returned to Lansing, Illinois, where he began his financial career with Dial Finance (now Wells Fargo Finance), in nearby Hammond, Indiana. By 1979 he was a district manager in the Minneapolis-St. Paul area. He stayed there when Norwest Bank bought Dial.

But in a few years, "tired of the upper Midwest," in 1983 he went south (and west) with his wife and two children to Phoenix to join the newly opened Liberty Bank, heading up its loan-production office (LPO) in the medical-practice part of town and making excellent contacts in the process.

He had been at this two years, when in August, 1985, a local banking tycoon, Bob Withers, talked him into joining another bank, the Biltmore Investors Bank, in a key role, as senior credit officer. It was an exciting time for banking, Homco recalled. He welcomed the opportunity.

He served 10 years at the Biltmore bank, five of them under Johnson Wax Company ownership. The Johnson Wax deal was negotiated in 1989 by an old friend of mine from Milwaukee, Dick Jacobus, who had sold his Milwaukee bank to Sam Johnson and had become its president.

Homco's time at Biltmore ended with his succumbing to the lure of a headhunter, who came to him in August 1994, with an offer to help Joe Reid start Valley Commerce, Reid's first Arizona bank. He took the offer and went with Reid and a group of private investors. He later concluded it was not a good choice.

Valley Commerce opened in April 1995, with Homco as president and seven employees, five of whom had followed him from Biltmore Investors Bank. It got off to a strong start. Homco brought in $12 million in loans in the first 60 days. The bank turned profitable after a mere four months. Homco called it "the rebirth of joy [in] a banking relationship."[2]

---

[2]   In letter to the public, on the bank's Web site, www.valleycommercebank.com/about/letter.html

But there were problems with the chairman and CEO. In a February, 1996, meeting of Valley Commerce directors, 70 percent of them agreed that Reid had to go. In April "a substantial majority" of shareholders put it in writing, in an April 18, 1996 letter to directors from their lawyer, Michael Lewiston, of Bodman, Longley & Dahling, in Detroit, saying, "We ask the board of directors to remove Joseph P. Reid as chairman and CEO of the bank."

They also wanted no connection with Capitol Bancorp. "Our clients do not have significant interests in Capitol and desire no relationship between it and Valley Commerce Bank," Lewiston said for them in his letter.

In early February, 1996, Lewiston continued, "we and several shareholders met with Mr. Reid, at which time we asked him to voluntarily resign his positions with the bank." In a letter to shareholders September 30, 1996, Fishman said, "Mr. Reid's employment as chairman and CEO terminated." Reid had resigned on September 6, 1996.

Shareholders Dykstra and Collins promptly sued the bank and its directors. The suit was decided on March 4, 1999. Homco finally had respite from a major distraction.

So did Jay Fishman, who had led the charge against Reid. His involvement with Reid had begun in 1991, when Reid's Capitol Bancorp bought a Farmington Hills, Michigan, savings and loan of which Fishman was chairman. Fishman, owner of an international investment counseling firm, Jay A. Fishman, Ltd., joined the Capitol Bancorp board.

A Michigan native, raised in Benton Harbor, with an MBA from Western Michigan University, where he briefly taught finance, he had spent two years at National Bank of Detroit as an investment analyst before starting his firm in 1970. He was co-author of a 1970 book, *Corporations In Conflict: The Tender Offer*. Dapper, successful, he manages over half a billion dollars for clients in 16 states, including some high-profile Detroiters and Chicagoans.

He had helped Reid start Valley Commerce, raising much

of the capital. Reid had suggested he help start an Arizona bank because he had an office in Phoenix and clients in Phoenix, Scottsdale, and southern California. He resigned from the Capitol board when Reid resigned from Valley Commerce.

Meanwhile, by year-end 2003, Valley Commerce was doing well. Its loan-to-deposit ratio was about 90 percent. None of the deposits was brokered. The DDA (demand deposit account)-to-total-deposit ratio was a whopping 30 percent. That demonstrated, said Homco, the ability to promote relationship banking. Much of this success stemmed from Homco's own relationship with the local medical-professional community, which accounted for 65 percent of the customer base. It's Homco's niche.

He is rightly proud of the bank's loan losses' totaling only $50,000 since opening. The bank has a 1.2 percent loan loss reserve.

The bank's efficiency ratio is high at 61 percent, but a major effort is underway towards lowering that. With 35 employees, Homco considers the bank somewhat overstaffed.

The directors are quite active. There's an audit committee; a loan committee on which all take their turn; a strategic planning committee; and a business development committee of nine directors, of whom three or four are active. Three directors live outside the state.

Directors are paid $750 a meeting and $250 a committee meeting. They receive no stock options.

Back room, audit review, and other services are outsourced.

Loan review is handled by a retired banker who comes in quarterly and charges $100 a month.

A new compliance officer has been hired.

Asset and Liability Management Committee (ALCO) work is done in-house.

Marketing is done internally by the board and a staff member. Bob Homco is active in this.

Human Resources work is done in-house by the officer who handles accounting.

The bank uses three to four local law firms, specialists in the areas needed.

As for expansion, the board is looking at two new loan production offices, one in southern California and one in the Phoenix area.

They use a courier service, "but you really need people out there," on site, says Homco.

The bank's Internet services, launched in 1999, have been very successful. More than 40 percent of commercial customers use Internet for banking transactions, Homco reports.

Their hundreds of local ATM locations are handled by Wells Fargo.

A new branch was opened October 1, 2003, in North Scottsdale. In the fourth quarter of 2003, a holding company was established, Valley Commerce Bancorp, Ltd., with a one-for-one stock exchange. Also in the fourth quarter, the holding company issued $5 million of trust preferred.

The key to successful community banking? "The president has to wear two hats," says Homco, credit and marketing (business development). "If the president can handle marketing and nothing more, the bank will get into trouble."

Moreover, "the smart president" wants checks and balances and establishes a niche. "Without a niche the bank will fall. You can't be everything to everybody."

The Valley Commerce board:

- ☐ Jay A. Fishman, Chairman, president of Jay A. Fishman, Ltd.
- ☐ Robert A. Homco, president and CEO
- ☐ Gregory S. Anderson, Investor
- ☐ H. Samuel Greenawalt, consultant with Standard Federal Bank N.A.
- ☐ Carolyn J. Johnsen, attorney
- ☐ Richard A. Rector, Chairman, Realty Executives

☐ David F. Righi, M.D., Chief Financial Officer, Valley
  Anesthesiology Consultants
☐ James A. Sharp, Jr., vice president, City Management
  Corporation
☐ Fredric G. Weber, Investor
☐ Anthony T. Yeung, M.D., president, Arizona Institute
  for Minimally Invasive Spine Care

Fig. A, History since founding:

	Net Loans	Deposits	Assets	Profit/Loss	Equity
1995	$14.5 mil	$42 mil	$46.6 mil	$<368> thou	$4.8 mil
1996	21.0 mil	54 mil	59.6 mil	476 thou	5.2 mil
1997	24.0 mil	58 mil	63.8 mil	511 thou	5.7 mil
1998	21.0 mil	65 mil	74.2 mil	622 thou	9.4 mil
1999	58.5 mil	74 mil	85.0 mil	751 thou	10.0 mil
2000	73.3 mil	93 mil	105.0 mil	1.20 mil	11.3 mil
2001	64.8 mil	87 mil	100.0 mil	900 thou	12.3 mil
2002	86.3 mil	88 mil	137.0 mil	1.40 mil	14.0 mil
2003	90.4 mil	103 mil	152.4 mil	1.58 mil	16.7 mil

In 2003 the ROAA was 1.08 percent. The ROAE was 10.96 percent.

Chapter 19

Napa Community Bank, Napa, California

I thought I was retired and out of banking when I sold First Colonial Bankshares to Firstar Milwaukee in January 1995 and moved to Napa, California, in 1996. I was content with a small winery that I bought, Astrale e Terra, making great red wine.

That changed slightly when a friend, Congressman Mike Thompson, called me in early January 2000. Mike is our congressman, representing California's first district, a huge district extending south of Napa, just north of San Francisco, all the way to the Oregon border.

A moderate Democrat who draws heavily from the Republican side, Mike had previously represented California's second district in the state senate, where he chaired the powerful budget committee. He serves currently on the U.S. House transportation, agricultural, and budget committees. He's a Purple Heart Vietnam veteran of the U.S. Army, having served as staff sergeant and platoon leader with the 173rd Airborne Brigade.

I had called Mike shortly after I arrived in Napa, on the suggestion of my friend Carlee Leftwich, former mayor of Yountville, California. Mike invited me to have coffee with him at Pacific Blues Café in Yountville. Carlee said he and I would relate, and we did, politically in our approach to most social issues and in our fiscal conservatism.

I liked him personally and immediately sensed him to be the person of his reputation, honest and dependable. That sense has been fortified over the years. He and his wife, Jan, and my wife and I have become good friends.

When Mike called in January 2000, from his office in Washington, he said, "Paul, as you may know, Wells Fargo Bank recently purchased one of the two remaining community banks in Napa, Napa National Bank. What you don't know is that because of the sale of Napa National several potential investors want to start another community bank. I told them about you, that you were a successful community banker with excellent credentials and experience with whom they might like to partner. Would you want to talk to them?"

I said, "Sure, I'll talk to them, Mike. But I'm not sure I want to get totally involved because I'm retired and having great fun with my new winery."

Mike replied, "Nothing ventured, nothing gained. Why not meet with Paul Krsek and Andy Bartlett, of St. Helena?" I said I would.

Paul and Andy and I met with Mike Thompson on January 20, 2000, in Mike's office in Napa. I found them to be nice guys. Paul had come to St. Helena several years before and started his investment company, Krsek and Andrea, building it into a modest but respected company. Andy is a bright, well-educated, enthusiastic lawyer and entrepreneur.

Paul said he could raise the required capital, which I estimated to be about $7.5 million, from his own client base. Andy said he would do the legal work and might like to be chairman or CEO.

Two days later, I sent Mike and Andy a memo saying, "I'm certain that if properly set up and administered, the community bank idea in Napa Valley would work." At that time we were thinking the bank would be in St. Helena, because that is where Andy and Paul lived, as did many of the potential investors.

In that memo, I introduced questions and made suggestions.

1. What kind of charter do we want, state or national?
2. What would be the composition of the board? How many directors? How would they be picked and who would be chairman?
3. How much capitalization would the California Department of Financial Institutions require? (My estimate was $7.5 million.)
4. About staff: I told them there were four key positions:
   4.1 President-CEO: He or she must have experience in community banking and sales and (preferably) be an experienced lender.
   4.2 Chief credit officer: Must have solid lending experience.
   4.3 Operations officer.
   4.4 Chief financial officer.
5. About the facility: To lease or to buy? And where?
6. Name for the bank? It should have "community" in it.
7. Estimate of preopening expenses: $300,000.
8. Earnings projections: $300,000 loss the first year, break even in the second, make back the initial loss in the third.
9. What kind of marketing niche to fill?
10. What services to be outsourced?
11. Develop a time line, get application in soon before other potential applicants.
12. Get four or five key backers together right away as an organizing committee, to start the process.

At first I thought we could form a conventional de novo community bank, outsourcing audit, legal and loan review services.

I also thought Paul Krsek could raise the capital we needed—$7.5 million—from his investment clients in a private placement.

I anticipated an independent loan review service like the

one we had for First Colonial—a group of retired FDIC and state banking commission examiners.

We also would need an audit oversight group, asset-liability assistance, and compliance counsel.

I figured we would have a good lawyer on our board who, through his firm, would provide most of the bank's basic legal work.

I presumed that one of several good California investment banking firms would help on the charter application and that like almost all de novo bank organizers we would hire someone to help put the bank together, a firm such as Carpenter and Company or the Findley Group.

As for outsourcing services, however it became apparent that Napa was no Chicago, where you had your pick of competent providers.

It also became apparent early in the process that Paul Krsek was overly optimistic about his capital-raising capabilities. Largely because of that question of raising capital, I decided we had to consider an alternative, namely partnering with an established bank to provide capital and "back room" services.

I had no intention of staying with the bank for any extended time. I had "been there, done that" with First Colonial and didn't want to put in a lot of time and be tied down for any time with a small community bank in Napa.

My intent was to get the bank set up, opened and operating, then step down.

I suggested we pick as chairman a local businessman with a higher Napa-area profile than I.

Partnering would solve both problems—raising capital and getting backroom support.

I went to Chicago and saw my old friend, Mike Sammon, who was associated then with the St. Louis investment firm of Stifel Nicolaus. Mike had started the banking division of the investment firm, Chicago Corporation, in the 1980s and had helped in the IPO of my bank, First Colonial, in November 1984. Thereafter, he went to Howe Barnes in Chicago to start up their banking division, and then to Stifel. He now works for Friedman, Billings, Ramsey in its Chicago office.

Mike is a brilliant small bank analyst and bank stock counselor. Over the years he had been a tremendous resource for me in keeping track of bank values and activities, and we had become good friends. I told him about the Napa Valley bank project and asked about firms with which to partner, in case we needed financial backing and did not want to outsource everything.

"Paul," he said, "there are three firms I would consider— one headquartered in Chicago led by one of the smartest bankers around, one in Southern California, and one headquartered in Michigan."

The firm in Southern California I knew well. Its CEO, John Eggemeyer, a man known for his integrity, had done a wonderful job building a group of banks.[3] He was my first choice. I called and arranged a meeting with him in San Francisco for October 13, 2000, bringing Andy Bartlett along.

John was interested in what I told him, even if he was not generally interested in de novo banks, but was involved in the sale of one of his holding companies and did not have the time to consider our de novo. He did ask to be kept informed.

The Chicago banker, Mike Kelly of suburban Oak Park, whom I had met in the '80s, was building his group of banks, many of them in California, into a formidable company. But he wasn't interested.

I had heard of Joe Reid of Capitol Bancorp in Michigan through Mike Sammon. Reid had started his company with the purchase of Capitol Bank in Lansing, Michigan, in 1988. Through Mike, I got annual reports, SEC filings, and other material on Reid's company, which included several other holding companies—Sun Community Bancorp in Arizona, Nevada Community Bancorp, and Indiana Community Bancorp. The four holding companies had twenty-eight banks.

Reid had an interesting model which at the time looked

---

[3]   See Chapter 15

good to me. His company would provide 51 percent of what was needed for capitalization of a de novo bank and would provide most of the needed support—for a fee which Reid did not specify but said was reasonable.

I called and introduced myself. "I know of you, Paul," he said. "I modeled my community bank group largely on your model—a president for each bank and a local board of directors—just like you did with your banks in Chicago."

I told him of our plan, asked if he would be interested in talking about partnering. He said, "Sure, let's meet in Las Vegas next week at the Mandalay Bay Hotel. We're having a board meeting there." Andy Bartlett and I met him and had dinner on November 3, 2000. I liked him and was intrigued with his approach to community banking.

But I said we would not be interested in a minority position. He said it was how he did it: "I only do a 51 percent investment. I wouldn't consider a smaller percentage." I was skeptical. Andy Bartlett's interest cooled at the prospect.

Reid is affable and persuasive, however. He had been a lawyer in Lansing for years but had tired of it and decided to try banking. He bought Capitol Bank and started investing in de novo banks in Michigan.

Then he began doing the same in Arizona, where he and some friends helped Jay Fishman organize Valley Commerce Bank in Phoenix, eventually taking a 15 percent position in the bank. He became Valley Commerce's chairman and CEO but later resigned those positions when the board asked him to do so. I did not know about the Valley Commerce matter, which is discussed in Chapter 18, when we met. I found out about it later, after organizing Napa Community.

At our Las Vegas dinner, I said I would like to come to Phoenix on a due-diligence visit to look at his back room and meet his staff. I did that and liked what I saw. His operations staff appeared competent and experienced.

I said we would like to proceed with him if he was interested. He was.

Meanwhile, we needed directors. I identified four of my Napa Valley friends as excellent prospects—Dr. Geni Bennetts, a very bright, retired pediatric oncologist; Carlee Leftwich, a retired Yountville, CA, mayor who knew "everyone in the valley"; Doug Hill, an outstanding viticulturist who knows the vineyard and winery business and the people in it; and Harold Morrison, general manager of Bridgeford Flying Service at the Napa County Airport. Each said he or she was interested. I introduced them to Andy and Paul in June 2000. Paul wanted to be a director, but we planned to contract with him for investment services, and that ruled him out because the regulators wouldn't permit it.

Paul, Andy, and I sent an offering circular August 6, 2000, to thirty-five or so local investors. It announced a "proposal to form a bank holding company, Community Bank of Napa Valley, with facilities in Calistoga, St. Helena, Yountville, Napa, and American Canyon." This was Mike Thompson's original idea, which we supported.

But in November Andy, unwilling to affiliate with Capitol Bancorp, bowed out. Reid's insistence on 51 percent ownership was for him "a huge disadvantage," especially its being out-of-state ownership. "With 51 percent [held out of state]," he said, "it's not a community bank any more."

I had the same reservations but decided to go ahead with the Capitol partnership, in part because I did not want to put in the time setting up the outsourcing of services that goes with starting a de novo but that Capitol would supply as part of the deal.

The search for a president kicked off in the final quarter of 2000. I interviewed several candidates, including a top executive from the Bank of Marin, an outstanding candidate who was over-qualified. I also interviewed a very good candidate from the Mechanics Bank and an excellent credit officer who would come with him. He looked very good; but he decided later for personal reasons not to leave Mechanics.

Before any of these, the most obvious candidate was Jim Wright, of St. Helena, who had run Napa National's St. Helena branch. Jim was highly regarded in the community and well liked. In his sixties, he would have been good for a couple of years, if the bank were located in St. Helena. But he impressed us as not enough an entrepreneur, and in addition, he had a non-compete agreement with Wells Fargo, who had bought his former employer, Napa National. We decided he was not the man for us.

I also interviewed the chief credit officer of the Vintage Bank, the well-run local community bank, who had extensive experience and was very well qualified in loans. But I questioned how well she would relate in the community as president.

I heard good things about a banker with Wells Fargo, in its wealth division, Dennis Pedisich. He had been a Napa-area banker for many years, having earlier been with Napa National and having run a branch for Bank of America in St. Helena. I called Dennis. We met in February 2001.

I had some concern about his lack of experience in lending and operations but thought that by picking two good officers in those areas to help him, he could succeed. I introduced him to the other directors, who liked him. I offered him the position and suggested we fly to Phoenix to meet Joe Reid and his executives.

My wife Debra, who had been marketing director for First Colonial, my seventeen-bank organization in Chicago, came with us. We met Reid's senior staff and were generally satisfied.

However, during the visit it became clear that Reid had a different approach to community banking from mine. My banks each had a strong board of directors recruited from the community, and each board had considerable authority. Reid's banks, on the other hand, relied far less on their boards, I learned. In addition, the presidents of his banks had not nearly the autonomy and authority that I gave our presidents.

I decided Napa Community Bank would require much more autonomy than Reid's banks had. Otherwise, I wanted no part of Capitol Bancorp. My directors agreed and urged me to meet with Reid.

I did so, again in Las Vegas at dinner. I told him I had been a CEO all my business life, and a successful one, and would need substantial autonomy if I were to found the bank and serve as chairman. Otherwise, I wouldn't be interested. I also told him we wanted neither him nor any other Capitol Bancorp directors or officers on our board. We wanted all local directors, I said, and as chairman I would run the show.

He quickly agreed to this. "No problem, Paul," he said. "You run the show."

We agreed philosophically on many things. But he did not know how much time I would put in or how well I would do, and I did not know how controlling he might be or how competent his organization was. I decided it was worth the risk and after discussing it at length with my board decided to put the bank together.

First we had to raise the capital. Reid wanted to do it through a holding company he already had in place, First California Northern Bancorp. First California Northern would be capitalized with $4 million, 51 percent of that coming from another Reid holding company, Sun Community Bancorp of Arizona, the rest from the Napa-area community. First California Northern would then downstream most of its capital to our bank. Later, when we decided to increase the bank's total capital to $8.5 million, we increased First California Northern capital to $4.5 million.

We had our president, Dennis Pedisich. Now we needed a location, a board, and staff. Our excellent chief credit officer, Rich Hemming, whom Dennis had worked with at Napa National and recommended highly, was our major staff addition. Two other fine additions were Nancy Stetler and Sandra Re. The best location would be on the vacant lot at the corner of Trancas and Big Ranch Road, on Napa's northern side. The lot had a for-sale sign on it. "Call Bill Kampton at Collier and Company," it said.

It was "under contract already," Bill said. The buyer was a builder who intended to build an office building. I told Bill we would be interested in leasing space. The buyer and builder was Joe Rossi. He was ready to lease half the space to us. Dennis and I began negotiations.

Dennis was in on this and much involved with the rest of the process, including forming a board. We already had four directors—Geni Bennetts, Carlee Leftwich, Doug Hill, and Harold Morrison. We needed more. At my request, Dennis listed some three-dozen potential directors, detailing their backgrounds and businesses. He and I discussed them at length. We needed a cross-section of disciplines, I told him. But there was one overriding quality, and it was not money. It was how that person would get along with us and the others on the board. The kind of bank I envisioned, I told Dennis, the kind I had run in Chicago, would be a truly community bank, with staff and directors who got along with each other. I intended this to be an enjoyable and comfortable place to work. He and the board agreed.

We eliminated a dozen or so, then interviewed a number of his recommendations. Many fit the bill. We chose some very good people.

Dr. John Pappas, MD, DDS, an oral surgeon and a good friend of Dennis, is an enthusiastic, affable man with a crusher handshake. I could never figure how he can be gentle with a patient with those hands! He was a natural. In our first meeting at Silverado Country Club, many people came up to him to say "Hi" and visit. Obviously well known and liked, he has a refreshing candor and is very direct. These are good qualities in a director.

Another good friend of Dennis was Chuck Dickenson, a lawyer at Dickenson, Peatman and Fogarty, an established firm that his father Howard, a friend of mine, started. Diligent, bright and dedicated, with a good personality, Chuck was another good choice.

Every board should have a good accountant to head the audit committee and serve on the loan committee in order to decipher financial statements. Dennis' acquaintance Kevin

Alfaro, a CPA with a respected local accounting firm, G&J Seiberlich, fit the bill well. A serious, studious, and bright young man with roots in the valley, Kevin was another excellent candidate.

Dennis also suggested Bill Dodd, even though he didn't know him well. As a Napa County supervisor, he would be a good addition. Bill was highly respected and very visible in the community. He was also a successful businessman as CEO of a local business.

Another director came our way when Harold Morrison, who had already signed on, came to me one day and said, "Paul, a friend of mine would be an outstanding director. His family has been here for years, he is well known and well regarded, and he runs one of the largest, most successful wine companies in the valley, Napa Wine Company." He meant Andy Hoxsey, whom he later introduced to me as his friend and fellow airplane pilot. Introspective, thoughtful, fairly quiet, Andy is sometimes short on words but grasps problems quickly. He has been a great director.

Another was brought to me later in the process by Paul Krsek. This was Jeff Epps, a friend of his and a great marketing person, who had built a thriving business, Epps Chevrolet in St. Helena. Jeff is personable, candid, and a man of solid integrity. He would offer his opinions with conviction. He was a natural to be chairman of the marketing committee.

Yet another director presented himself one day, when I got a call from a very good friend of mine—and since I too had been an air force fighter pilot, a hero of mine—the renowned test pilot and breaker of the sound barrier, General "Chuck" Yeager. In his usual gruff, straightforward manner, Chuck said, "Hey, Paul, I understand you're starting a bank. 'Bout time you got into something you know something about!" referring to my being in the wine business, which I knew nothing about.

"How many directors ya gonna have?" he asked.

"About twelve to thirteen," I replied.

"Too many," he says.

"You're probably right, Chuck, but that's what we're going to have."

"Who are the directors going to be, all bankers?"

"Heck no, we're gonna have folks from all walks of life. Lawyers, accountants, winery owners." Then teasingly, I added, "And test pilots."

"Okay, I'll be a director."

"You're kidding. Would you? You know how much time you need to put in?"

"Not really. But you gotta tell me what I'm supposed to do."

"Fantastic. We'd love to have you."

That's how Chuck Yeager became a member of the Napa Community Bank board. We planned a pilots' club of potentially a thousand members (customers). As its chairman, Chuck would obviously be a huge asset. And as a no-nonsense guy, he would never be intimidated. Not by anybody!

The Napa Valley *Register* headlined, "Banking on Chuck." The article about his joining the board helped our stock sale a lot.

Andy Hoxsey called with another candidate, a relative newcomer to the valley, an accomplished lady who had been quite successful in real estate in Minneapolis and had bought some excellent vineyard property on Howell Mountain and Mount Veeder and was starting her own winery. Harold Morrison also knew her, he said. They both had great respect for her.

This was Betty O'Shaughnessy. Dennis and I met with her at Bistro Don Giovanni. Betty came across as charming, attractive, and obviously bright. Her success in commercial real estate, her knowledge of the wine business, and her confident style would make her a valued director.

Meanwhile, our bank director applications were going through the Capitol Bancorp legal department on their way to the FDIC and the state regulatory institution, the Department of Financial Institutions, or DFI. This is how Capitol wanted it, but the process was taking much too long, especially as regards the Chuck Yeager application.

In his usual style, Chuck had submitted his financial statement with only one figure entered twice, for assets and liabilities. No detail, no net worth. For income he had "Enough"! The lawyer at Capitol called to say she would not submit his application. He would have to fill in the entire financial statement. I said he'd never do it. So, in fact, I'd handle his application and anyone else's from then on.

In Chicago a week later, I went to see an old acquaintance of mine with the FDIC, "Woody" Graham, an examiner on our application. I told Woody about the Yeager application and the lawyer's balking at it. He laughed and said, "I don't presume you're bringing General Yeager on the board for his financial capacity anyway. No problem, Paul, we'll pass him if he passes the FBI background check, which he should."

A week later Woody called and said, "Paul, legal has a problem with Yeager."

"What's that?"

"He put down as his place of birth a town in West Virginia that doesn't exist."

I called Chuck and asked what was going on.

"Hell, Paul," he said, "my hometown in West Virginia had four houses, a bar, and a gas station. The town isn't there any more!"

No problem. He was approved.

Betty's application was next. I had her send it directly to the DFI, our state regulatory agency, and to Woody Graham at the Chicago FDIC. It was approved in two weeks.

The directors were now in place, and I was very pleased. I started to set up the committees, deciding who would fit best with each other and provide the most expertise.

I formed a marketing committee, apparently the only one in Capitol's system at the time. I appointed an audit committee, though Capitol's "model" called for an "audit liaison," a local director who would report directly to the holding company.

Our board said no to that. An audit committee reports to the bank board, we all agreed. Checking with the Department of Financial Institutions, we found, sure enough, that California banks are expected to have an audit committee. I named Kevin Alfaro chairman of ours. He has done a splendid job. He's independent and straightforward and speaks his mind—an ideal audit chairman.

Jeff Epps took on chairmanship of the marketing committee, which filled a big void because the Capitol marketing assistance was very limited and our president had little experience in that area.

Geni Bennetts, one of the smartest and most diligent of our directors, took on chairmanship of the asset/liability committee—a job few would care to take on. She mastered it quickly. I counted on her taking her directorship seriously, but had no idea how dedicated she would be.

I appointed Bill Dodd chairman of the compensation committee. We also formed a human resources committee and had Geni Bennetts chair it.

Our loan committee was strong, as it had to be. I appointed Dennis to chair it. As an ex-officio member, our strong chief credit officer, Rich Hemming, does the major work of that committee. Several of its members, particularly Doug Hill, Kevin Alfaro, and Chuck Dickenson, have been a big help.

Our biggest challenge was that no director had experience in lending or overseeing the loan process. I took it on myself to do some serious director training in these matters, spending many hours at it. I also wrote for the directors a fairly inclusive "loan primer," included in Chapter 28, on starting a de novo community bank. It gives the dos and don'ts of lending, danger signs, areas to avoid or be careful in, etc. I sent a copy of the loan primer to Capitol's top Arizona credit officer, Pat Stone, in Phoenix, at her request, asking for comments. She changed a few minor items and asked if they could use it in their system.

To help finance Napa Community Bank, as we have seen, Capitol used a holding company, First California Northern

Bancorp (FCNB). FCNB was capitalized at $4.5 million. Paul Krsek, the directors, and I raised approximately $2,160,000; and Sun Community Bancorp, a subsidiary of Capitol Bancorp, put in approximately $2,340,000. So Sun Community had 51 percent, local investors 49 percent.

Then $4.335 million was downstreamed into Napa Community Bank, and we raised $4.165 million more from 477 local investors. Thus the bank was capitalized at $8.5 million. So for an investment of $2,340,000 or 26 percent of an $8.5 million bank, Capitol through Sun Community Bancorp gained control of 51 percent or $4.335 million.

Capitol's model, which calls for buying 51 percent of the initial capitalization at book as I have noted, also calls for buying out minority shareholders' 49 percent at 150 percent of book after three years. That makes Capitol's total investment *125 percent* of book price of a profitable bank, usually of a size between $50 and $75 million of assets.

I'm reminded of Ed Carpenter, interviewed in another chapter, who said, "One of the biggest mistakes made by a group planning a de novo bank is they don't think they can raise the required capital in their own communities. But if you don't raise the capital in your own community, you won't have a roaring success."

Our capital-raising went this way: We began selling stock on October 2, 2001, when we received our permit to organize. We had decided we wanted as large a shareholder base as possible, all of whom would be potential customers. I knew that in a community like Napa, hundreds would like to be "founder shareholders." So we set a very low minimum investment of $1,000.

We needed publicity. So five months before we could begin selling, we contacted the *Register* and interviewed with the managing editor, Frank Hartzell. Out of it came a front-page story on May 3, 2001, "New Locally Owned Bank to Open in Napa," with Dennis's and my picture.

Then we got another front-page article with photo,

mentioned above, about our celebrity director, Chuck Yeager, headlined "Banking on Chuck." I had urged reporter Kevin Courtney to read Chuck's autobiography, *Yeager*, before the interview. Chuck, impressed by Kevin's knowledge of his story, gave a great interview, and the article increased interest in our stock substantially.

We got another story on November 16, 2001, "Interest High With Napa Bank Stock Offering." It was. We were rolling.

We held two seminars for prospective shareholders at the Embassy Suites in Napa. I introduced the local directors and Dennis, then made a presentation and answered questions. Our staff manned tables with stock information. Both were well—attended and successful. We've had a number of shareholders tell us they bought stock because of those meetings. Our stock sale took off. Our board was an enormous help bringing in dozens of investors.

There soon was a problem, however. We were not aware of a five-hundred-investor ceiling above which we would enter a new category of reporting. By the time we learned of the ceiling, we had sailed past the five-hundred shareholder level and our targeted $4.25 million and were oversubscribed.

Finally apprised of the limit, several of us directors cut back on our investment and then had to tell a number of would-be purchasers, "Sorry, you didn't make it in time," even though time hadn't run out. Naturally, there were some very ticked-off people, including us.

So we cut back to 477 shareholders, almost all local, a majority of whom invested only $1,000, though the average investment was about $17,500.

Our opening was delayed, partly because of a problem with the DFI in processing our application. Dennis Pedisich, the president-CEO, and I, the chairman, were not directly involved in the process, though we were only an hour away from DFI's office in San Francisco. This is unusual. A bank's chairman and CEO are usually directly involved. But Capitol wanted to handle everything from Michigan.

This procedure delayed our opening, as shown in comments by the DFI general counsel, Rosemarie Oda, in response to our asking how we should have done it. "On two separate occasions," she said in an April 17, 2002, letter to me, after our opening, "your attorney [in Lansing] specifically requested Mr. Patten (DFI) to deal only with them," not with anyone in Napa. "Mr. Patten complied with their request."

As for what we could "do better the next time [we] organize a bank in California," she said, "We believe it would be helpful if you consulted with local counsel, who may better understand the requirements of California law."

In any case, we opened for business on March 1, 2002, in a 896-square-foot trailer at Trancas and Soscol Avenue in northeast Napa. At our grand-opening ribbon-cutting ceremony, we had Congressman Thompson, Chuck Yeager, DFI Commissioner Don Meyer, Napa Mayor Ed Solomon, and other notables.

I had convinced Dennis and the board that a trailer would serve us well for the 18 months it would take to build the permanent facility. I had done this in Chicago several times. We got the trailer from Idaho, built to our specifications. Those 896 square feet were a challenge to operate out of, but the trailer sufficed.

Meanwhile, several problems arose with Capitol Bancorp after the bank's opening. One had to do with who decides our president's compensation and to whom he reports. When Dennis Pedisich accepted the presidency on May 1, 2001, he signed a contract with First California Northern Bancorp, which paid his salary until the bank opened in March 2002.

My understanding was that the bank would assume the contract once it was operational, and Dennis would report to the bank board. Rather, Capitol told us, Dennis would report to First California Northern, who would handle his compensation. Our board rejected that approach and went to the FDIC in Chicago and the DFI in San Francisco for advice in the matter.

The FDIC said it assumed Dennis was an employee of the bank and not of a third party or holding company and said it preferred that the president report to the bank board, who would be responsible for his compensation. California's DFI responded similarly. A new contract was effected between the bank and Dennis, with Dennis reporting to and being compensated by the bank board.

There was the matter of stock options. President and CEO Pedisich was to get 20,000 options at $10 a share or $200,000 value, according to our November 7, 2001, offering circular. This is very reasonable for a CEO. His well-deserved increase in stock value will be $100,000 if the bank is "rolled up" into Capitol Bancorp on March 1, 2005, when he would receive, at 150 percent of book, $300,000 of Capitol stock.

As "proposed chairman" and founder of the bank, I was to get 15,000 options. I voluntarily forfeited these a year later when I resigned from the board, to make room for future bank officer needs. Joe Reid, as "strategic planning officer and advisory director" and chairman and CEO of Capitol Bancorp, got 30,000 options. Later Rich Hemming as chief loan officer got 10,000. The total covered almost 10 percent of total shares outstanding, toward a target limit of 15 percent. The bank reached this limit at the end of the first quarter of 2004.

Reid's options meant that he would receive on March 1, 2005, at the same 150 percent of book, $450,000 of Capitol stock.[4]

On September 11, 2003, eighteen months after opening in the trailer, the bank had another grand opening in its new quarters—6,500 square feet. The new building was to lead to a considerable increase in personal retail deposits and business. It always happens that way, because many people draw the

---

[4] None of these options were expensed, as is standard among Capitol Bancorp banks. See Chapter 30, "Compensation Issues," for how this affected Napa Community's earnings for 2003.

line at banking in a small trailer that looks as if it could be hooked up and driven away some dark night.

The new building's interior was designed by Marsha Gabbert, of Chicago-based Creative Interior Design, a firm that did interiors for most of my Chicago banks. It's lovely and functional and came at the right price. Betty chaired the building committee and did an excellent job.

The bank has done well. It broke even in its thirteenth month. The new building encouraged deposit growth. Loan demand has been good, thanks to the directors, who have been a great source of loans and deposits, and to Dennis, our president and CEO, and Rich, our senior loan officer, and their dedicated staff. In 2004 the bank added two more good directors.

A year after opening, still in the trailer, the bank had assets of about $39 million. Ten months later, at year-end 2003, it had $53.5 million. The new facility had raised shelter costs substantially, from $5,800 a month to $23,000—an increase that shows how working in the trailer, which had been a tight squeeze, had contributed to the bottom line by keeping the cost of shelter down.

Staff was fifteen, up from a starting eight. Salaries were running somewhat higher than projected, but this is not unusual for a young bank. Loans were $35 million, deposits $45 million. The loan-to-deposit ratio was comfortable at 78 percent; the loan loss reserve was 1.34 percent; capital to assets was a strong 20 percent; and year-to-date net interest margin was a respectable 4.17 percent.

The first quarter of 2004 showed continued strength. Total assets were $58.641 million; loans were $40.926 million; deposits were $50.311 million. Earnings for the quarter were $67,760; loan loss reserve was 1.37 percent. The ratio of DDA to total deposits was 23.4 percent. Capital-to-asset ratio was 14.07 percent.

While the ratio of demand deposits to total deposits was relatively good at 23 percent, its $13 million in idle cash and federal funds constitutes a major challenge faced by every bank today, how to get the best return in a time of low interest rates. Alternative investment opportunities or a faster pace of booking loans will help. In any case, total assets are over $58 million; and the bank is earning money. That's an excellent start.

Meanwhile, Dennis, enjoying competition with other Capitol banks, has pointed out that one of Capitol's Nevada banks, the Bank of Las Vegas, a month older than Napa and doing business in a much more dynamic area, had only $35 million in assets, compared to Napa's $53.5 million, and in its second full year had a loss of $8,000, compared to Napa's profit of $290,000.

In any case, I came to realize that my style of banking clashed with Joe Reid's; and in November 2002, after eight months as chairman and a year before that spent organizing the bank, I resigned. I didn't want to continue working with Reid's organization, and he clearly did not want me in his organization.

Betty O'Shaughnessy was elected chairperson. She has been a good one. The directors are independent, talented people of integrity who enjoy being directors. The president and CEO, Dennis Pedisich, learns quickly, has developed well, and is thoroughly community-oriented.

The loan situation is healthy and promises to continue that way, thanks to a solid and thorough senior loan officer, Rich Hemming, helped now by several new loan officers, and the loan committee, an excellent group.

I enjoyed founding Napa Community Bank, and I'm glad I did it. I accomplished what I set out to do. It was fun, for one thing, and I have enjoyed friendships developed with the board and staff and with some of the Capitol staff. More important, the bank fills a need, and it's rewarding to do something well and contribute to the community.

The bank faces stiff competition from Napa's other community bank, Vintage Bank. But it should prosper, in large part because of its excellent board, drawn from the community and dedicated to enhancing shareholder value, and its very competent president-CEO.

The key to its success is its independence, the issue that has been backdrop to much of what's been discussed here. If the bank keeps its independence, its future is bright.

Chapter 19a

Dennis Pedisich, President-CEO

Dennis Pedisich has had two good years as president and CEO of Napa Community Bank. I am doubly glad about that, because as founding chairman of the bank, I recommended him for the job. I did so knowing he had not much lending and operational experience and had never been a bank CEO but knowing too his other qualifications.

For one, he has the perfect community banker personality, as demonstrated by his multitude of friends and contacts in the Napa Valley, where he was well known, liked, and respected.

For another, he's a hard worker, eager to learn, and willing to listen to people he respects. The time I spent with him as a sort of tutor I consider well spent.

For another, he's sharply competitive, which means he takes pride in the bank's performance that compares so favorably with other banks held by Capitol Bancorp.

I interviewed Dennis some eighteen months after the bank opened and shortly after it had moved into beautiful new quarters—at 6,500 square feet a far cry from the 896-square-foot trailer where we started.

Looking back, he recalled his hesitation at taking on a job that was new to him in that he had worked only for large banks. He recalled overcoming it by concentrating on the encouraging factors: the high quality of people he would work with, including those he brought with him from his previous position, and the clear need for a second community bank in the Napa Valley, where once there were three before big banks acquired the others.

The trailer part was certainly new. He hadn't counted on that. Neither had he counted on the complexity of the job, its combination of being banker, salesman, and community leader—he's on five civic boards and participates in a number of other activities, from local hospital board to Chamber of Commerce to children's services. But out of it all came his once in a lifetime experience of never working so hard and never having so much fun.

This went for the challenge of working with a mix of directors, and thirteen of them at that, when he was used to nine or ten. But this group was different, from other boards and from each other. He looked on them as business developers—women and men, older and younger, competent in a variety of disciplines. There was doctor, lawyer, and merchant. They included a CPA, physician, dentist, wine grower, county board member, auto sales executive, former mayor, and president of a flying service operation at the local airport. Those thirteen represented as many disciplines, no small advantage to a growing bank.

The first four formed the core—Dr. Geni Bennetts, MD; the former mayor (of Yountville) Carlee Leftwich; the flying service president Harold Morrison; and the vineyard manager Doug Hill. Every bank needs a financial expert on its board, which is where Kevin Alfaro, partner in a local CPA firm, comes in.

Bankers have to decide how to regard regulators. "We welcome them with open arms," Dennis said. "The DFI and FDIC—state and federal regulators—are allies, not threats to us. I would never get into an adversarial position with them. An FDIC examiner from San Francisco popped in the other day to 'see how things were going,' he said. That's nice!"

There are cyclical challenges, such as current interest rate compression. They meet the challenge of compression by reducing liability costs. Napa Community has the lowest cost of funds in the Capitol Bancorp system. Strong control of the cost of funds and a good banking environment have produced good results. The cost of interest-bearing deposits has been reduced from 1.53 percent at year-end 2002 to 0.8 percent at year-end 2003. The cost of funds has come down year to year from 1.73 percent to 0.86 percent, and the net interest margin has increased year to year from 3.51 percent to 4.69 percent.

The bank also not only lowered costs of funds but it also raised its net interest margin, from 3.54 percent in August 2002 to 4.4 percent a year later.

Banks commonly supply ancillary financial services. How important are such services for Napa Community? One such service, supplying home mortgages, makes a "huge" profit difference. The bank warehouses mortgages on the books for about thirty days, after they are approved for sale in the secondary market but before the sale is completed for a fee.

The loan is locked in: it goes on your books as a short-term loan, earning income. Then you sell it for a commission. In August 2003, for instance, the bank had $6 million in mortgage loans on the books yielding 5.5 percent, before they had sold the mortgages. Then they sold them and booked the points, that is, put them on the books. That pointed to a hefty $50,000 in fee income for September. For this short-term mortgage lending, Dennis gave credit to the bank's recently hired residential lending manager.

Banks are nothing without their people. Napa Community began with nine staff and had grown to fifteen by September 2003, with more help needed in lending.

As a relatively freshly minted CEO, Dennis has advice, beginning with the importance of not getting "hung up" on expenses. Focus rather on revenue, he said. "If you think you can get a top-notch loan officer, for instance, grab him, even if the timing is not quite right. Invest in good people."

That's been another surprise for him, the higher than

expected salaries required to attract "good people." In the credit department, for instance their four lenders and three support staff are still not enough, he said.

All in all, Dennis Pedisich is very happy he took the Napa Community Bank job and would do it again, in a California minute.

Chapter 19b

Chuck Yeager, Director

One can only admire the courage, dedication, and contribution to country and aviation of Chuck Yeager. He was a double ace in World War II, bailing out of his flaming P-51 over occupied France and escaping to Spain with the help of the French underground; broke the sound barrier in 1947; became the best test pilot ever at Edwards AFB in the 1950s.

At his retirement at Edwards Air Force Base on October 14, 1997, he broke the sound barrier fifty years to the minute after he had done it in 1947 in the Bell X-1, this time in an F-15. General Engel at the ceremony cited "three defining moments" in aviation history—the Wrights' flight at Kitty Hawk, Yeager breaking the sound barrier in 1947, and Neil Armstrong walking on the moon in 1969.

Responding with only a hint of emotion, Chuck said, "Everything I've done I owe to the United States Air Force."

Chuck is the epitome of a patriot and a sincere man whose head has not been turned by fame. He was my personal hero when I entered the air force after graduation from Michigan State University in the fall of 1953. I entered "in grade" as a second lieutenant. After six months of primary pilot training at Bartow AFB in Florida, I entered basic training at Bryan AFB in Texas and in November 1954, won my wings as a single-seat jet fighter pilot. I was going to become an ace by shooting down five Korean Migs, like my hero Chuck Yeager nine years before. But the war had just ended in Korea. I was devastated.

In our ready room at Bryan AFB we had two items on the wall, the poem known by heart by most air force pilots, "High Flight," by John McGee, a nineteen-year-old RAF pilot killed in 1941, and a picture of Chuck Yeager next to the X-1.

I was tempted briefly to remain in the air force after my tour and fly some even hotter fighters, but decided to start my business career and to continue flying privately, as I have for forty-six years. I presently own and fly a Cessna 414.

It was thirty-four more years before I met Chuck. In the spring of 1988, living in Chicago and chairman and CEO of First Colonial Bankshares, I was invited by Bob Galvin, chairman of Motorola, to be a guest for dinner to meet then Vice President George H. W. Bush, who was campaigning for president.

It was at Galvin's condominium on Lake Shore Drive. I arrived a little late but in time to go through a dignitaries' receiving line before meeting Bush and being photographed with him.

The line included Galvin, Illinois Governor Jim Thompson, and others. As I made my way, a smiling guy stuck out his hand and said, "Hi, I'm Chuck Yeager!"

"My hero!" I exclaimed, too loudly I'm sure.

"You're a fighter pilot!" Chuck said, laughing.

That's how we met. To be honest, meeting the vice president and having my picture taken with him was anticlimactic after meeting Chuck Yeager. I tried to find a seat at Chuck's table but couldn't.

But I quickly followed up, sending him a letter saying I hoped to see him again. And it happened, by chance, a few months later, in September, at the world-famous One Shot Antelope Hunt in Lander, Wyoming.

I'd had a cattle ranch near Lander since 1972 and though not a hunter had regularly attended this wonderful event where politicians, sportsmen, and dignitaries gathered from around the country to form teams of three to see which team got its antelopes first. I was not on a team, but Yeager was. We struck up a conversation, recalling our meeting with Galvin and Bush. From that time we have been the best of friends.

He would stay at my Wyoming ranch house when he came for the one-shot event, and we would get together at his home in Grass Valley, California, at mine in Napa, and at events around the country.

When we'd fly to Lander I'd pick Chuck up in Grass Valley. Once we took off, I'd ask if he'd like to fly, to which I invariably got an enthusiastic yes. I'd land the plane, not that he wouldn't do it better, but I love to fly and like to get my time in.

In the air force, we, jet pilots, would try to stall out and land smoothly as close to the far end of the runway as possible, on the hash marks. Now I'm older and wiser and get in only one hundred hours or so a year, the minimum to stay tuned to the process, and have adopted a more cautious landing procedure.

I've adopted the old rule, that altitude and air speed are your friends. So I've become accustomed to coming in on my landing approach a little higher and a little faster just to have the extra element of safety. I always land a little long.

Well, one beautiful autumn day I was flying back from Lander with Chuck and his World War II P-51 buddy, Bud Anderson, and I was going to drop them off at Grass Valley. As Chuck and I changed seats so I could land, he said, "Okay, Paul, now land on Runway 25. It's uphill. Come in lower and slower than you usually do and put it down on the hash marks."

Well, I was determined to make the perfect air force landing! And I screwed up. Undoubtedly a little tense and obviously trying to do my best, my traffic pattern was too close. I didn't throttle back soon enough, didn't use enough flaps, and sailed down the runway and landed a third of the way down.

Embarrassed doesn't describe it. I pulled up to the apron, turned the engines off, and, while everyone got off except Chuck and Bud, Chuck said in his West Virginia twang, "Hell, Paul, I could smell those brake linings back here!" Bud chimed in: "Geez, Chuck, give him a break. He only flies one hundred hours a year!"

I was devastated! It took me days to get out of a severe funk.

Several days later I got a picture in the mail of an X-1 and Chuck's comment, "Bell X-1. Over the fence at 130 knots and always landing on the hash marks." Cute!

I mailed back to him a picture of my Cessna 414 with tail number 797 Romeo Alpha, with the caption, "797 Romeo Alpha, a 414 specially rigged to land long!" He got a kick out of that. But every time I land now, I say either "Geez, Chuck would love that one" or "Man, I'm glad Yeager wasn't with me on that one!"

Coming back from Lander one day and stopping at Grass Valley for a visit, I called Chuck and gave him an estimated time of arrival. He drawled, "When you get twenty-five miles out, give me a call on frequency 122.5. I'll be at five thousand feet in my Husky," referring to his single-engine plane, "and we'll land together. But you'll have to throttle back and drop your flaps and slow down, so I can keep up."

No problem. Twenty-five miles out, I got him on the radio, and sure enough, he spotted me first and said he's going to pull up on my wing and "fly a little formation." Wow! Okay. I put my gear and flaps down and slowed to about 120 knots, and he came in under my right wing, steady as can be. We were flying tight formation! Me for the first time since 1954. What a kick. I shot a picture of him out my right window in his yellow Husky, to prove for posterity that Chuck Yeager once flew my wing!

I got a call from Chuck in Grass Valley one day in 2003. My son Chauncey was three years old. Chuck had seen him growing up.

He said, "Hey, Paul, I've got a neat P-51 model that a guy I met at the Oshkosh air show built for my granddaughter, Amanda. It has a prop that goes around as you pedal it. It's got my squadron's colors, and it's a really neat plane. Amanda is ten years old and has outgrown it. I'm bringing it over and I'm giving it to Chauncey!"

I said, "Chuck, you can't give that away. It's a Yeager heirloom. I can't accept it."

He responded very slowly and deliberately, "Paul, I'm coming over tomorrow in my pickup and I'm giving it to Chauncey. What time is good?"

Well, he brought it over and gave it to Chauncey, and we got a great picture of Chauncey in the cockpit wearing a flight jacket and scarf and Chuck and me kneeling behind him. Talk about generosity! The little plane sits in the "robbers roost," a great 1880s stone room in our Napa home, which was built around the roost, with the picture of Chuck, Chauncey, and me behind it.

Several years ago I heard on my car radio that General Chuck Yeager had had an accident and was in intensive care at an air force base in San Antonio, Texas. I rushed home, tracked the hospital down, and called. "Airman First Class Brandt" answered, "How may I help you?"

I said, "This is Paul Johnson, and I want General Yeager's room or the nurse's station."

He said, "I can't put you through, sorry."

I said, "Airman Brandt, I'm a very close personal friend of General Yeager's, and if he finds out I couldn't get through to him, I guarantee you'll end up in Thule, Greenland!"

"Yes sir, Mr. Johnson," he said. "I'll put you right through to the nurse's station!"

The nurse told me Chuck had fallen off a ladder while cutting a limb with a chain saw at a friend's house and was seriously injured, but they were quite sure he'd recover.

Of course he'd recover, I thought. Can you imagine Chuck Yeager buying the farm by falling off a ladder?

I admire many things about Chuck, but one of those I admire most is his devotion to Experimental Aircraft Association's Young Eagles, whose mission is to introduce young people to flying. Since 1992 Chuck, who is chairman of the Young Eagles, has recruited pilot volunteers to take young people up in their planes to encourage them to become pilots. Appropriately, in December 2003, at the Centennial of Flight celebration in Kitty Hawk, North Carolina, the millionth kid was taken up for a flight by Chuck.

This is typical of him. I have watched him at public events like Safari Club meetings, where he is stopped by dozens of people. "Hi, you're Chuck Yeager," they say, their admiration showing. "Can I get an autograph?" Unlike many famous athletes and movie stars who brush past such folks, Chuck almost always stops and signs.

He also donates his time in speeches for causes he likes. As a speaker for hire, he could make a lot of money. But that has no appeal for him. He gives time and makes appearances for his foundation, his pet projects, and various charities but would much rather be fishing for salmon in Alaska or for goldens in the high country in the Sierra Nevadas or hunting elk in Colorado than attending functions.

He's an American hero, whose fame has not gone to his head, devoted to his Young Eagles, his friends, and to many good causes—proud of his accomplishments but not living on his laurels.

He has been my hero since my air force days, my friend for less time than that. My admiration has done nothing but grow over the years.

Chapter 19c

Geni Bennetts, Director

I approached my friend Geni Bennetts, MD, early in 2000 about becoming a Napa Community Bank director because I considered her ideal for the position. I had known her for four years and had developed great respect for her. We had become close friends. Specifically she fulfilled these criteria which I had discovered over many years of recruiting community-bank directors.

She's smart, one of the smartest people I know.

She has an excellent business background, which is unusual for a doctor.

She's a positive person with excellent social skills.

She has a drive for excellence that is greater than almost anyone I've known.

She had numerous contacts and was widely respected among local doctors and other medical professionals, which made a logical marketing target.

It's no wonder I asked her to serve.

She wanted to do it, in fact was excited at the opportunity, but questioned her qualifications, protesting that she had no banking experience. I told her that as chairman I would tutor the directors and get them up to speed. That satisfied her. She accepted.

For this book I wanted her perspective as a director in order to help bank organizers looking for one. I asked her why she took the job.

"Besides the stimulus you provided, Paul, as a friend, I saw it as a way to contribute to the community in a new way. I knew we needed another bank, particularly because of Wells Fargo's purchase of Napa National. And personally, I liked the idea of learning a challenging new discipline. That's something I enjoy."

I asked her how it worked out.

"Very well. It's certainly been more time-consuming than I thought. The responsibilities were more than I thought too."

Were you upset about the level of regulation?

"No, banking needs a high degree of regulation, if only because of the savings and loan debacle and more recently the bankruptcies of Enron, Worldcom, and others. The Sarbanes-Oxley legislation refers specifically to banks $2 billion and larger, but smaller banks are encouraged to adopt its provisions, and we are doing that.

"I'm glad we have solicited a broad base of investors in the bank—almost five hundred shareholders. So large a number is more cumbersome, but it's important that we did it. Such widespread involvement meant the community came together. We directors have had to focus all the more clearly on our responsibilities to watch out for investors and enhance shareholder value."

What about the regulators as such?

"I have no problems with regulators. I am used to them from practicing medicine. Banking has been well served by its regulators. I would never take an adversarial position towards them. Dealing with them is time-consuming, as in our internal audits that prepare us for examiners. But I agree with [investment banker] Joe Stieven when he says they help keep banks solid."

You are vice chairman of the board. What committees do you serve on?

"I'm chairman of the asset-liability committee [ALCO],

and I'm on four others—audit, executive, loan, and the newly combined human resources and compensation committees."

I appointed Geni ALCO chairman. The asset-liability area is very important and one of the hardest to grasp. She grasped it quickly.

The bank's earnings and loan portfolio?

"The bank is coming along as envisaged. We'll be profitable in the third year; and I believe, compared to other de novos, we're doing well. We should be very cautious with our lending, but we have a lot of liquidity that I'd like to see working at better rates than the investment portfolio gives us."

What's your advice to a group putting together a de novo community bank?

"The board choices are very important. I'd be very concerned about picking directors who work well as a team. Pick people who will get along with each other well. Tell them that being a director is a big responsibility, that they must put in time, not just dash in for a monthly meeting, and keep learning. I've been to several seminars on banking finance and oversight. Many good one-day seminars are available. We at Napa Community will also have a retreat in November. We have done this before. They have been very helpful. I'd also be sure to emphasize the need to be business-gatherers for the bank."

What were benefits of being a bank board member?

"First, the camaraderie. I like everybody on the board. They all want the bank to do well. We have the same vision and we enjoy each other. I've developed new friendships.

"Our relationship with the CEO is good. You have to learn how to work with a CEO. We being a bunch of entrepreneurs, sometimes it's challenging."

There are fourteen of you on the board. Is that too many?

"Well, it's somewhat on the high side. The benefit is we have more to share the workload. If we had six or seven, the meetings might go more quickly, but some directors put in a day a week to the job as it is."

Geni learned the basics of banking quickly, a fellow director told me. He was astonished at how quickly. She's a quick study, to be sure.

I asked her about her background. It's impressive. She got her BA from Columbia Union College, in Takoma Park, Maryland, in psychology and chemistry in 1967. After attending Virginia Commonwealth University for a time, she moved to Andrews University in Michigan, where she got her master's in clinical psychology, summa cum laude, in 1969. In 1973 she got her MD at Loma Linda University in California. Her certifications and honors fill several pages, as do her professional memberships.

She got her business experience as chief of hematology-oncology at Children's Hospital of Orange County. In this capacity she ran clinical programs for kids with blood diseases until 1996, overseeing seventy medical personnel while building the organization.

In Napa she does some medical management consulting and is president of Family Services of Napa Valley, which provides mental health services for low-income people. She is on the family services committee for developing mobile dental and health access for uninsured kids.

Dr. Geni Bennetts is a concerned and caring citizen who has contributed greatly to the less advantaged. Her involvement and time commitment to Napa Community Bank has been an inspiration to her fellow directors. The bank is lucky to have her.

Chapter 19d

Andy Bartlett, Organizer

One of the first people involved in starting Napa Community Bank was Anderson "Andy" Bartlett, a lawyer in St. Helena, just north of Napa, who did not like what the purchase by Wells Fargo of Napa National Bank would do to its branch in St. Helena.

He and Paul Krsek, a St. Helena investment company owner, got together with Congressman Mike Thompson, who also foresaw a big loss to the Napa valley community from the demise of Napa National as community-owned. The three talked about starting a de novo community bank in St. Helena.

Neither Paul nor Andy—Dartmouth College '62, Harvard law '65, holder of a Le Cordon Bleu (Paris) cooking certificate—had banking experience. Mike had a solution for that. "I know a retired banker in Napa with excellent background in community banking," he said. "His name is Paul Johnson. You two should talk to him"

Mike called and asked if I'd be interested in "helping some investors start a bank in the Napa Valley." I said I would. We three met Mike in his Napa office to consider whether we could raise the required capital and hire a qualified staff. We decided we could.

"The focal point was to be St. Helena," Andy recalled in a 2003 conversation. "Paul Krsek and I visited three banks in northern California to get a feel for community banks. We found that only three or four of the many de novos started in the past ten years in northern California survived to the late '90s, each of them plugged into their communities. We thought we could do that.

"We thought we knew who should run the bank, Jim Wright, branch manager of what was Napa National's but was now Wells Fargo's branch in St. Helena. We thought he would be ideal for developing banks in St. Helena and 'up valley' in Calistoga and beyond, basically in Mike Thompson's Congressional District, as Mike had urged us to do.

"But Jim had a noncompete contract with Wells Fargo and wouldn't be available for some time. That was one problem. Another was that there appeared to be no good location for a bank in St. Helena.

"Then you and I went to Las Vegas, Paul, to meet Joe Reid of Capitol Bancorp, who looked good to you, with his successful cookie-cutter deal, with its advantages and disadvantages.

"A huge disadvantage, from my vantage point as a business lawyer, was that Reid insisted on 51 percent ownership. As you know, I had no interest in 51 percent out-of-state ownership of our bank. That made me hesitate, being controlled by a Michigan banker. With 51 percent owned out of state, it's no longer a community bank."

So Andy dropped out. But he helped us very much with ground work for Napa Community Bank and getting interest up.

It became apparent that it made sense to locate the bank in Napa, not St. Helena.

"Now," said Andy, "Napa Community has its work cut out for it, competing with a very well-run, locally run bank, Vintage Bank. But it has a great board who hired good management; so I think it will do very well.

"We laugh now at what a St. Helena old-timer said, 'St. Helena used to have eight bars and one bank. Now it has eight banks and one bar. It was more fun before.'"

Chapter 20

Bank of Tucson, Tucson, Arizona:

Mike Hannley

Tucson, Arizona's second-largest city with almost a half million people, several miles from the Mexican border in southern Arizona, has about eight hundred thousand in its metropolitan area. The city was established in 1775 by a Spanish commandant with an Irish name, Hugo O'Conor. It became part of the United States with the Gadsden Purchase in 1854. Arizona became the forty-eighth state in 1912.

Tucson is more comfortable—usually 10° to 15° cooler— than Phoenix, ninety miles to the north, because it's higher (2,100 feet vs. 1,100 for Phoenix) and is surrounded by mountains. In addition, it does not have Phoenix's miles of canals and pavement.

Bank of Tucson, one of the most successful in the country of its size and the best-performing bank in Joe Reid's Capitol Bancorp group, is headed by its president, Mike Hannley. Mike has lived in Tucson most of his fifty-five years. He keeps himself in great physical condition by working out daily and pursuing his passion, horseback riding.

This has its problems. On a trail ride early in 2001, he fractured his leg in many places and acquired some eleven picccs of repair hardware that sets off alarms on airport metal detectors. The leg is a patchwork of scars, but he's been back trail-riding with his buddies. No competing in rodeos, however. His wife made him promise.

Bank of Tucson opened for business in July 1996, with six employees, $5 million in capital, and $2.3 million in assets—$314,000 in loans and $2 million in deposits.

In seven and a half years, to year-end 2003, it grew to $158 million in assets—$102 million in loans and $146 million in deposits. Its noninterest-bearing deposit ratio was a handsome 29 percent.

In 2003 it earned $2.8 million—a strong 2 percent on average assets and a whopping 25 percent on equity, with an efficiency ratio of 49 percent. Bank of Tucson is one of the high best-performing banks of its size in the country, Mike says. As said above, it is surely the best performing of Capitol Bancorp's thirty banks.

Mike Hannley and his staff have done this while maintaining a relatively conservative loan-to-deposit ratio of around 70 percent and very little "time" money (time deposits, as thirty-day CDs) and no "hot" money (brokered CDs, money that arrives and leaves quickly). He works constantly toward two goals: a high interest margin, at or near 5.5 percent, and an efficiency ratio of about 45 percent. He ran the bank in 2003 with a full-time staff of only twenty-eight.

CHARTING TUCSON GROWTH

The bank grew quickly and steadily. In its first year, it charged off $290,000—$150,000 organizing expense and $140,000 operating loss. In the tenth month, it turned a profit. At that point they had a grand total of eleven full-time employees.

At the end of the second year, in June 1998, with thirteen full-time and five part-time employees, the bank had $51 million in deposits and $29 million in loans averaging $119,000. Loan-to-deposit ratio was only 55 percent; the lending limit was $885,000. Earnings were $400,000 for the year.

A year later, with eighteen full-timers and two part-timers, deposits were $69 million, and loans were $41 million, with a loan-to-deposit ratio of 67 percent. The lending limit was up to $1 million. Net interest spread was approximately 6 percent. The efficiency ratio was down to about 50 percent, mainly because of increased staff size. Earnings were $837,000.

The fourth year closed with deposits of $81 million, loans of $65 million, for a loan-to-deposit ratio of 78 percent. The lending limit had been raised to $1,300,000. The efficiency ratio was down again, to 46 percent, thanks in part to the adding of only one employee. Earnings were $190,000 a month.

By the end of year five, with twenty-two full-time employees and three part-timers and an efficiency ratio of around 48 percent, the bank hit the magic $100 million mark in deposits. It had $83 million in loans. Equity had risen to $9,200,000.

The sixth year, 2002, began with a bang. The January profit of $228,000 made it the bank's best month to that point, and this in a flat economy. The year's profit came to $2.7 million. The bank had $11 million in capital at year-end. Its capital-to-asset ratio was a comfortable 8 percent. The ROE was 24.5 percent. The ROA was 2 percent. The efficiency ratio was lowest yet at 43 percent.

The bank charged off five loans during 2002 totaling $330,000. This was the first loan loss of any size. But reserve-to-loans ratio climbed, from 1.36 to 1.62 percent, well over Mike's goal of 1.5 percent and considerably more than the 1.25 percent he had run most years, with addition of $200,000 to the loan reserve, bringing it to $1.5 million.

The bank's efficiency ratio is one of several factors that have made for Tucson Bank's profitability. Others include its 8.83 percent loan yield, 5.6 percent net interest margin, and whopping 44 percent ratio of demand deposits to total deposits.

These deposits are mostly in business accounts running in a number of cases average balances of $300,000 to $400,000. The bank has no public funds.

A conservative approach to lending is another factor. The bank's loan-to-deposit ratio was recently a comfortable 75 percent.

TUCSON JEWEL IN CAPITOL CROWN

Capitol Bancorp is lucky to have Bank of Tucson among its nineteen southwestern banks. "It produces 66 percent of the earnings of the nineteen (once it was 78 percent)," says Mike, a Capitol Bancorp director since 2002.

Three directors are Capitol people from Lansing, but most are local. One of them, Rich Flynn, grew up in southern Oregon, where his father owned a drug store. He got his accounting degree from the University of Oregon, then joined the navy and went to OCS, then served three years on a destroyer. After the navy he went to San Francisco to be a stock broker from 1970 to 1976, when he got an offer to move to Tucson for a year to work in an auto business. He stayed in Tucson running car washes for eight years, then got into real estate development industry in the '80s.

He was one of Hannley's first shareholders when Mike started the bank in 1996, and one of the largest. The two had known each other since 1985. "Mike has gotten extraordinary results from ordinary people," he said.

Mike had been recruited by Capitol's Joe Reid to start the bank. To capitalize the bank, Mike found investors who put up $2.5 million to match Reid's $2.5 million. The investors exchanged their shares for stock in Sun Community Bancorp, later folded into Capitol Bancorp, on their third anniversary. This was their "liquidity exit," carrying with it a 50 percent bump in their investment—not a great return, all things considered, as is made clear elsewhere in this book.

In any case, Bank of Tucson is an example of seizing the

tried-and-true community-bank opportunity that opens when big banks buy smaller ones and ignore the demand for personal banking. Mike demonstrates that. He learned the ropes at well-run larger banks, including National Bank of Arizona, establishing contacts and a customer base which he took with him to his own bank.

He knows how to motivate people and has a keen appreciation for the bottom line. Customers pay him well for his services. He believes in "spread, net interest margin, loan yield, loan fees," he says. "That's where it starts." He controls expenses. The net result is an enviable ROE, the key to a shareholder's heart. His is a conservative balance sheet, with strong loan reserves, few charge-offs, and no hot money, or brokered CDs.

Thanks in part to contacts made through Rich Flynn, Mike and his staff generate a high quantity of loans in commercial real estate and construction. Mike takes pride in what he's paid for them. Indeed, loan fees over all account for $50,000 a month for the bank, whose average yield, with fees, is around 7 percent.

Mike is proud too of his cost reductions. He negotiated and bought his own furniture and equipment at bargain prices and shows off a beautiful directors table that looks to be worth ten times the $2,500 he paid for it. He is tight with his marketing budget but spends $72,000 a year on radio advertising that pays off. He is generous with salaries and bonuses and humble about his own banking skills, giving ample credit to his lenders.

For services such as electronic data processing, marketing, audit work, investment, human resources, and assets and liabilities management committee (ALCO) services, he relies in part on what's offered by Capitol Bancorp.

He stays alert to what needs changing. Among his innovations is locating computer screens below the desk top, so customers do not have to talk over a monitor. He considers the drive-up window of "critical" importance: "Moms," he said, "don't want to get out of their cars if they have kids with them."

He's a casual, down-home guy, without pretense, who by

the way hates early morning meetings. He's straightforward and takes guff from no one. He's a likeable guy whom you trust instantly.

As an alert and innovative CEO, he is in my Exhibit A category in how to run a community bank. For instance, he recently opened a small loan production office in nearby Nogales, on the Mexican border, staffing it with an experienced Hispanic loan officer. The goal is to make Export-Import Bank-guaranteed loans to packers and distributors of produce, Americans and Mexicans, this in a town that combined with the much bigger Nogales, Sonora, across the border, its "sister city," has grown into a metropolitan area of four hundred thousand.

Seventy percent of North America's produce comes through Nogales, Mike says. He saw his opportunity, and he took it. In the five months Bank of Tucson has been in Nogales, it has averaged some $6 million to $7 million in loans, averaging 6 to 7 percent interest. A very profitable move indeed.

Competing against Bank of Tucson in Nogales are Wells Fargo and Bank One, but Mike expects his bank's personalized service to do very well there. That's community banking, after all, outdoing the bigger with the best.

Chapter 21

Butte Community Bank, Chico, California:

Keith Robbins

Keith Robbins started Butte Community Bank, now in Chico and other Butte County, California, towns, when he was forty-seven. It was the right age for the CEO of a de novo community bank, according to the bank consultant Ed Carpenter. Equally important was that he had worked entirely in community banks.

The rest of his life, including what I call his PSD degree, "Poor, Smart, and Driven," seemed also to prepare him. He joined the army out of high school in Bakersfield, California, where he grew up, a "true mustang," untamed. Out after three years, he took some college courses at night, married, and went to work as a loan officer for an industrial bank. He moved to a finance company in 1963 as an installment loan officer.

He went to California Republic Bank in Bakersfield in 1971 as a loan officer—a bank with some $60 million in assets, overloaded with branches of only $5 million to $10 million each. Those were "days of excessive branching," he mused. Promoted to manager of one of them, he was told to "light a fire" there. It was an opportunity to study commercial loans. He taught himself by studying files.

In 1980 he left California Republic, well before it was acquired by First Interstate of California, for a new bank being started near Palm Springs, California, three hundred miles away. This was Yucca Valley Bank. It was two months before opening. Invited by a president he had worked for earlier, he came as executive vice president, leaving ten years later as president, when the bank's capitalization had risen from $1.25 million, all raised locally, to $65 million. The bank had four branches and had several times been given a top FDIC CAMELS rating of 1. He enrolled at the Pacific Coast Banking School, at the University of Washington. He was forty-two. It was tune-up time.

Not for long, however. He hankered after his Northern California home area, and when a friend asked him to run a trade school in the North Bay, he took the position, even though it meant leaving banking. The young-mustang response pattern was still operating. His school career was over in short order, however, when the place was sold soon after he joined it. It would be back to banking, he decided.

That's when he got a call from Gary Findley about a position with the not yet formed Butte Community Bank. Wells Fargo had bought the seven-year-old Bank of Paradise (California). Starting a new bank to fill the community-banking gap had proven troublesome. The man first chosen as president left town. The second stood in the way of FDIC approval, and investors could not be found.

Would Robbins, the third choice, take the job? He would, and the buyers' logjam gave way. Investors began coming aboard in Paradise and Oroville, twenty miles apart. In the seasoned Robbins, supremely well versed in community banking, they had chief executive and chief loan officer and marketing officer all in one. He stayed in Paradise. The senior lending officer went to the Oroville branch to double as its manager.

When stock sales fell $300,000 short of the targeted $3.5 million, the directors signed a note for that amount jointly and individually. The bank opened in mid-December 1990, with seventeen employees, three of them part-timers. Eight of the fourteen full-timers still worked for the bank after thirteen years, when the bank had 181 employees. Senior managers have been with the bank from the start; no executive or manager has left for a competitor. The original directors have all remained.

The bank has begun hiring second-generation employees. It trains them as high school students, so they learn and understand "what Mom and Dad do." Six to eight had been hired by mid-2003.

In any case, he does not hire officer-level people for the business they bring, but for the business he expects them to bring as people who share his philosophy. It's a rule with him.

As for the $3.5 million to start, Robbins would not consider that enough in 2003. Closer to ten times that would be necessary. "How do you leverage with even $10 million?" he asks. "How do you invest so little at a profit? It's not easy."

Directors at Butte Bank do not borrow from the bank, as Robbins insisted from the start. Neither are they privy to borrowers' financial statements, because the bank operates in small towns, where people are more likely to know one another. Robbins also insisted on having right of approval for small loans.

As for investing in the bank, he put in the same amount as everyone else, so he would be an equal partner and not a "hired gun." The same went (for the same reason) for the other officers, who were expected to buy stock.

OVERALL SUCCESS

At year-end 2003, Butte Community Bank had deposits of $342 million, a 1.56 percent return on assets, a 20.8 percent return on equity, and no loan loss. In 2003 it made $5.27 million on $27 million income—$21.5 million in interest income and $5.4 million in noninterest income. By year-end 2003, it had $385 million in assets, $246 million in loans, $329 million in deposits, and $25 million in equity—up from that $3.5 million at the start, remember.

It is the only bank to rate as Super Premier Performing for eleven consecutive years in the Findley Reports—every year since the bank began to be rated in 1992. It ranked among the top twenty community banks as reported by the FDIC in *Independent Banker Magazine*. And it was named a top ROE (Return on Equity) Subchapter C corporation (all community banks before 1997) in the June 2002 issue of *American Banker* magazine—the only California community bank so named in the category of banks worldwide with assets between $150 million and $300 million in 2001.

Indeed, the bank earned a healthy over 20 percent ROE for each of the seven years, 1996-2002.

As a top-ranked community bank in the state's poorest county, which Robbins said was "almost bankrupt" when the bank was started, Butte Community Bank verifies Gary Findley's contention that a bank with the right ingredients can be successful anywhere. It was Findley who told me about Butte Bank and urged me to talk to Robbins, the architect of its exemplary success.

The bank opened a full-service operation in Chico in 1996. After ten years it had six offices in five communities. In 2002 the board formed a holding company, Community Valley Bancorp, with a view to making an acquisition to be funded with $8 million in a trust-preferred security.

For EDP Robbins went with popular ITI Internet Services, of Tacoma, Washington. For merchant-card processing, he chose Fiserv. The bank did its own (transaction) processing. But as a rule of thumb, he recommends farming out such operations for a bank's first few years, to save money.

Robbins made credit quality a major emphasis, convinced as he was of the need to avoid substantial credit losses in the first few years. Loan charge-offs never topped $500,000. A $113,000 charge-off for 2001 was wholly recovered in 2002.

The bank does a good deal of short-term lending. About 50 to 60 percent are concluded in a year. He's for "loan velocity" over loan volume because of the points to be earned at the start of each loan.

In any event, "you have to be flexible," he said, "and a community bank can be flexible." When interest rates dropped, for instance, the bank got into secondary-market financing and construction lending.

All in all, funds are kept busy with loans. This keeps the bank's investment portfolio "very short and fairly small, because we're also usually 85 to 88 percent loaned up."

THE BOARD

All but one of the ten directors (Robbins) are outsiders. For the first five years, they served gratis except for stock options. Since then they get $800 a month. The chairman gets another $500 per meeting. The usual committees are operative: audit, loan, compensation, and fixed-asset. Committee meetings are open to all directors. What business directors bring to the bank amounts to not much. The bank's success, said Robbins, has been "CEO-driven."

Robbins rates employee communication very highly. The "cornerstone" of the bank's success he says is regular written employee communication by way of a newsletter, "What we are all about."

Another major factor is employee training. Almost all attend leadership school at bank expense. The goal is to help break down the "fear of rejection" that too many feel, said Robbins. Of the more than one hundred who have attended, the vast majority (86 percent) have so valued the experience that they have sent members of their own families, paying their tuition.

Robbins is like a coach. He wants people on his team who are willing to work, in contrast to the many who "think too much about hours spent at work." He wants "A-team players," not also-rans. Customer, shareholder, and staff are equally important, "but staff is where success starts."

Motivation becomes a major issue, of course. "It's a matter of risk and reward," he said. You want investors on your team, people with something to gain and something to lose. Salary, when all you have to gain is keeping your job, isn't enough. Commitment requires stock ownership and stock options, so that people act like owners, working "to increase stock value."

When he started the bank, he put the eggs of his $63,000 IRA into a basket of bank stock that today is worth an IRA of more than $1 million.

He also took a reduction in salary in exchange for options on 7 percent of outstanding stock, 24,500 shares of 350,000 sold. His exercise price was $1.77. At $27 in mid-2003, his stock was worth $3,737,000, for a stunning 1,500 percent price increase, not counting dividends, for all original shareholders, including his CFO and chief lending officer, whom he stipulated should also receive options. Investing $10,000 in 1990 got you $150,000 in 2003. That's motivation!

ANCILLARY (NONINTEREST INCOME PRODUCING) SERVICES

The bank draws considerable noninterest income from a variety of ancillary financial services. Secondary loan financing, the packaging and selling of loans, earned about a million in 2002 and was expected to do better in 2003, if only to judge by one midyear month, when it netted some $230,000—this by a division of eleven employees.

In B&I (Business and Industry) loans—SBA-style lending in rural areas—the bank is #1 in California and #5 in the country. On a recent deal, financing of a $5.5 million retirement home preapproved by B&I, the bank earned seven points, or over $350,000, plus a one-point construction fee.

The bank also sells mutual funds and does merchant-card processing. Both are profitable. Merchant-card processing, which employs nine, was netting $35,000 or so a month in mid-2003.

WORKING WITH REGULATORS

Regulators, "an industry in their own right," do an excellent job, far better than when he started in banking, partly because for historical reasons—a new group came in some years back and has stayed on—California examiners are more experienced than they used to be. He has "very good" relationships with them, both state (Department of Financial Institutions) and federal (the FDIC).

The secret is to look on them "as human beings" and "don't always roll over," while being attentive to their priority concerns—"hot buttons." He asks in advance of their coming what these are and prepares with an audit by a Sacramento CPA firm that does thirty or so other community banks. In any case, he says, the banker must get along with regulators and realize that they provide "a good discipline."

Chapter 22

Macatawa Bank, Holland, Michigan:

Ben Smith

Another community-bank success is the Macatawa Bank Corporation in Holland, Michigan, which like other home-grown operations has leaped into the yawning market gap that follows big-bank acquisitions of local banks.

Since opening in November 1997, Macatawa, named after Holland's Lake Macatawa, has become one of the nation's "fastest-growing banks," according to Stifel Nicolaus, profiting mightily from what the analyst calls "customer dislocation caused by recent acquisitions of local, Michigan-based banks by out-of-state rivals."

Fast-growing is right. In six years Macatawa shot up from $11 million assets to $1.4 billion and from two locations to twenty, in three west Michigan counties—Kent, Ottawa, and Allegan.

Macatawa has completed two public offerings—1.5 million shares in April 1998 and 1.6 million more in June 2001.

This community-bank company happened a little differently from others, in that its driving force was an investment banker, Benjamin A. Smith III, who spotted the need for a new influx of community banking.

Ben Smith, president since 1992 of Smith and Associates Investment Management Services in Holland, had put in twenty-one years at the venerable First Michigan Bank (founded in 1900 as Zeeland State Bank) and its subsidiary in Zeeland, a town of 5,800 people that is six miles east of Holland, a city of thirty-six thousand people.

A Detroit native with no interest in staying there, he joined First Michigan, a $60 million bank, as its first trust investment officer in the early 1970s. His assignment was to set up a trust investment operation within its trust department, which itself dated only from the mid-1960s. Consolidating the trust department with investment services, he introduced mutual funds and a broker-dealer operation and oversaw the department's marketing, operations, and accounting, in Holland and Zeeland. In Zeeland the First Michigan branch, which enjoyed home-office protection because Michigan was not yet allowing multibank holding companies, had the only trust department in town.

First Michigan, "progressive" in its approach, became a "premier, profitable community bank" proud of its earnings and its customer service, Smith recalled.

Then Michigan laws changed to permit multibank holding companies, and First Michigan expanded. It formed a holding company that bought the Community Bank of Dowagiac, some fifty miles to the south, and another in Muskegon, about the same distance to the north. Eventually First Michigan was to buy seventeen banks in all. Smith was to handle investments for all seventeen.

Meanwhile, banking as such was becoming a "dead business," as the First Michigan chairman, Robert Denherder, put it. As the economy faltered, loan demand decreased, and noninterest income (fees) rose in importance. The focus was shifting to customer relationships. But big banks, competing solely on price, were not making the shift.

First Michigan did make the shift, establishing its own trust company, captive life insurance company, mutual funds, and investment advisory subsidiary. Internal growth followed—15 percent—and external, to the tune of seventeen banks. But it veered from the required new focus, in Smith's view, and was sold in 1997 to $20 billion Huntington Bancshares, of Columbus Ohio. The sale effectively called a halt to First Michigan's community—bank posture.

Into the void Smith inserted Macatawa Bank. He raised $8.6 million in a private placement and opened with two branches in 1997, the first in a Zeeland storefront in November—1,300 square feet at $800 a month—the second in a rented building in Holland in December.

He kept an eye on expenses. Opening costs were a paltry $50,000, including the very low Zeeland rent. Neither branch had ATMs, parking, or drive-up facility. In almost no time, the bank was opening 1,500 accounts a month and was growing at $10 million a month, and this with no out-of-market large CDs. This bank was funding itself.

Its growth was aided and abetted by the clumsy way in which Huntington Bancshares handled its conversion and assimilation of First Michigan. It was "the worst" such assimilation that Smith had ever seen. It left First Michigan staff disillusioned, for one thing. Smith quickly hired the best of them, as he had hired as his founding president a refugee from big-bank environment, twenty-five-year veteran Phil Koning, who had been "community president" in Holland for Kalamazoo-based First of America.

By June 2001, two-thirds into its fourth year, Macatawa Bank Corporation did a secondary offering, already mentioned, of 1.6 million shares. These sold at $16 a share. Dain Rauscher Wessels and Stifel Nicolaus handled it. By now shareholders' equity was about $40 million. Assets were about $530 million. The bank had thirteen branches in three counties in western Michigan.

There was more to come. In April 2002, Macatawa bought

fifteen-year-old, $250-million-asset Grand Bank, in Grand Rapids, Michigan, a city of more than 190,000 and center of an $8.5 billion market, where dominant Old Kent—"one of the better large community banks," said Smith—had just been bought by Cincinnati-based Fifth Third Bank.

Macatawa Bank Corporation now had two wholly owned subsidiary banks, Macatawa Bank and Grand Bank, with approximate combined *pro forma* assets, projected to year-end 2001, of $962 million, deposits of $750 million, and loans of $769 million. It had become profitable in its second full year, 1999, earning $693,000. The next year, it earned $3.3 million. In the first quarter of 2001, it earned $1.1 million, compared to $527,000 in the first quarter of 2000. Net income for 2001 was $3,349,000. For 2002 it was $9.5 million. For 2003 it was $11.78 million.

They did it (or would do it), according to the May 2001 prospectus, "by opening de novo branches, hiring experienced bankers with existing customer relationships in our local market, providing outstanding customer services and *capitalizing on customer dissatisfaction resulting from bank acquisitions in our markets.*" (Italics added)

Old Kent's sale to Fifth Third contributed to this dissatisfaction. As has been said, Macatawa succeeded largely because Huntington in the Holland area and Fifth Third in Grand Rapids were unable to assimilate banks in competition with Macatawa. Nor could they get a handle on community banking.

It's a pattern. Big banks make staff and customers unhappy, presenting opportunities to Ben Smith and his like who open their own banks, staffing them with experienced *community bankers* who concentrate on personal service. The big banks seem unable to understand that.

Macatawa success has run through the immediate past year, as seen in these figures:

Year-end 2003:

Return on Assets	.94 percent
Return on Equity	9.90 percent
Net Interest Margin	3.60 percent
Reserve for Loans	1.39 percent
Nonperforming Loans	.14 percent

1997-2003 (000s)

	Assets	Branches	Shareholders Equity
2003	$1.40	20	$130 mil
2002	$1.18	17	$114 mil
2001	$670 mil.	14	$66.5 mil.
2000	$499 mil.	13	$38 mil.
1999	$345 mil.	13	$34 mil.
1998	$189 mil.	8	$19.6 mil.
1997	$11 mil.	1	8 mil.

The Macatawa directors receive an annual retainer of $5,000 and are paid $500 per board meeting attended and $250 for committee meetings attended.

At year-end 2003, directors and executive officers owned 845,000 shares, of which Ben Smith owned 309,000 shares, for a combined total of 10.1 percent. The stock closed at $28.39. Six weeks later, on February 17, 2004, the stock closed at $26.70 with a yield of 1.7 percent and a multiple earnings of 19.21 on earnings of $1.39 per share.

Chapter 23

Community Bank of Oak Park and River Forest, Oak Park, Illinois: Marty Noll

Marty Noll, the quintessential community banker, has taken advantage of the wave of mergers and the inability of big banks to compete against a well-run community bank.

He opened his community bank in November 1996, in Oak Park, Illinois, with $5,250,000 in capital. Its net worth on December 31, 2003, was $12 million, with $1.8 million in loan reserves. He has reached his seventh anniversary with total assets of $163 million, loans of $132 million, an ROA of 1.6, and an ROE of 22.11 percent with earnings of $2.8 million. It's a great de novo community-bank success story.

His background was ideal. He started at Chicago's American National Bank in 1968 as a management trainee, after graduate work in economics at Indiana University following undergraduate work at Catholic University in Washington, DC.

In four years, as a second vice president in the correspondent division, he was helping me accumulate Colonial Bank stock after I had borrowed $4.5 million from American National so I could buy a controlling block of Colonial. This is when I met him.

Four years after that, in 1976, he began a community-bank

career that included presidency of Security Chicago Corp. and divisional presidency for First National Bank of Chicago in Oak Park.

I hired him in 1993 as president and CEO of our $100-million-asset Avenue Bank of Oak Park, where he served for two years, until shortly after it was purchased by Firstar. He had an important mission at Avenue Bank, which under its previous president had received an unsatisfactory CRA (community reinvestment) report from the FDIC which effectively stalled our approval from the Federal Reserve for acquisition of two banks.

He did a great job, drawing on his extensive Oak Park experience and his excellent people skills. In a year we got our satisfactory grade and completed our acquisition of the two banks. In January 1995 we sold First Colonial to Firstar Bank. Not long afterwards, he availed himself of the "walk away" clause which was part of the severance package we had negotiated for our staff, whereby an officer could walk away from Firstar with an attractive package.

He knew he wanted to start a community bank to go head to head with what was now Firstar's branch—the bank he once headed. In early 1995 he contacted an acquaintance of us both, Jim Haugh, a financial consultant, to help him put together a group that would apply for a state banking charter.

They decided to sound out a group of friends with a presentation. About fifty people attended. At the end of the meeting, Marty handed out cards where each could check "I'm not interested" or "I have some interest" or "I am interested and could be interested in investing" a given amount. Marty walked out of the meeting with $4 million in interest. He eventually raised about $2.5 million from that group out of $5.5 million total raised.

They got an organizing group together. Marty approached three of the best of our old board of Avenue Bank—Rich Gloor, a local real estate executive; Hank Pearsall, former Sanford

Corporation CEO; and Chatka Ruggiero, a local real state investor. They added Dr. Arthur Morris and Dr. Eugene McEnery shortly thereafter.

They started their application process for a state bank in the fall of '95, having sent out a book to prospective investors during the summer.

Marty put $50,000 of his own money into a holding company—Oak Park River Forest Bankshares—to cover expenses. They received their permit to organize in early '96 and had a $5.5 million sale of stock completed by the end of June. Then they downstreamed $5.25 million to the bank and waited for the charter. On November 6, 1996, they got it and opened their bank with approximately $3 million in loans, $6 million in deposits, and $5.25 million in capital.

After a first-year operating loss (par for the course), the bank went on a steady upswing, from a 1998 profit of $298,000 to a 2000 profit of $1.66 million. Loans and deposits rose from $33 million and $42 million respectively to $62 million and $78 million in the same period.

By the fifth year, 2001, loans were $77 million; assets were $110 million.

At year-end 2003 shareholders' equity had more than doubled in seven years from the $5.25 million initial investment to $12 million. Assuming a market value of 1.75 to 2 percent of book, the bank is worth $21 million to $24 million, or about four times that initial investment.

The bank, Community Bank of Oak Park and River Forest, opened with nine employees in 7,500 square feet of space in an old S&L building, Great American Federal Savings. They had two drive-up lanes which Marty calls "critical" to their success.

There are just three community banks left in the Oak Park area, down from twelve banks or branches in the early '90s, most of them purchased by larger banks. They are Forest Park National Bank, which had $125 million assets at year-end 2001;

First Bank of Oak Park, $183 million at year-end 2003; and Marty's bank, $163 million, also at year-end 2003.

Major-bank competitors are First Chicago, Firstar, Fifth Third, Citicorp, Corus, and Charter One.

The bank has only seven directors, including Marty and the chairman, Hank Pearsall. They have three committees, loan, audit, and personnel and compensation. They have no marketing committee. That function is outsourced to the George Morvis firm, Financial Shares Corporation. There is no executive committee, explains Marty, because "there are only seven directors," which is darn few. Directors get no cash stipend but receive stock options at the end of the year.

The bank now has a small staff of thirty-five, including six lenders. The staff is small because they have outsourced "everything," Marty says. They have no proof machines: First American Bank, Tom Wells's organization, performs "back room" operations, including proof, cash letter, and Web master debit cards, for approximately $30,000 a month.

They outsource external auditing, loan auditing, compliance, and marketing. But they handle internally investment, asset-liability, and GAAP function. They have Internet banking.

The bank has been conservatively run. The loan-to-deposit ratio has always been between 80 to 85 percent, and they have never suffered a loan loss. They charged off $26,000 about three years ago and collected it within sixty days.

Deposits of $100,000 and up account for only about 18 percent of deposits; what's more, these depositors are all customers. That is they have no brokered CDs and none of their mere $1 million in municipal deposits are in the $100,000[+] category.

Their loan portfolio breaks down as follows:

Commercial Real Estate	$48,600,000
Home Equity	$29,400,000
Personal	$18,900,000

The mortgage loans are all short term, none exceeding three years.

Reserve for loans is 1.3.

Future plans? "We'd like to buy a money manager, but they're tough to come by. We want to consolidate our presence in our market, with a branch in every part of it. For instance, we'd like to branch into south Oak Park and enlarge our branch in River Forest.

"We'll continue our conservative lending practices. Our loan loss reserve of $1,813,000 is still untouched. We charged off a small loan seven years ago, but it was fully recovered. Our budget calls for $200 million in assets in 2004. We feel we can become a $500 million bank in this market and still maintain a high profit."

What is the bank worth today seven years after starting with $5.2 million in capital? At 225 times book, $27 million; at fifteen times earnings $30 million. That would be five to six times the investment. Not bad.

One of the reasons Marty has been successful is his extraordinary involvement in community affairs.

His wife, Mary Lou, is active in many community affairs. Health care and children's causes are among her favorites. They have two daughters, both college graduates.

Hank Pearsall, chairman of the bank, has been very important to the bank. A bright, outgoing, experienced CEO, he served on our board at the Avenue Bank of Oak Park.

I asked Marty why his bank has done so well.

"First of all," he said, "we answer the phone with a human being. We have no machine-answered 800 numbers.

"The bank Firstar bought, our old bank, and turned into a branch lost focus. It has had two to three managers in the last five years. It has no direction. Credit decisions are all made elsewhere. They have a centralized 800 number. We hired away three of their best people who wanted to be with a community bank.

"For example," he said, "a woman came in recently and opened an account with a significant balance she had just closed at the [once] Firstar [now U.S. Bank] branch. She said the branch manager had asked where she was going. She told him. He said, 'We can't compete against them.' We're successful because we relate to people and the community. The branches don't know how to do that."

Chapter 24

First Bank & Trust, Evanston, Illinois:

Bob Yohanan

Robert R. "Bob" Yohanan's career path was typical for a community-bank founder. He went from large-bank training to entrepreneur, helped by an exquisite sense of timing, a clear vision of what he meant to achieve, and the need to call his own shots.

A 1962 Naval Academy graduate, he won the Bronze Star with Combat "V" and the Air Medal in Vietnam. Leaving the navy in 1967, he got a master's degree in international relations from the University of Chicago and in 1968 was recruited by the First National Bank of Chicago, for whom he went overseas, serving variously as area head for the British Isles and Scandinavia, regional manager for the Caribbean, general manager of the Dublin Branch, and a credit manager in Beirut, Lebanon.

Returning to Chicago, he worked on integrating with First National its newly acquired banks, including American National Bank of Chicago. From this he gained experience that he thinks probably helped him most in starting a bank of his own.

In 1987 he left First National for Chicago's high-performing, billion-dollar Lake Shore National Bank, on Michigan Avenue, where as president and chief operating officer he honed his skills in commercial lending, retail banking, and trust and investment. All would prove vital to his work as a community banker.

First National bought Lake Shore in 1994, and the time was at hand for him to start his own bank. He looked about him and liked what he saw in north suburban Evanston, where big out-of-state banks were buying up community banks and creating a vacuum for the personal service and local accountability that is the hallmark of community banking. He looked right off at two experienced community bankers, both once orphaned by acquisition, Howard Kain and James Lytle.

Kain had headed First Illinois Bank and Trust of Evanston, bought four years earlier by Bank One, which was later to acquire First National of Chicago. Lytle had been senior vice president and senior lending officer at State National, bought in 1988 by NBD of Detroit. Lytle went then to Pioneer Bank and Trust, in Chicago, another community bank. He had also been mayor of Evanston. He and Kain each had his following, each had a high Evanston profile.

Evanston was ripe for a new bank, what with those two highly regarded community banks recently out of the picture. It was a city of seventy-six thousand whose banks had $2 billion in deposits. It had no manufacturing but a concentration of not-for-profit organizations, including Northwestern University, Kendall College, two big hospitals, and Rotary International, whose headquarters is in Evanston.

First, they had to raise money. To attract investors from within the community, Yohanan, Kain, and Lytle did an intrastate offering, further limiting buyers to five hundred and requiring a $10,000 minimum investment. They aimed at $8 million but raised $10 million in four months at $50 a share and had to give back $1.5 million.

Corporate structure was another issue. Instead of the usual chairman-CEO and president-COO titling, he, Kain, and Lytle at the start became "managing directors," Bob's philosophy being that ego has no place in bank titles and structure. Later

Bob took on the CEO title, for the bank and for its holding company, First Evanston Bancorp, Inc.

The bank, First Bank and Trust of Evanston, opened in September 1995, with thirteen employees and the motto, "We put Evanston first." In eighteen months it broke even. Assets rose yearly: $96 million, $147 million, $196.5 million, $232.3 million, by September 30, 2001, $273.4 million, and by year-end 2003 more than $300 million.

Deposits did too: $78 million, $128 million, $174 million, $195.7 million, and $240.2 million by the 2001 date. The largest deposit category was money market accounts—a consumer standby—of $126.4 million. There were also "very substantial" deposits by not-for-profit organizations—institutions of higher and lower education, medical, and "a wide variety of other," according to Yohanan.

And loans: $72 million, $105 million, $157 million, $196.4 million, and on September 30, 2001, $224 million, the largest category being consumer loans of $113.4 million. Loan loss reserve was $3.3 million.

And interest income: $8 million, $11 million, $15.3 million, and $13 million in three quarters of 2001. On September 30, after only three quarters, net income was $1.414 million, up $554,000 over the whole previous year for a 60 percent increase.

The high noninterest income—$1.4 million before expenses—was the work of the bank's new trust-investment-management department, started late in 2000. This department—a division, not a subsidiary, of the bank—had $100 million under management by late 2001 and was sending $33,000 in fee income to the bank each month.

Consumer loans—almost half the total and almost all indirect auto loans—loomed big. Yohanan had a good deal of experience with auto dealer loans in the late '80s and early '90s at Lake Shore Bank, where were very important. But these were floor plans and indirect paper. First Evanston was not in the floor-plan business, however. Instead, Bob built what he called "a very strong indirect team," including the chief auto-loan buyer from Lake Shore. First Evanston also had several car dealers as shareholders.

The bank's net interest margin was a respectable 3.96 percent, its return on assets 0.76 percent, and its return on equity 8.92 percent. It operated with an efficiency ratio of 61 percent. "We are still increasing market share," Bob commented. "We haven't raised fees in six years, and they were low then! Now is the time to build our customer base."

The bank made another stock offering in November 2000, selling $3.3 million in stock at $100 a share—twice the price of five years earlier and 140 percent of book value, which was $72. There were 450 buyers, up from 250 in 1995. Shareholders' equity, $12.6 million at the close of 1998, reached $14.7 million.

The staff, skeletal in 1995 at thirteen, by 2002 was a still skeletal sixty-five, only one employee per $400,000 in assets.

By 2002 there were three locations—the original, main location, in downtown Evanston, another on Central Street in northwest Evanston, a third in a suburb to the north, very affluent Winnetka.

The bank had twelve directors by now (thirteen at year-end 2003), not counting Yohanan, who was managing director and CEO. He was also chairman and CEO of its holding company, First Evanston Bancorp, Inc., and since 1998 had been a director of the Federal Reserve Bank of Chicago.

There are five directors' committees—a loan committee which meets every two weeks; a trust committee and an audit committee, both of which meet quarterly; a compensation committee which meets annually; and an executive committee. Directors were paid in stock options (two hundred shares a year) for the first five years, rather than cash. Since 2000 they have been paid $200 a meeting.

I asked Bob why First Bank and Trust of Evanston had been so successful.

"Our products and services are excellent. Our people are experienced and service-oriented and involved in the community"—in the Evanston Chamber of Commerce, for instance, of which Howard Kain is a past president, and in Evanston Inventure, a local economic development partnership, of which Yohanan is chairman. "We know the community," said Bob, "and the community knows us."

There was another element, their timing. "Frankly," he said, "we got a boost from the competition. We came along when the big banks were reducing services and chasing people away. They became our sales force! We told people, 'Merged Bank Victims Welcome Here.'"

Chapter 25

Bank of Stockton, Stockton, California:

Tom Shaffer

For Thomas H. Shaffer, executive vice president and chief operating officer of the Bank of Stockton, a bank's success starts with "communication with customers and staff." And the customer is "always right." And rates and fees have to be market-sensitive. And your staff better stay around a long time and be loyal to your bank.

"That longevity and loyalty is critical. You have to take care of the people who got you there. I mean the employees. One of ours has been with us fifty-three years. Many have been here twenty, twenty-five, thirty years. We have a family environment."

Shaffer joined the Bank of Stockton in June 1995, from the just-sold First Los Angeles Bank, which as its new president and CEO two years earlier he had found "in terrible shape." His job was "to fix it up," which he did.

He had earlier been at California Republic Bank, in Bakersfield, as a vice president, executive vice president, and then CEO, and at Bank of America, working in agricultural lending and branch management. He was a Fresno State graduate, class of 1971. At this writing he was chairman-elect of the California Bankers Association, set to take office June 1, 2004.

Another quality of a good banker is to recognize the beneficial role of regulators. "Examinations are a good discipline," Shaffer said. Furthermore, examiners are getting better at it.

As for FASB 91 and when to charge loan fees, he said, "We amortize loan fees over the life of the loan and follow regulations to the letter of the law. I don't believe banks should distort earnings by trying to take fees up front."

Currently, the Bank of Stockton is doing nicely. Its deposits were up 18 percent in the first half of 2003. "Low interest rates will slow that down, however," he said in July of 2003, "as depositors put money where it will earn more. But deposits will still continue to grow at 11 to 12 percent. Net interest margin has been 5.5 percent, but lately has fallen below 5 percent. We're keeping short on our investments. We're not reaching out long. We also have a very strong 12.5 to 13 percent capital."

The bank operates in a market of 325,000 people. The area is a bastion of community banks, with three established billion-dollar community banks and two de novo banks. In fact, it's the last such bastion in the state, and it's very competitive. The two new banks—Service First Bank and Community Bank of San Joaquin—are each about two years old, with $80 million to $90 million in assets.

Bank of Stockton has $1.7 billion in assets. Its parent, 1867 Western Financial Corporation, is owned by the Eberhardt family. Doug Eberhardt is chairman and CEO of the holding company. Tom Shaffer is its president. The bank's charter is California's oldest.

The bank is active in the community, making philanthropic donations of over a million a year, the largest amount to University of the Pacific, where Doug Eberhardt is on the Board of Regents. Shaffer has served on the board of its business school.

The 1867 Western is the new owner of Modesto Commerce Bank. It was looking in Modesto, which they considered vibrant and promising, in early 2003, with a view to expanding by starting a de novo bank. They heard Modesto Commerce was for sale and bought it in June.

Shaffer considers Modesto Commerce "the biggest de novo success story in California," with its 84 percent business accounts, 16 percent retail—"a mix we like," he said. And it fit their requirement of at least $250 million in assets. "You need that big a bank to get good talent," he said, in this case referring to Jeff Burda and his staff. Modesto, for its part, liked the offer largely because Stockton would keep the Modesto Commerce name and the talented Modesto Commerce employees.

Chapter 26

Wyoming National Bank, Riverton, Wyoming:

Kent Shurtleff

A town is important in Wyoming, our second-highest state, to the extent that its population exceeds its elevation. Riverton, with ten thousand people at 4,956 feet, qualifies. In a state said to have more antelope than its half-million people, Riverton is definitely important.

Founded in 1906, Riverton has always been in competition with its neighbor twenty-five miles to the southwest, Lander. Riverton has the regional airport, the regional college—Central Wyoming College—and the regional weather station, which until recently was in Lander. The town has clout!

It's in Fremont County, which is named after the explorer and Oregon Trail blazer, John Charles Fremont, who came through nearby South Pass on his way to California. Farming, ranching, and mining are its economic mainstays. The area raises good timothy hay, alfalfa, hay, malting barley, sugar beets, silage corn, and pinto beans. Large ranches date from the late 1800s. The town is in but separated from the Wind River Indian Reservation, one of the largest in the country, in which live Arapaho and Shoshone tribe members.

It's not a boom town. Population rose from 9,200 in 1985 to 10,000 in 2000. The town suffered, as all Wyoming did, during the farm and ranch recession of the mid-1980s. Banking fared according to the small-town pattern: several community banks sold out to larger chains in the '90s.

Nor is it affluent. The average weekly wage is $391. But the 5 percent sales tax is the only nonfederal tax in town. There is no state income tax, no business inventory tax.

Best of all, Riverton has an average of 347 sunshine days a year!

And it has a new bank, Wyoming National. On Saturday, August 4, 2002, I met with Kent Shurtleff, its president, and Bill Garland, its board cochairman, who started it and have on their hands a model of community banking, what I call the wave of banking's future.

Kent Shurtleff had been a senior lender and executive vice president of the Riverton State Bank, a community bank. A rancher himself, he had made numerous agricultural loans in the area. Amid rumors that the Riverton State Bank would be bought by Wells Fargo, he got a call from the chairman of Rawlins National Bank 150 miles to the south and east. Would he come to work with them and set up a loan production office in Riverton?

When Kent said he had in mind starting his own bank in Riverton, the man said he would help him do that. So Kent resigned his Riverton job and joined Rawlins National Bank. He began putting together a board of directors and applying for a national charter for his own Riverton bank. Meanwhile, he made loans which the Rawlins Bank warehoused until he and his team got their bank started, at which time they would buy them back.

They got their charter on June 14, 1999, and opened with only $3 million in capital—it was all they thought they would need. They were wrong about that. Surprised by success two years later, they would have to go back to the original investors with a capital call, so much had their bank grown.

But why a national charter, with its lower lending limit and supervision by the Controller of Currency? For the very practical reason that they were familiar with the Controller of Currency people and felt that would expedite the process.

The bank grew far faster than the board thought it would. They budgeted for $25 million in assets after four years; in four and a half years they were at $44 million. They had $38.7 million in deposits and $32 million in loans, of which $17 million were real estate, $8 million (26 percent) were agriculture loans, $7 million were commercial loans. Their loan-to-deposit ratio was 80 percent.

Shurtleff had originated these loans while still at Rawlins National Bank, with the understanding that the Rawlins bank would "warehouse" them there until his bank opened, when he would buy them back. These early loans supplied a quick-start $5 million.

Earnings kept pace with growth. The bank broke even in its thirteenth month. It made money (about $80,000) in its third year, 2002. By mid-2003 it recovered its entire preopening expense of $400,000—which it had written off in its first year. The loan reserve reached $390,000 in 2003. The bank was at first budgeted to make $120,000 in 2003, but at year-end earnings were $224,000, for an ROA of 0.6 percent.

At year-end 2003, they had deposits of $41.7 million—$15.7 million in time deposits, $13 million in savings, $10 million in demand deposits, and $3 million in other deposits. An unusual 90 percent of the time deposits were for less than six months. Demand deposits were over 25 percent of the total. Total assets were $46.8 million, up 13 percent for the year.

Most of the operating loans, agricultural and commercial, are variable and tied to money-center prime—without the bank's legal limit of 15 percent of its capital since September 2001, when the U.S. Controller of Currency allowed more than that in states where state-chartered banks had a higher limit. The legal lending limit for Wyoming National in 2003 was $525,000. Shurtleff's own limit, board-imposed, was $100,000. Loans over $100,000 were referred to the loan committee, which worked hard at this responsibility, as has been noted.

The startling growth of Wyoming National was nothing to pull back from. "When we saw [the asset total] growing, we wanted to keep it growing," said Bill Garland. "When we hit $35 million, we had a good foothold."

They did it all for two years out of a trailer they picked up from First National Bank of Niwot, Colorado, for $30,000. They fixed it up for $22,000, connected it to Riverton water and sewage, and that was it. After two years they moved into a new building on Route 26 (Federal Boulevard) as it ran through Riverton, on ten thousand square feet they got at $150,000 an acre. The new building cost $1.8 million.

The bank has thirteen directors—farmers, ranchers, businessmen, including Tom Youtz, a Ford-Lincoln-Mercury dealer across the street, who dropped in while I sat with Shurtleff and the chairman, Bill Garland. Each director owns roughly equal amount of stock. The thirteen work hard at seven committees. The six-member loan committee, for instance, meets weekly. Eight serve on the executive committee. The other committees are the standard batch—compensation, marketing, assets and liabilities management (ALCO), privacy, and building committees.

At year-end 2003, the bank had a twenty-six-person staff, including three at the recently opened Lander branch, which was approved in June 2003, with $2 million in assets. The bank had begun in 1999 with eight, six of whom came from what had been the Riverton State Bank but had become the Riverton Branch of Wells Fargo Bank Wyoming. Rumors had proven true, and Wells Fargo had bought Riverton State. The six much preferred working for Wyoming National, a community bank.

The bank's four competitors are all branches of super-regional banks—the Wells Fargo branch ($35 million in assets, down from $60 million before competing with the new Wyoming National); U.S. Bank, a branch of U.S. Bancorp ($20 million); First Interstate ($75 million); and Central Bank and Trust ($56.7 million in deposits).

They expected significant synergies from a five-person brokerage business purchased in mid-2002 that they moved to a Main Street office, in downtown Riverton. Then next to it, they opened a branch.

The bank is a stand-alone, true community bank, performing its own proof (listing and recording of checks and the like) and bookkeeping. Not surprisingly, it outsources audit and legal work—to Denver firms—but not asset-liability or marketing. For compliance they use a part-timer who does the same work for three other banks.

Its thirteen directors are all local except two experienced bankers from Rawlins. One, Richard Chenoweth, is president of the Rawlins National Bank. The other, Tim Borden, "a real player," is Rawlins National's chairman, cochairman of another bank, in Steamboat Springs, and chairman of a third, First National Bank of Wyoming in Laramie.

Shurtleff considers the board very important, especially its two banker members, who have helped "dramatically." Earnings have lagged because of unexpected rapid growth and the compressed interest rate. Kent, admittedly "green," relied "heavily" on the two bankers, he said.

Wyoming National is a story of mostly inexperienced bank investors who realized their town, dominated by ineffectual large-bank branches, needed its own bank. Among them Kent Shurtleff, a long-time resident with solid contacts and good reputation, became the key element. He brought customers and key staff from his previous bank. The hardworking board has also been crucial. All worked together to make Wyoming National Bank a prime example of community banking as the wave of the future.

Chapter 27

Granite Community Bank, Granite Bay, California: Richard Seeba

Outsourcing bank services isn't always necessary, says Richard Seeba, CEO of Granite Community Bank, in Granite Bay, California. You just have to know what you're doing.

He has proved it at Granite Bank, which opened for business in June 2002 and after eighteen months had $53 million in assets and was poised to make about $100,000 in its first full year in business. For Granite Bank, Seeba outsources—to the industry standby, Fiserv, Inc., of Brookfield, Wisconsin—only EDP and item processing.

These go by courier each evening to Fiserv's center in San Leandro. Fiserv then delivers them to the Federal Reserve in San Francisco, transmitting the data to the Fiserv computer center in Chatsworth. Statements come out of Fiserv in Atlanta. They are received the second day of the month.

The cost to Granite Community during the first year was $2,500 a month for item processing (not a flat fee but based on items processed) and about $7,000 a month for data processing.

"If I had done this in-house," said Seeba, "I would have needed two and half FTEs [full-time-equivalent staff], costing $100,000 a year, and would have had to spend another $250,000 for equipment such as proof machines, which would have cost me forty to fifty thousand a year in depreciation. Outsourcing these services is practical and cost effective."

Not so when it comes to other services, in his view. He will need just a little help in human resources and some help with ALCO, he says. His annual financial statement, done by CPA Perry Smith of Sacramento, will cost about $30,000. He did most of the work himself on the bank's charter application, hiring a lawyer for the legal work.

That's it.

It takes experience to figure this sort of thing out. Seeba, a University of San Francisco 1960 graduate and onetime credit union executive, got his experience as a community-bank CEO in banks in Visalia and Paradise. When the Bank of Paradise, which he joined in 1984, was sold to Wells Fargo in 1989, he joined another institution, a thrift and loan in Roseville, again as CEO. This became Roseville First National, a community bank, in 1992. It was sold in 1999 to Western Sierra Bank for about 1.8 times book—a somewhat low multiple, Seeba admits, but the stock has almost quadrupled, rising from $12 to $47 a share. He stayed on as CEO until June 2001.

In August he joined others in organizing Granite Community, which at year-end 2003 had eleven board members serving on four committees: executive, which handles compensation; loan, which meets weekly; ALCO; and audit.

Seeba and the staff are compensated modestly. Rich started at $120,000 salary and has recently been increased to $130,000. He was granted ten thousand options. Board members were awarded five thousand to ten thousand options each, and staff members up to five thousand options.

Seeba and the others raised $7 million in a public offering to capitalize the bank at $10 a share. Investors had a $25,000 minimum purchase, a $300,000 maximum, or 5 percent of the total. The offering took ninety days. Some $400,000 in start-up costs were expensed. The board intends to raise $3.5 million more in a private offering in April 2004 at $10.50. To the original 140 shareholders will be added thirty or so more.

The bank began with eleven staff, at year-end 2003 had seventeen full-time equivalents (FTEs). More staff were to be added in March 2004, when a branch was to be opened in nearby Auburn.

The bank has done well. Demand deposits are roughly 20 percent of total deposits, which are $46 million. Net interest margin is about 5 percent; loan yield is 6.5 percent. An ROA of 0.6 percent to 0.7 percent is forecast for the second full year, 2004.

To what does Seeba attribute this success? "We had a great board. Smart guys! The key, though, is knowing your customers. At Granite Bank, they know us. We get on a first-name basis fast.

"Another thing, we went into a community where a big bank had bought out a community bank. We're doing that again in Auburn, where Auburn Community Bank was bought by Western Sierra and Belvedere Bank was bought by Placer Sierra. The two local banks are gone. We'll do well in Auburn!"

PART III

STARTING A DE NOVO

COMMUNITY BANK

Chapter 28

Starting a Bank: An Overview

Some 1,416 banks with assets under $1 billion were chartered since 1994, for a total of "roughly 8,900," according to a March 2003 *Barron's* article citing the American Bankers Association. These banks are "seeking in part to fill the void created by the industry's consolidation," said *Barron's*. The chartering of new banks peaked in 1999 with 271. In 2000, 223 were chartered, in 2001, 146. About as many national banks were chartered as state banks.

This proliferation of de novo community banks has been stimulated by the awareness among bankers and bank customers that big banks, because of their mind-set, cannot offer community-bank services. Wells Fargo, Bank of America, and others buy a community bank or group of banks, then fail to come even close to replicating the community bank's success.

A de novo community bank is started by either a banker or some bank customers.

The banker: A veteran senior manager loses his position or has to work for a large, faceless organization that has gobbled up his bank.

The customers: Several customers of means become unhappy with the new big bank because of a loss of personal service.

I have been involved in banks started by both. This book's previous section gives examples of both. Here are a few, recapped:

The Community Bank of Oak Park and River Forest got its start when Firstar bought the Avenue Bank of Oak Park in 1995 with the rest of my seventeen Chicago-area community banks and Marty Noll lost his job as president to a (lower-paid) Firstar branch manager. Noll promptly gathered three of our top directors as nucleus of a new bank, which they started within four blocks of Avenue Bank.

Wyoming National Bank in Riverton, Wyoming, was the brainchild of Kent Shurtleff, a senior lender and executive vice president of the Riverton State Bank, which was bought by Wells Fargo. Shurtleff got a local rancher, Bill Garland, to be chairman of a new bank. The two put together a board who raised the $3 million needed to start it, a half mile from the Wells Fargo branch.

First Bank and Trust of Evanston, Illinois, was formed mainly by Bob Yohanan, who was president and chief operating officer of Lake Shore National Bank, a larger community bank in Chicago. When First National Bank of Chicago bought Lake Shore National in 1994, Bob joined forces with two experienced community bank executives, also orphaned by acquisition. The three put together a board, raised capital, and started their bank, taking a number of key personnel from Lake Shore.

The Bank of Tucson was started a little differently. An out-of-state banker wanted a presence in Tucson; so he hired a headhunter to find a president and CEO. The out-of-stater provided half the capital, a local board the other half. Mike Hannley, the president-CEO, became the key ingredient in this bank's success.

Macatawa Bank, in Holland, Michigan, another investor-driven bank, is the work of Ben Smith, who ran a successful investment management company in Holland. Smith raised $8.6 million capital for Macatawa Bank, his first of many, and hired "all the best people" from a local community bank that had been purchased by Huntington Bancshares, a large Ohio-based big bank.

The Valley Commerce Bank in Phoenix, Arizona, was also started by an investor who used a headhunter and found Bob Homco, an experienced community banker, to head up this bank.

Napa Community Bank, which I founded in Napa, California, was also investor-driven. When Wells Fargo bought out Napa National Bank and converted it to a branch, several possible investors were brought to me by our congressman, Mike Thompson, with a view to starting a new bank. This situation was somewhat different from most in that I was not only an investor but an experienced community banker who qualified as the bank's chairman.

Regardless of how a bank is started, by investors or by bankers, the challenge is the same. Organizers have to approve of the president-CEO.

OVERVIEW

Community banks are here to stay and will continue to multiply. If well run, they always do better than their competitor big bank branch.

A community bank can be an excellent long-term investment. A de novo bank's president-CEO can do very well financially over time by acquiring stock and stock options, far better than he would do as "hired gun" for a big bank.

Community bank work gives the well founded feeling of contributing to the community. Time spent as a community bank director is a learning opportunity of the first order. Starting and running a de novo community bank is satisfying and usually enjoyable.

THE PROCEDURE

Organizing a bank is not a complicated procedure. Here's how it's done:

Gather four or five community leaders, substantial investors who can become the foundation of your board.

Decide whether to be a national bank, chartered by the U.S. Office of Comptroller of Currency (OCC), or a state bank, chartered by a state banking commission and the Federal Deposit Insurance Corporation (FDIC).

Find a president-CEO, get a commitment.

Find an investment banker with de novo experience to help you get your charter.

Develop your board, aiming for ten to twelve directors. Decide on a chairman.

Working with your CEO, identify and hire a senior credit officer, an operations manager, and a chief financial officer—the staff you must have to apply for a charter and open as a bank.

Working with directors, president-CEO, and regulators, develop a business plan that details capitalization and expected growth, the bank's type (business or retail), location, market niche, and capacity for outsourcing services.

Obtain from your regulator a permit to organize.

Raise your capital with a private placement or public offering of $8 to $10 million. This is what most de novo banks raise, but consider points raised in a long note at the end of this chapter, demonstrating variations on this.

Hire staff, taking care not to have too big a payroll before opening.

Lease or buy space—usually 4,000 to 5,000 square feet.

Hire an experienced interior designer. How banks look matters, especially community banks.

Obtain your charter.

Have a great "grand opening"!

HOW TO SUCCEED

Hire the right CEO. Take your time in this. The right CEO is the difference between an average and a great bank. He or she has to be either an outstanding marketer or great loan officer. Like any successful entrepreneur, he must be ready to work hard.

Assemble a board of highly qualified people who will work hard and bring business to the bank. Without such a board, you cannot succeed.

Do not overestimate your ability to raise capital—how much and how soon. This is a common mistake.

Decide early whether you will obtain needed services by outsourcing them or by partnering with a larger bank. If you partner, *never do so* by surrendering 51 percent, that is, control, of your stock. Instead, partner with a 20 to 25 percent stock sale to the partner. Control your destiny, do not barter it away.

If you're lucky enough to start your bank in a community where a big bank like Wells Fargo or Bank of America bought out a local community bank, move in across the street from the big bank's branch. They won't have a clue about running a community bank. You'll clean up.

Instill in your bank a family atmosphere, reinforcing it through regular get-togethers of directors and staff. The staff has to know and like the directors and their families, and vice versa. Camaraderie throughout the organization is very important.

Make sure that directors and staff are active in the community. Each must participate by contributing time and effort to community affairs, preferably because he or she wants to.

Be careful about expenses, especially pre-opening expenses, which cannot be capitalized and take a long time to earn back. The average de novo should be able limit them to $450,000 or less.

Develop good relations with regulators. Examiners want to help, as do regulators in general. It's what they are here for. Your life as a banker will be much easier if they like and trust you. They are not your enemies. They want you to succeed.

They work so hard at it, in fact, that failures of de novo (less than five-year-old) banks are rare—two out of thirty-four failures in the U.S., 1997 through 2003, which includes the 2002 uptick to 11 failures. Acting on what the FDIC considers "commonly believed," that "newer enterprises have higher failure rates," regulators give de novos special attention in getting their charters and in using them.[5]

Develop a market niche. Do not try to be too many things to too many people. On the other hand, as a community bank you have to provide a variety of services. Your hours have to be longer. Your staff has to be friendly, helpful, enthusiastic. Your motto should be First Colonial's, "Kiss them on the lips until they chap!"

Be sure your chairman is a motivator and inspirer, especially since he frequently acts as de facto CEO until your president gets his or her feet on the ground.

Form an active and competent compensation committee, keeping in mind the importance of incentive-based compensation for key staff in which a modest base salary is paired with results-based cash bonuses and stock options.

Make sure that your directors, most of whom have had no experience in banking, attend as many educational seminars and conferences as possible. The president and CEO must do the same to keep up with developments.

---

[5]   Bruce Wedel, Examiner Specialist, "Fourth District Conditions," Federal Reserve Bank of Cleveland, Supervision and Regulation Department, Volume 4, issue 1, 2003

Keep in mind that the most important board committee is its loan committee, which protects the bank from an overly aggressive president-CEO and his or her tendency to load up on weak loans—apparently at the root of nearly half the above-mentioned thirty—four bank failures.[6] A board may lack lending experience at its start; so this committee should consist of its members who are most experienced and successful in business in general.

With this lending-experience problem in mind, in August 2002, I composed my "Loan Primer" for Napa Community Bank directors, none of whom had lending experience—a summary of what experienced lenders keep in mind as they pursue the goal of safe, sound, and profitable lending.

The primer answers the three main questions about lending: What's the money for? How will it be paid back? ("Capacity" in the lender's lexicon) Will it be paid back? ("Character")

THE LOAN PRIMER

Begin with **capacity,** the first and most important of the "three C's" of lending. It's the capacity to repay debt, as judged by the borrower's cash flow and overall income.

"Capacity is king. It trumps collateral," the regional manager of U.S. Bancorp (Illinois) and former president of one of my banks, told a recent directors meeting.

Collateral is secondary. The best collateral is land or property improvements—bricks and mortar. The worst is what can be moved quickly out of the area—cars, planes, boats, cases of wine, computers and the like. Leasing companies accept this kind of collateral; it's why they have larger losses than banks. This type of collateral works when the lender has a relationship with the borrower, and the borrower lives in the area, as for us the Napa Valley.

---

[6]   Ibid.

A conservative approach to evaluating collateral is always warranted. Continental Bank went under in the 1980s after buying large participations in loans from several Texas banks for which oil in the ground was collateral. When oil's value plunged from $30 a barrel to $13, Continental's aggressive approach spelled disaster.

Also in the 80s, banks and savings and loans, particularly savings and loans in the Southwest, made aggressive real estate loans in a booming real estate market. Then came a major real estate devaluation and bankrupting of the savings and loan industry.

No conservative, well-run community bank makes loans for which collateral or borrower is not in its market area. A rule of thumb is this: collateral must be no more than a half day's drive away—a half day to get there and look it over, a half day to get back. The same goes for the borrower. You don't want to have to track the borrower down in New York or Miami or Frankfurt.

Neither do you want to make loans that do nothing for the area or for you. As a community banker, you want to develop relationships. How can you do that if the borrower neither lives nor works in your area and so has no account or other business relationship with you?

Most banks will not lend to someone who has had a **bankruptcy**, and for good reason. The issue is whether someone who has asked a court to protect him from creditors, who usually settle for less than the amount borrowed, will do it again.

I do not rule it out, however. If I were to lend, I'd get a copy of the bankruptcy file from the court to corroborate what the borrower told me, and I'd ask these questions:

What caused the bankruptcy? More debts than assets? Not enough cash flow? Severe economic downturn?

What came of it? Did creditors get paid? How much on the dollar?

At whom was the bankruptcy aimed? A supplier? A contractor? A bank?

Why did this borrower take a bankruptcy instead of choosing to work out repayment with creditors?

For years, making a stock loan, lending 50 percent against a listed stock, was a "no brainer." Fellow brings in $500,000 of IBM stock and you lend him $250,000, the most you can lend per Federal Reserve Board Regulation U. Plenty of coverage, right? Used to be. But what if your banker had lent 50 percent against the darling of Wall Street several years ago, a company called Enron, or against a dot-com company? This is what would have happened:

Your $500,000 value dropped to $300,000, and you had to make a margin call to stay at 50 percent. The borrower had to pay off $100,000 or come up with more collateral. He couldn't, as sometimes a margin player can't. Like many banks in this predicament, you felt fortunate just to be paid interest. But you still had to allocate 15 to 25 percent of the loan to a special reserve. The experience shook your confidence in the stock loan.

Avoid **brokered loans**, sold by a broker who earns a commission in the process. The broker has an interest in your taking on the loan and is probably not objective. The borrower cannot get a loan from his own bank and is probably not a good loan customer. It's not a good deal for you the lender.

Beware of lending to the **not-for-profit borrower**. Not-for—profit organizations are called that for a reason; they are frequently not profitable. Look at the organization's borrowing history if it has one. If it does not have one, be particularly careful. Then look at the size of its endowment, the investment portfolio that is extremely important to pay-back capacity.

In the end, even when everything looks good, you make this loan for public relations purposes, to be and to be recognized as good citizens. Which means you do it only in your market territory. You get no publicity or compensating business from 1,000 miles away. Again, the message is "relationship banking."

Restaurant loans are quite risky. Banks often shy away from them, because well-run, profitable restaurants almost always feature and depend on a notable personality or outstanding chef. Napa restaurateurs Donna and Giovanni Scala (Bistro Don Giovanni), Thomas Keller (French Laundry), and Greg Cole (Cole's Chop House and Celadon) come to my mind. If something happens to that person, you usually have a problem. If a restaurant goes down and the only collateral is the restaurant, you'll get back about 10 percent on the dollar from the equipment.

A bank should be very selective making restaurant loans and should always get some other collateral.

Guaranteed loans may be guaranteed, but they are not risk-free. One bank made a $3 million loan, of which $2.4 million was guaranteed by the U.S. Dept. of Agriculture. If the borrower should fail, the bank would get the guaranteed amount only after suing, foreclosing, and establishing the deficit. And then USDA would have to clear the bank's loan documents. In the meantime, the interest income would have been cut off.

As for the $3 million loan, the bank found its exposure excessive and sold off the $2.4 million guaranteed part at a nice profit.

Construction loans are profitable but risky and eat up a lot of time. They call for a construction-loan specialist who knows the developer has deep pockets and the contractor is very reliable.

Two important lending standards to keep in mind:

One, maintain a conservative loan reserve, allocating to it 1.5 percent of every loan. This reserve is an asset "bucket" to be dipped into when a loan is charged off. It is to be replenished when that happens, kept at the 1.5 percent level. The replenishment obviously affects earnings.

Two, set up a system for reporting this information to the board:

☐ Past due loans of 30, 60, and 90 days

☐ Non-accrual loans, on which the customer cannot make

interest payments and booking of income to the bank is stopped

- ☐ Watch list loans, identified as potential problem loans usually based on the borrower's weakening financial situation or a slowing down of a borrower's revenue flow
- ☐ Sub-standard loans, deteriorating for one of a number of reasons and identified by the examiners as possibly requiring allocation of 15 to 25 percent of its amount to a special reserve
- ☐ Doubtful loans, classified by you or the examiners as not likely to be collected in full and requiring allocation of up to 50 percent of its amount to a special reserve
- ☐ Charge-offs, what you do when a loan is not paid, as when the borrower goes bankrupt or the value of the collateral disappears or if you face a long legal battle to collect on diminished collateral value. Regulators probably will ask you to charge off such a loan, if you haven't done so already.

The key is to understand the primary focus of successful community banking, namely *relationship banking*. Every loan that is contemplated should raise the question, what kind of relationship can I build with this customer, what kind of compensating balances or deposits can I generate with this loan customer? Can I develop a relationship that can earn us some non-interest income? Can I do a home mortgage or a consumer loan for that customer?

Always go in trying to sell *all* your services. If you conclude that there is little or no chance for a relationship, you should probably take a pass on the loan request.

That's my loan primer. Your loan portfolio is the bank directors' responsibility. Your loan committee must have whole—board approval of its decisions, because it is no more than an extension of the board, appointed because they are best qualified to review loans.

When a loan goes on the books, it's always a "good loan." A loan does not usually go bad overnight, but deteriorates over time. The loan portfolio must be subject to continuous management oversight, and reporting to the board must be timely, honest and objective. This is imperative.

There will be past due, non-accrual, and charge-off loans. It is directors' responsibility to head off large charge-offs and build the loan portfolio in a safe and sound manner. It is their obligation to shareholders.

The right president-CEO is pretty much the difference between an average and a great bank. I liken it to the wine business. It is virtually impossible to make bad wine with Napa Valley grapes, but great wine calls for an excellent wine maker. It's that way with a bank's president-CEO.

A CEO must have "curiosity," says Allen Stults, a former president of the American Bankers Association, who called it "the one common character in successful CEOs." It's "the ability to ask the proper questions." He or she has to be an excellent loan officer or an outstanding marketer, says Bob Homco, president and CEO of Valley Commerce Bank.

I'll agree with both propositions, based on my working with dozens of bank presidents and interviewing some of the best for this book. The best had this in common: They were bright. They worked their tails off. They had intellectual curiosity. They always wanted to learn more about the business and were not afraid to ask questions. They were excellent motivators.

Starting a community bank is challenging, fun, and frequently financially rewarding. This book tells a number of successful CEO and investor stories. Talk to some of them if you can. Pick their brains. Bankers are usually a friendly group willing to share information and advice.

Community banking is here to stay. America is known for its entrepreneurship; and as bank mergers start picking up again, more opportunities will arise for well capitalized, well-run community banks.

NOTE TO CHAPTER 28:
THE LARGE DE NOVO CAPITALIZATION
PHENOMENON

Most de novo banks, in California about 75 percent, capitalize at $8 million to $10 million. The rest come in at more than $10 million, John Fleming, president of Irvine-based Carpenter and Company, estimates. These large-cap de novos are motivated largely by de novos' success and responsiveness of investors. They make a more ambitious business plan, staffing with twelve to eighteen employees including several highly paid executives rather than five or six and aiming at growing to $500 million in five years rather than $75 million or $100 million. They capitalize up to $25 million.

These banks, all but one of California, are typical.

* **Orange County Business Bank, NA**, Newport Beach, opened for business on December 26, 2002, started by J. P. Gough with a public offering of $19,840,160. The bank could have raised $40 million, Gough is convinced; but the FDIC capped him at $20 million. His public offering, with no underwriter, took him one hundred days and several hundred meetings. It attracted six hundred stockholders and was oversubscribed by $8 million. The stock came at $10 a share on October 2, 2002. By April 2004, when the bank had assets of $50 million, it had hit $16. The bank started with a twelve-person staff, strictly a business bank, taking no CDs, just checking accounts. Its first-year loss was $2.1 million. Carpenter and Company assisted them.

* **Pacific Mercantile Bank**, Costa Mesa, started by Ray Dellerba, its president and CEO, closed its IPO on February 20, 1999, for $8.4 million; a secondary on November 2, 1999, for $11 million; and a tertiary in June 2000 for $21.4 million. After that, it had three issues of trust preferred of $5 million,

$7 million, and $5 million. At year-end 2000, it had $119 million in assets, which grew by year-end 2003 to $724 million, all in growth of the de novo. Stockholders equity, $16 million at year-end 1999, was $70 million at year-end 2003. Book value grew from $4.31 to $7.10.

* **Bridge Bank, NA**, Santa Clara, discussed at length in Chapter 14, raised $19.2 million in April 2001 at $5 a share and fourteen months later another $14.4 million at $6.50 a share. There were commitments in the second offering for $19 million, but the bank was prevented from exceeding its stated goal. Preopening expenses of $1.1 million and operating losses of $5,119,000 presented quite a hurdle, but the bank became profitable. By April 2004, its stock is selling at about $13 a share, which is about 2.9 times book. Market capitalization was $78,610,075.

* **Private Bank of the Peninsula**, Palo Alto, raised more than $18 million at $100 a share from nearly three hundred local investors, for an average investment of about $60,000. The brainchild of Jim Wall, a thirty-plus-year commercial banking veteran—with Silicon Valley Bank and others—and Bill Phillips, a Morgan Stanley Dean Witter veteran, opened October 1, 2003, with a staff of six, including Wall, age fifty-eight, as chairman and CEO and Phillips as vice chairman and executive vice president. It's basically a wealth management bank, located next to a very wealthy area—the Stanford University campus, with average individual and household income of $138,000 and $214,000 respectively and average house price of $1,587,000. There is no other community bank in seven miles.

There were about $1 million in preopening expenses. By the sixth month, April 2004, the bank had $35 million in deposits and $10 million in loans. Organizers expected to break even in their ninth month. The bank outsources almost everything, sending EDP and data-capture to Fiserv, with which they are very satisfied, says Phillips, who cites its ability to customize products and provide great service at low cost. There are nine directors, including Wall and Phillips. Another of the nine, Hugh Barton, has extensive de novo experience—important for a director, as discussed elsewhere in this book, especially in chapter 14 about Bridge Bank—having worked with six other de novo banks.

* **Commercial Bank of California**, in Costa Mesa, California's largest-capitalized independent start-up bank, raised $27.4 million in a private placement to only thirty-nine stockholders before its opening with a staff of seventeen on May 15, 2003. Assisted by Carpenter and Company, organizers had just three meetings with investors in January and February 2003. The offering took only forty-five days. It is strictly a business bank, which focuses on small-middle-market companies, local real estate developers, and individuals in the community.

The chairman is veteran home-builder General William Lyon. The president-CEO and cofounder is K. P. "Bala" Balkrishna, a fifty-eight-year-old experienced banker. In April 2004, the bank had approximately $79 million in assets, $47 million in loans, and $56 million in deposits. The Bank was aiming for $100 million in assets after thirteen months and at breaking even after fifteen months. The bank outsources almost all services, including EDP and data-capture to Fidelity Information Service. There are five other directors.

* **Bank of the Internet** in Del Mar (San Diego), as the name indicates, has a fascinating business plan—selling loans on the Internet. It is the brainchild of fifty-five-year-old Gary Lewis Evans, president-CEO, who, while president of the La Jolla Bank in 1994, introduced one of the first Internet capabilities in a bank in the country. He and Jerry Englert, the bank's chairman, and eighteen other organizers did a private placement of $14,250,000 in June 2000, at the time a U.S. record for a

newly formed bank. They did another in September 2001, of $8 million, and were raising yet more capital in April 2004.

The bank opened on July 4, 2000. ("Born on the Fourth of July" is its byword.) At year-end 2003, it had $28.3 million in capital. In April 2004, approaching its fourth anniversary, it had $365 million in assets, $330 million in loans, and $262 million in deposits. It had turned profitable in fourteen months and had $200 million in assets in eighteen months. Starting with fourteen employees, it had twenty-three in April 2004, for an astounding $17 million in assets per employee, compared to the national-average $4.8 million.

* **First Century Bank**, Century City, organized by Alan Rothenberg, age sixty-four, a prominent Los Angeles lawyer who founded Major League Soccer, raised more capital than any other start-up bank in Los Angeles County history. It set out to raise $22 million in December 2003, but got permission from the OCC to increase that 20 percent to $26.4 million because of strong demand. The offering was oversubscribed, with 470 shareholders, and more than $7 million had to be returned.

The bank's president-CEO, Richard S. Cupp, age sixty-three, a former executive at First Interstate Bancorp and at California Federal Bank, has been a bank-turnaround specialist at five other banks. First Century will target small-and medium-sized businesses and professional organizations. Rothenberg chairs the ten-member board, of which five besides Cupp have bank experience. The bank opened with fourteen employees. It outsources everything. Carpenter and Company assisted this bank too.

* **Texas Capital Bank**, Dallas, the non-California bank in this group, set the record for de novo capitalization in December 1998 with a staggering $80 million sold in a private placement to some 430 individuals. This bank was organized by Joseph

M. "Jody" Grant. On its fifth anniversary, it had total assets of $2.2 billion and shareholders equity of more than $171 million.

Grant, age sixty-five, a thirty-five-year Texas banking veteran and onetime chairman of Texas American Bankshares of Fort Worth, has a PhD in economics from the University of Texas and is author of two books, *The Development of State Chartered Banking in Texas* (1978) and *The Great Texas Banking Crash, An Insider's Account* (1996). He was *American Bankers Magazine* "community banker of the year" in 2000.

Chapter 29

Required: Outsourcing

Starting a de novo community bank, you will need to outsource some services, getting others to do for you what is too expensive to do for yourself. This means contracting for some or all of these functions:

Electronic Data Services and Item Processing
Human Resources
Asset-Liability Consulting
External Financial Statement
Internal Audit Control
Credit Analysis-Note Department
Investment Advisory Services
Compliance Oversight
Community Reinvestment Act Assistance (CRA)

These are the things you should have others do, because you do not want your staff diverted from their main work of gathering deposits, making loans, and servicing customers. It is not cost effective. Such services are available for $150,000 to $175,000 a year.

Almost all de novo banks contract out for EDP and item-processing, for instance, rather than buy proof and bookkeeping equipment to do it in-house. If you feel you should do it in-house, various servicers will sell you a good software package, but doing it that way takes a lot of man-hours. There are a number of good EDP servicers in the country. These three are good to mention here:

- ☐ Fiserv, headquartered in Brookfield, Wisconsin, services over three thousand U.S. banks, mostly smaller and mostly community banks. Fiserv uses the excellent ITI software, out of Montreal, to provide basic services and all the "bells and whistles" you'll want or need. The company is professional and experienced. Costs range from $3,000 to $6,000 a month.
- ☐ Metavante, a subsidiary of M&I Bank in Milwaukee, has more than 3,500 clients, including the largest twenty U.S. banks.
- ☐ i_TECH, a subsidiary of First Interstate BancSystems of Billings, Montana, is smaller and more regionalized.

WHAT ARE TYPICAL FIRST-YEAR EDP AND ITEM-PROCESSING COSTS?

The just-named i_TECH, which has 150 smaller-bank clients in Washington, Idaho, and Oregon and will have clients soon in California, charges only for items processed, whether in core processing or ATM and card processing, as is the common practice.

For instance, four i_TECH clients paid $1,500 a month in their first year for core application but varying amounts for item processing, depending on use.

- ☐ "Bank A," which had $20 million in assets at year's end, averaged $1,764 a month, for a total of $21,500.
- ☐ "Bank B," which ended the year with $15 million in assets, paid $1,417 a month, $17,000 for the year.

- ☐ "Bank C," which ended with $25 million, paid $2,740 a month, $32,880 for the year.
- ☐ "Bank D," which ended with $16.3 million, paid $2,002 a month, $24,000 for the year.

Fiserv, serving eleven northern California client banks of $7 million to $501 million in assets, averaging $112 million, charged more, again in a bank's first year—from $3,000 a month for basic EDP and item processing to $6,000 for its whole package, including ATM and Internet banking. In each case, the bank in its first year paid $1,500 a month for check processing.

- ☐ "Bank A," capitalized at $5.5 million and growing to $12 million, averaged just over $3,000 a month in its first year for data processing, which included basic processing, telephone banking, document-management software, network support, and data lines. In its thirteenth month, it paid just over $4,500 for data processing.
- ☐ "Bank B," capitalized at $6 million and growing to $21 million, averaged $4,600 a month for starting data processing, which included basic processing, telephone banking, Internet banking, Internet cash management, document-management software, teller-platform software, network support, and data lines. Its thirteenth-month data processing cost was $6,000.
- ☐ "Bank C," capitalized at $6 million and growing to $49 million, averaged $3,200 a month for starting data processing charges, which included basic processing, telephone banking, document-management software, shareholder-accounting software, network support, and data lines. Data processing in its thirteenth month cost $7,085.25. This bank added Internet banking after it opened.

Fiserv has a variety of service-delivery models. For 1,316 bank clients, it processes accounts in service-bureau settings. For 1,442 banks it does so in account-processing data centers in twelve U.S. cities. For 1,937 banks that process in-house, it provides software. For 1,442 banks it does item-processing in data-collection centers in fifty U.S. cities.

For instance, for Granite Community Bank, Granite Bay, California, near Sacramento, with assets of $53 million after eighteen months, Fiserv handles checks, deposit, and data off-site. The bank sends a nightly "bag" by courier to the Fiserv Service Center in San Leandro, near Oakland, where its contents are processed. The checks and deposits are delivered to the San Francisco Federal Reserve. The data is sent to Fiserv's data center in Chatsworth, in southern California. The bank gets its financial statements on the second day of each month.

Fiserv costs seemed quite reasonable to us at Napa (California) Community Bank, by the way. When we got estimates for basic services, Fiserv came out looking very good. Napa's parent was charging $6,750 a month. Fiserv estimated $3,000 a month—$1,500 each for core account processing and item processing plus more for additional features.

Nothing better demonstrates the value of outsourcing than this case of Napa's paying $81,000 for basic services in its first year, contrasted with Wintrust-owned Northbrook (Illinois) Bank and Trust's payment to Metavante of $63,900 in its first year. And this for a bank two and a half times Napa's size, $90 million in assets to $36 million for Napa after ten months. And for bells-and-whistles (not basic) EDP and item-processing services, to boot. It obviously paid Northbrook to outsource.

Finding good service providers at reasonable prices is not hard. The thirty-page directory in Western Independent Bankers' *Western Banking* is a good source, as are other bankers' organizations. Services listed include Asset-Liability Management, Audit-CPA Firms, Bank and Data Processing Systems, for which Fiserv and Metavante are noted as providers.

Consultants are also listed, Bill Isaac's Secura Group among them. So are providers of Correspondent Services: Credit Card and ATM Services and Investment Banking, among which are named Friedman, Billings, Ramsey and Company; Hoefer and Arnett; and Keefe, Bruyette and Woods, all consulted for this book. So are Legal and Regulatory Services, for which Gary Steven Findley and Associates are listed.

When we at Napa Community Bank considered outsourcing, we contacted Mary Rhodes, of Community Bank Consulting, Sonoma, California, who suggested several California firms:

For human resources work: HR Central, in Seattle and Sacramento, would charge $500 for setting up a program and $500 a month.

For asset-liability-interest-rate risk analysis and sensitivity analysis: ALX Consulting, in Redmond, Washington, would charge $650 for setting up and $142 a month for the first year, $300 a month for the second.

For external audit: Perry Smith LLP, in Sacramento, would charge about $25,000 a year.

For internal audit: Bank Audit Associates, LLC, in San Jose, which services some sixty community banks of $40 million to $50 billion assets, would charge a starting fee of $1,627 a month for work in compliance, credit review, risk assessment, note operations, information systems, and accounting-finance administration.

For credit analysis: St. George Integrated Financial Solutions.

For investment advisory-ALCO consulting and interest-rate risk analysis: Mike Higgins and Associates, in Aliso Viejo.

Consultants can be a big help. Two Californians whom I quote in this book, Ed Carpenter and Gary Steven Findley, provide advice on outsourcing as part of help in organizing a de novo bank.

Bank directors should make sure their CEO finds the best outsourced services for the best prices. They owe it to shareholders. This is so even if a bank has partnered with another bank or parent company that provides capital and intends to supply EDP and other services.

Directors should be alert in this case to the tendency to lump services together and being charged for all of them, whether used or not. They should insist on individual pricing, for comparison with other providers, making sure the cost of services is not more than the cost of what an alert CEO can find on his own.

Legal, marketing and human resources, for instance, should probably be supplied locally. Make the parent company prove its costs and compare them. Then decide.

Chapter 30

Compensation Issues

Initial contracts with a de novo bank's CEO are usually for three to five years. Directors will want to consider five compensation items—base salary, annual incentives (cash bonus), long-term incentives (stock options, equity, or other long-term plan), benefits (retirement, nonqualified and qualified benefits), and perquisites (employment agreements, country club, car).

The base salary for an experienced, well-qualified CEO will generally be in the range of $100,000 to $150,000 per annum. In some cases it could be more.

Minneapolis-based Clark Consulting's Banking Practice and Compensation Group, a top compensation consulting firm, provided comparative information on a number of California banks ranging in size from $41 million in assets to $169 million.

The CEO in the fiftieth percentile made $144,000 in salary. Average bonus was $6,000, for total cash compensation of $150,000.

The seventy-fifth percentile (upper 25 percent) received $178,300 total, the twenty-fifth percentile $145,600.

Compensation differs between rural and urban banks. State banking commissions have good information on this. The FDIC is another good source. So is a recent study by the Independent Community Bankers of America (ICBA), which found that the average community-bank CEO earns $151,400 in salary and bonus, up from $124,500 only two years earlier.

Stock options are usually very attractive to the de novo CEO, who has an entrepreneurial bent in the first place, or would not want to be part of a business starting from scratch. Indeed, the emerging stories of considerable community-bank stock appreciation are a lure.

De novo CEOs are frequently given a one-time grant of $50,000 to $200,000 in stock options to vest in three to five years. In some cases a straight stock grant of some size might be appropriate.

Directors should be aware of several important features of any stock option plan. For instance, regulators do not like to let outstanding options exceed 20 percent of the total outstanding shares. Most banks stay with 15 percent.

There are two types of options, qualified (incentive stock options) and nonqualified (NSOs). For the present, qualified options have no tax consequences to bank or individual when exercised. Only bank employees may receive qualified options, but they can also get nonqualified.

A board should encourage a CEO to buy stock in the bank and a CEO should be given a sizeable option grant. So should every employee receive at least a modest stock-option grant, because it makes them feel like owners.

Expensing of options is a current hot topic. Until 2003 a bank (any company) could choose to expense the cost of options, or not. In 2002, investor Warren Buffet and Fed Chairman Alan Greenspan, among others, weighed in on the side of expensing options, with a view to giving more accurate earnings' figures to shareholders.

"The failure to expense stock options has introduced a significant distortion in reported earnings," said Greenspan.

"When a company gives something in value to its employees for service, it is clearly a compensation expense," said Buffett.[7]

---

[7] *New York Times,* July 24, 2002.

I agree. A number of companies have gone to more conservative accounting procedures on their own and are expensing options. Aggressive accounting misleads shareholders regarding earnings. That practice will almost certainly change soon, and banks will be forced to expense options.[8]

My advice is, do it now. Your shareholders deserve accurate earnings' figures.

The International Accounting Standards Board already (as of February 19, 2004) requires companies following its standards to make their financial statements reflect stock option expenses. This "throws down the gauntlet to its U.S. equivalent, FASB, to speed up the forcing of companies to expense stock options," said Reuters.

Goldman Sachs expected option expensing to become mandatory in 2005 or 2006. "We believe," they said in a research publication dated March 10, 2004, "that the fair value of ESO's can be reasonably estimated in many cases" and "the share price reaction will not be significant for most firms."

Not so for Napa Community Bank, for which expensing options would have meant a near-30 percent reduction in earnings—an $86,717 chunk out of $290,497.[9]

My advice is, forced or not, be honest with your shareholders and do not use aggressive accounting.

A CEO's fringe benefits include automobiles, country club memberships, expense accounts, and other perks.

Retirement benefits take several forms. The CEO will probably want a plan. One of the most innovative to be

---

[8]   The Financial Accounting Standards Board (FASB) in March 2004 urged regulators to require businesses to expense stock options in their earnings' statements beginning January 1, 2005.

[9]   "No stock-based compensation expense is recorded upon granting," say the bank's accountants, BDO Seidman, LLP, in the bank's financial statements for the year 2003 (p. 8), noting that "certain pro forma disclosures . . . are required." From these disclosures come the figures given.

developed in the last fifteen years is the BOLI (Bank Owned Life Insurance) Plan pioneered by Clark Consulting's Robert Gallivan in the mid-eighties.

BOLI has emerged as one of the most efficient employee benefit financing vehicles available to banks. It is used by close to 85 percent of California's 286 banks for their CEO, Gallivan told me.

Clark Consulting is banking's largest provider of BOLI portfolio services, administering nearly 100,000 individual BOLI policies for more than 1,900 financial institutions. Several other large, competent firms also administer BOLI plans. BOLI coverage neither replaces nor interferes with other (group term) insurance provided by a bank.

Here's how BOLI works. The bank purchases life insurance on the CEO and frequently on other staff. The bank pays the premium, owns the cash value of the policy, and is its beneficiary. The policy's cash value growth and death benefits are not taxable if the policy is held until death.

A policy is part of a bank's general assets. It informally finances the cost of benefits. Normally, BOLI life insurance proceeds are earmarked to offset specific employee benefit liabilities.

A bank can choose from several types of BOLI plan. Of special interest to bankers in these times of low interest rates, BOLI is designed to provide higher after-tax yields than most bank-eligible investments. For instance, payments would cover a fifteen-year retirement plan for a forty-five-year-old CEO who would receive $60,000 per annum at retirement.

The single premium payment for this plan would be $1.25 million. The balance sheet asset would be $1.303 million. If the $1.25 million were taken out of 2 percent T-bills ($12,500 in after-tax earnings), there would be a net of approximately $6,000 to earnings because of the BOLI's higher yield.

Among banks using BOLI are Vintage Bank, of Napa, which has six people in an executive retirement plan backed by BOLI; Napa Community Bank, which has a BOLI-backed plan for its president; and Bank of Tucson, which has the same.

Whatever plan a board adopts, it should be determined by a compensation committee that understands its responsibility to shareholders and is independent of the CEO. When it comes to compensation, a CEO must not control a board, especially when his compensation is in question.

PART IV-A

OUTSIDE EXPERTS: INVESTMENT BANKERS, CONSULTANTS

Chapter 31

Joe Stieven, Stifel, Nicolaus & Company:

Why Start a Bank and How to Do it

Joe Stieven swears by small regional banks, which he says are better investments than money-center banks or major-company stocks. He should know. He heads a Stifel, Nicolaus and Company research team that covers sixty-eight such banks in twenty-two states from North Dakota to Louisiana and New Mexico to Ohio.

Those banks did far better in four of the last six years than those in the SNL Midwest Bank index, which covers all Midwestern banks, outperforming them usually by 50 percent or more. In six of the last eight years, they outperformed the S&P 500, in four of those years by more than 50 percent.

In the little guys vs. big guys, it was no contest. Of sixty-eight banks with assets of $200 million to $15 billion, more than 10 percent scored a two-hundred-fold (!) return over the last fifteen years. Stieven believes and vouches for the results but still calls them "unbelievable."

We should believe them. Stieven's firm puts money where its mouth is, financing small Midwest regional banks. Between 1999 and mid-2003, for instance, it managed $510 million in equity offerings for fourteen banks and close to $1.5 billion in trust-preferred (debt-like) offerings for thirty-two others.

Among these have been two de novo Michigan banks that Joe Stieven considers the two best-run banks in the Midwest—Macatawa Community, in Holland, and Mercantile Bank of West Michigan, in Wyoming, each with $1 billion in assets after five years, without growth by acquisition.

Both banks were started in the immediate aftermath of the 1997 acquisition of First Michigan Bank Corporation by Huntington Bancshares, of Columbus, Ohio. When Huntington pursued what Stieven calls "the old scorched-earth model, the cram-down—overhead routine," including 35 percent expense-cutting, and made other mistakes, the two new banks were handed the opportunity to fill in gaps in now-missing services. Shareholders approved the sale September 9, 1997. Macatawa was started in November 1997. The two banks' success developed in large part from Huntington mistakes, but also from opportunistic management.

Macatawa grew almost $900 million without acquiring another bank, pursuing a branching strategy—fourteen branches by mid-2002—with a mix of retail and business deposits. It made its first acquisition, of a bank in Grand Rapids, in April 2002. The driving force behind Macatawa, its chairman and CEO, Ben Smith, was chief financial officer of First Michigan. Presently he also runs his own investment company. Smith emphasizes trust department work as crucial to growth, says it will account for 30 percent or more of Macatawa's total income.

Macatawa has "great figures," says Stieven, including a first-quarter-2003 ROA of 0.96 and ROE of about 10 percent.

More telling is its low nonperforming asset ratio of 0.24 percent (compared to the average 0.67 percent), a reserve-to-loans ratio of 1.4 percent, and a very high reserve-to-nonperforming ratio of 491 percent, compared to the peer-bank average 171.4 percent.

Mercantile, based in the Grand Rapids area, is another success story, but in a different way. It uses far fewer branches in the belief that branches cost too much. It also frequently uses brokered CDs. But its asset quality is "excellent," says Stieven, with fewer than 1 percent of its loans nonperforming, a reserve-to-loans ratio of 1.40, and a reserve-to-nonperforming-loans ratio of 2,140 percent! Mercantile reached its first billion dollars in assets in May 2003, in its sixth year, with no acquisitions! Providing key impetus to this excellent work has been founding chairman and CEO Gerald R. "Jerry" Johnson, Jr.

JOE STIEVEN AND I TALK

Joe Stieven has been measuring banks since 1985, when he left the Federal Reserve after two years as a bank examiner to join Stifel Nicolaus. His time at the Fed, spent examining banks for problem loans, gave him an edge: spotting problems as an examiner prepared him uniquely for spotting them as an analyst. For Stifel Nicolaus clients he has found "great companies who need money" and along the way inspired his sales staff as few analysts do. He rose rapidly at Stifel to a top executive position.

Joe and I have known each other for more than fifteen years. Stifel participated with Dean Witter, Chicago Corporation, and other Midwestern firms in the IPO of my firm, First Colonial Bankshares. He helped us raise capital, and we returned the favor by making a substantial return on the money.

Born and raised in St. Louis, forty-two years old, he has his MBA in finance and his undergraduate degree from the University of Missouri. He and his wife Mary have six kids ranging from a freshman in college to one who just graduated from kindergarten.

In June 2003, in Chicago, where he had flown up from St. Louis to meet me, we talked about community banking.

He has a list of what to look for. At the top is a bank's management. If he likes what he sees, he and the others at Stifel "take care of the capital," though new rules that forbid research for investing clients will put a crimp in that, he says.

Of banks he has chosen for researching in the last ten years, community banks have grown the most—10.9 percent a year in compounded earnings per share—in part because they do not dominate their markets and thus have had room to grow. Money-center banks such as Bank One in Chicago, on the other hand "max out." They are "done growing," except as gross domestic product (GDP) and inflation grow. Banks with biggest market share, therefore, "are *not* the most profitable," he said with emphasis.

His banks' profit comes mainly from fees and capital management. Overhead is important. "But you can't just cut expenses, as by controlling loan losses. You have to manage capital. When your capital is growing, you should buy stock back. This is where your profit comes from."

NICHE, FOCUS AND ALL THAT

A bank can't be everything to everybody. Community banks have to be focused. It's a matter of market niche, whether it's a lending specialty, fee-based income strategy, credit-card operation, mortgage servicing, or whatever else the bank does well, as long as it involves personal service. Customers must be known to the bankers and must know it. They must have access to them.

This is the core strength of a community bank, of course. First Colonial's senior citizens' Doers Club, for instance, nourished and drew on high customer loyalty. Slightly lower rates on deposits mattered less than the satisfaction people got.

(In those low-cost deposits, I reminded Joe, was $500 million that brought our cost of funds down to one of the lowest in the Midwest.)

"You focused on that," he said. "It was your niche, and you filled it, tapping into the price people were willing to pay for service. Love has its price," he said with a laugh.

"But the price is higher now. Customers now will sacrifice only about twenty-five to maybe thirty-five basis points [one hundredths of a percentage point] for the personal touch. Senior citizens will accept 2.5 percent on deposits vs. 2.75 percent at a big bank, for instance." It's in this sort of service-for-a-price that "the big banks can't keep up" and community banks can "pick up table scraps and do well."

Such an approach requires full attention of staff and management. But this won't happen unless supported by "the culture of senior management," which must look to customers (30 percent of their attention), employees (another 30 percent), and shareholders (the rest). "All three have to gain, but shareholders take the biggest risk" and deserve the highest consideration.

HOW A BANK GROWS

What about potential shareholders, investors? They see that a *de novo* bank is not quite a sure thing. As their representative, he's "very selective." What does he look for?

How it grows, for one thing. Not by asset acquisition, which disrupts focus, impairs culture, and jeopardizes asset quality and risk management. Forget acquisition as a growth strategy. It's "a seller's game." Forget market share. In a ten-bank market, he has no use for the top three. Fourth through tenth are his cup of tea. Internal growth is the goal.

How fast? "Plan on making no money for a bank's first two years. Look at least to five, and convince investors to stay that long. You don't hit your stride for five or six years.

"Not until then is your price best if you want to sell—not

three years, which is the Capitol Bancorp way. The only reason you'd go with a three-year sell time is for help in raising your initial investment. This is what Capitol does for you."

SELLING PRICES

"Investment bankers and commercial bankers are quite different. In investment banking you 'eat what you kill.' commercial banking is a continuum of earnings. You can't bring these two cultures together overnight.

"Analysts and investors look at earnings per share, asset quality, balance sheet strength, management track record, and franchise value. Take care to preserve asset quality and capital position. Strong common stock valuations and ready access to capital markets are crucial."

Bank sale multiples "are influenced by two factors: stock prices of buyers [what sets the pricing mechanism] and the competition. Currently [mid-2003] multiples are down. There are fewer buyers. The big three in Chicago [Bank One, La Salle Bank, Northern Trust] are not buying, so there are fewer buyers. Acquisition prices have dropped but are still high. We're seeing them fifteen to twenty times earnings, from two times to three times book—down from their peak but still healthy. Mississippi Valley Bancshares, a $2.5 billion bank, for instance, was just purchased by M&I Bank for over three times book."

BLESS THE REGULATORS

Along the way, regulators help. "Banking, the most regulated industry in the world, has the world's most independent set of bookkeepers. These are the regulators, who are also investors' best friends, because they protect investment."

They are "the police on the banking highway," trained to ask tough questions and demand facts, analyzing the industry and individual companies on a daily basis. "Like parents, they are sometimes annoying. But if you earn their respect, you have all the flexibility you require."

Thanks largely to regulators, there hasn't been a major U.S. bank failure since the Bank of New England in 1991.

"We are thankful for them. And so are CEOs. I can't recall one complaining about them. It doesn't mean they alone can prevent all abuses or even bank failures."

Joe and I agreed it's a fool's game to battle regulators on issues such as aggressive accounting and loans classification. Only a few banks do so. Of these banks, investors should be wary.

CEO AND BOARD

What of management? Start with the CEO. For your new bank, get a proven commodity like John Dubinski of Mark Twain Bank or Paul Johnson of First Colonial, "not someone in flight from a merger who is looking for a job. Get one who learned banking in a community bank and watched it grow to, say, $2 billion in assets, wearing many hats and using lots of shoe leather, and then learned the good and the bad about big banks from the one that bought them out. I would not pick a fifteen-year veteran of a mega bank like Wells Fargo or Bank of America. It's too specialized an experience."

He likes CEOs with "a little arrogance," deciding how important the chairman should be, for instance. They should know what they are doing, of course. He applies an "arrogance-to-competence ratio." The man has to be enthusiastic, "like you were, Paul," he said, and I was flattered. But arrogance must not outstrip competence.

"'It's not braggin' if you can do it,' as Michael Jordan said. I like guys who focus on a few things and push hard. Lose focus, and bad things happen," he said, citing Chicago's Continental Bank, which closed, and First Chicago, which was sold.

REVENUE VS. EARNINGS: THE PETER LYNCH MOMENT

"Son," Peter Lynch once told Joe, "don't talk about revenue growth. Tell me about EPS growth!" Investment expert Lynch was talking in his "safe room," called that because the table top was a bank vault door, to a young Joe Stieven, who had been granted time with the master. Lynch was polite, but forty-five seconds into their conversation, as Joe talked of revenue, Lynch interrupted. Joe never saw things the same after that.

Not revenue but earnings were the thing, he realized. He left the "safe room" having absorbed the investment principles that would guide his career.

"Give me two things in a bank," Joe says, seventeen years later, "10 percent or higher earnings growth and 14.5 to 15 percent return on equity." Most of all, give him earnings growth.

"Do I want $200 million in five years?" he asks today. "No, $500 million. I want an important bank. And I don't have to sell to achieve it. I can stay independent forever if I want."

PROFITS AND LOSSES

"An environment in which interest rates rise slowly is best. It's something a better economy brings. With increased loan growth, just drag your heels on deposit rate increases, and you'll do well on the margin."

As for noninterest income, "fees from asset managers are great, but investment banking is highly cyclical. Insurance fee income has good potential. There is similarity in that you gain annuity income just like banks interest income."

IN GENERAL

What else? As for a bank's location, "bricks and mortar are not the franchise," he said. "They're just a tool. There's a successful bank in Columbus, Ohio, for instance, with just an office—and a great courier service!"

As for attention to shareholders, the annual meeting is "a great tool for shareholder communication." In fact, "when you have a pulpit, use it," Joe says.

He loves to quote a letter to shareholders from Clement L. Buenger, chairman of Fifth Third Bank, in 1987, in which he closed with the comment, "As always, we owe you a better year in 1988," after noting that "a generation of young people [had been] shocked" at the year's near-disastrous stock market collapse culminating in a fourth-quarter near trillion-dollar loss. The young had discovered, Buenger wrote, "that what goes up does come down," joining "the rest of us who know that."

"Banking is like football," Joe said. "Everyone runs with the same play book. You mustn't think yours is the best. What you have to do is take a page and do it well, like the Green Bay Packers did their 'sweep' in the Lombardi era. The other teams knew it was coming, but they couldn't stop it.

"At the same time, you have your niche. Stay on the page with the plays you run very well, that niche. It's a way to satisfy the customer in a way no one else can, or not as well."

Every bank wants the same thing. The key is to execute. It isn't complex. "In football terms four yards and a cloud of dust will do it."

CUSTOMER FIRST

"Let me tell you a story about customer satisfaction," he said. "My wife and I had an account with the private bank department at the Commerce Bank in St. Louis. One day Fran [at the bank] called and said, 'Mr. Stieven, how are you doing? How's your new home coming? How's your wife? Is she doing well?' As she talked, a light dawned—maybe my wife was doing too well! 'Am I overdrawn?' I asked Fran. 'I wouldn't tell you that,' she said. She didn't have to, of course. I asked how much I should deposit to cover the overdraft.

"What a way to tell a customer you're overdrawn. What a way to take an unpleasant situation and get a laugh out of it." He told the bank's board about it, calling it a case of excellent banking that showed the huge difference between big-bank and community-bank banking.

Chapter 32

Ed Carpenter, Carpenter & Associates:

How to Start a De Novo Bank

You want to start a bank? If so, you are most likely already a banker, because two out of three *de novo* (new) banks are started by bankers, one out of three by investors. In the early '80s, before the savings and loan industry was brought down by a imprudent investing of deposits combined with rate deregulation—what also created problems for commercial banks—"it was the other way around," says Ed Carpenter, veteran and highly regarded California bank consultant.

The chief organizer of today's bank is usually a community banker who has been bought out by a big bank. There are many more of these than there used to be. In 2003 in California, for instance, there were two hundred banks, down from 485 in 1992. It's a huge net loss largely attributable to 51 percent attrition among community banks. Indeed, in Ed Carpenter's experience, most community banks are good for fifteen years before they are bought up and consolidated into bigger banks.

An average twelve banks a year have been started in California in the last five years, but there have been some twenty consolidations, for a net loss of about eight banks a year, he tells us.

That imbalance is one reason community banks compete

302 | C. Paul Johnson with Jim Bowman

well with big ones. Consolidations have led to a dearth of community banks, so that only 9 percent of small business deposits are in community banks. But he figures *30 percent* of small business owners prefer their deposits to be in community banks. That spells opportunity for the new community bank.

For certain kinds of people—that is, those who (a) have the self-confidence to think they know their community needs a bank "where management laughs and cries because they know their customers," (b) have learned from bad experience with a big bank, and (c) have the urge to make money and know that a community bank can be very profitable. Ed Carpenter calls it "the EEG factor," for "ego, education, and greed."

These banker-organizers had not been CEOs of the banks that had been sold. So they have to look for an experienced management team—credit officer, CFO, head of operations, president, chief operating officer.

Advice from Ed Carpenter in these matters is valuable. His Carpenter and Associates does startup consulting and financing for 50 to 70 percent of California de novo banks. They do "about 70 percent" of first and second public offerings, for totals of "about $400 million" in new equity offerings, the same amount in trust-preferred offerings, and "about $200 million" in traditional debt offerings.

They have consulting contracts with two hundred of the California's 280 banks, having helped about 60 percent of the 280 get their charters. They have been "on one side or another" in two of every three merger-and-acquisition deals done in California, which comes to "fourteen or fifteen a year."

Indeed, they have been around the block a few times. Between 1974 and 1984, operating primarily as a de novo consulting shop, they did fifty or so charter applications a year. But in 1984 the DFI and the Controller put a moratorium on de novos, so they shifted to investment banking. In the aftermath of the savings and loan catastrophe, they sold $12 billion to

$18 billion of S&L assets, becoming "the largest contractors of such work west of the Mississippi."

In 2003 their business has three elements: (1) investment banking and advice, a thirty-banker department, (2) real estate joint ventures, and (3) investment in independent banks. They invest in "the vast majority" of banks they work with.

In their advisory work, they do "a lot" of investment banking, work with the regulators, put together applications, and do strategic "running," or consulting, for big and small banks.

"We even helped a large Korean bank pick a president," he said.

Carpenter calls his firm "a humble organization." They do no advertising and spend less than $20,000 on business development. They aim to be known as "best friends" to banks they work with. They have done well, he says, because they help people, including "displaced CEOs and officers, staying close to bankers and boards" and operating without "policy or procedure manuals" on a philosophy he attributes to President (and native Californian) Richard M. Nixon: "Be there when someone is down."

He loves the business and has no intention of leaving it, not even, he says with a smile, to indulge his passion for surfing or for mastering the art of flying a glider, which almost mastered him in a recent bone-breaking crash.

"We've been advisors to 517 banks and have helped raise capital for 450," he said. "In every case we try to be first, fathers [before the bank opens], then mentors [after it opens], and finally peers [after five years]."

THE CHARTER

The process starts with a charter, the "permit to organize," as Carpenter terms it. Obtaining a charter costs up to $75,000, including $10,000 in legal expense, and takes 120 to 150 days from filing. This is after four months or so of preliminary efforts with a consultant.

Getting which kind of charter, state or national, is an issue. A state charter is given by the state banking commission joined at the hip with the FDIC, which together regulate state banks. A national charter is given by the Office of Controller of Currency (OCC), which regulates national banks.

A state charter grants a higher lending limit than a national charter, and its fee is lower—only $5,000 in California, for instance, vs. (currently) $25,000 for a national charter. But the OCC staff is usually longer-termed and more experienced, and going national is worth the expense to some. A bank's organizer goes state or national, depending on which agency or agencies the banker is more familiar with. Indeed, for a variety of reasons, the choice is pretty much a toss-up.

Too many think they can't get a charter, as too many doubt their ability to raise enough capital. But if they can't raise the money, they are in trouble from the start. Their bank will never be "a roaring success," which in his book is the only success worth going for.

Some outside bank companies play on these fears and convince de novo organizers they need help, Carpenter said.

Ideally, two out of every three shareholders (375 in all on average, more than 500 if more than $15 million is being raised) become customers. It must be clear what each shareholder intends to do for the bank before shares are allocated. Minimum investment is $10,000 in 85 percent of cases. In most successful offerings, the average investment is $35,000. Secondary offerings are usually priced 25 to 50 percent higher than the first.

Bank stock is attractive. Of the forty thousand Californians who have owned it, about half still do. Over the last three years, the average small cap bank stock (under $500 million) has appreciated 157 percent.

Who runs the bank? Management evolves, he said. The CEO you start with can usually manage up to $150 million in assets. "Then the Peter principle kicks in." The next level of

CEO testing is at $500 million. Beyond this, three out of four banks need a professional manager; in only one of four do entrepreneurs remain in charge. Two out of three new banks have an outsider as chairman. The others have a banker as chairman and CEO.

Roughly half the CEOs are gone in, say, four years. (Not in eighteen months, as another consultant, Gary Findley, said.) Most get three-year contracts, and success can't be decided in the first few years.

As to rolling up a bank (buying it out) at the third anniversary of its opening, as Capitol Bancorp does, he said, when I asked him about it: "A bank should not sell early in the game unless it has to. It doesn't hit its stride for five to six years or when it hits $250 million. And there's no correlation of early earnings with ultimate success."

As for selling a bank when it has hit its stride in Carpenter's terms, most sales (about 64 percent) are of banks of $100 million to $200 million in asset size, and the highest prices are paid by competitors. "For example," he said, "of the class of '95 [banks started that year], 50 percent got to $250 million in five years. There is a value jump in the sale price at $250 million and another one at $500 million."

As for motivating a CEO, the offer of options on 5 to 10 percent of the offering is common, he said.

Meanwhile, "watch out for 'the ogre mechanism,'" he said, when one or more directors try to run the bank.

He believes strongly in strategic planning retreats for directors, every three years. That way, the consultant can give directors the direction they need.

HOT NEW BANK

He raved about a new bank which he and his associates helped, San Diego Trust, whose approval came in a record ninety days. It has a forty-year-old CEO, Larry Willet, who came out of a "new generation" of bankers trained in independent community banks.

This is something new. Up until 1995 more than half of new bank presidents came out of big banks, he explained. "But big—bank training is not conducive to success in a community bank. These new bankers are more passionate about their work. They aim to get and keep customers by raising the level of service and not by cutting prices, which is what big banks do."

Willet, he says, is "the perfect CEO," with operating experience in three of San Diego's largest community banks. He's what Carpenter calls a "displaced banker"—in flight from consolidation and big-bank practices. He was president and CEO of Peninsula Bank of San Diego when its 297 percent a year was the highest return on bank investment in the county.

He became chairman of San Diego Trust Bank. Two other top community-bank executives filled out the management, Dan Hurtley as president and Mike Holen as CFO. The three of them came out of retirement and bought into the new bank, forming what's known as the Willet Group.

Ed Carpenter is sold. "It will be an enormous success," he said in June 2003, when the bank was selling stock and aiming at capitalization of $13 million to $15 million.

MARKET

The future is bright for independent community banks because California has so few, but serving small business customers, not retail, which calls for twenty thousand customers. Carpenter contrasted that requirement with the recent achievement of CommerceWest Bank, in Newport Beach, has only fifty-three (business) customers and $41 million in loans after one year. CommerceWest was profitable in its ninth month. Its cost of funds is a very low 0.8 percent. Its net interest margin (NIM) is 5.75 percent!

Carpenter et al. did CommerceWest's first offering of $10.25 million and in mid-2003 was doing a second of $7.5 million, which would take CommerceWest to $200 million in assets. In its fifth quarter in June 2003, it was to have roughly $100 million in assets with about eighty customers by year-end. "This," said Carpenter, "is true core banking."

The extremely talented CommerceWest CEO is Ivo A. Tjan, a twenty-seven-year-old Indonesian refugee, who at nineteen was named Home Savings of America's best branch manager. It was Tjan who put together a board of "big hitters" with a plan to service only business accounts, said Carpenter, who is euphoric about opportunities in Orange County for de novos. He points out that within a mile of the John Wayne Orange County Airport (and from CommerceWest offices just across the street), you can find $5 billion in deposits; within eight miles, $8 billion.

Smaller towns are fine too, he is quick to add. Half of California's de novos are in towns with less than twenty-five thousand populations. He and his associates were helping to start a group who would open a bank in Eureka, a town of twenty-five thousand people, in fact, and another in Santa Cruz, a town of sixty-five thousand people.

His dream location? Tucson, Arizona. "It's one of the best in the country, the place to be," according to the Oregon-based management consultant Bill Seidman "the federal janitor hired to mop up the 1980s S&L scandal," as an editor at Boston-based *Fast Company* magazine called him. If Ed Carpenter were starting a bank there, he'd do an $8 million to $10 million initial offering and a second offering of $13 million. "Tucson is like the Midwest," he said, "like Minneapolis, with generations of deep roots."

COSTS

Expenses mount, of course. The average bank has $750,000 or so in capitalized expenses. De novo openers should plan to lose another million before their bank turns the corner. It should look for $60 million or so in assets at the end of the first year.

There are or should be preopening loan commitments to fund capital liquidity. This is where the CEO looks to board, shareholders, and other sources.

But those and any other loans over $100,000 in the first six months should be approved by the board, "even if it's after the fact," he says, so they get in the habit of keeping their eyes open.

He's down on aggressive accounting, of course, and sees little of it, what he calls "the edgy stuff," like taking loan fees up front in violation of FASB 91. He sees "a little" of upstreaming dividends to a holding company from money-losing banks, in violation of Fed regulations 23A and 23B, "but not much."

Most banks he sees are conservative and don't cut corners when it comes to accounting. California had a grand total of five "troubled" banks at the time of our interview, that is, with a rating of 4. Eighty percent are rated 1s or 2s. No California bank has failed since 1995.

Chapter 33

Gary Findley, Gary Steven Findley &

Associates: Rating the Winners

When Gary Findley enters a bank, he feels "'the vibes,' the sense of positive attitudes that spell success." Spending more time where the vibes are good, he finds high stability among senior managers and a close working relationship between them and the bank's board.

Findley is someone to listen to in such matters, as I did in June 2003. His firm, Gary Steven Findley and Associates, specializes in banks and other financial institutions—organizing and reorganizing them, helping them merge with and acquire each other. In 2003 the firm's lawyers were serving as special and general counsel to more than seventy banks in the Western United States.

His Findley Reports on California Financial Institutions, founded by his father, Gerry Findley, in 1968, publishes newsletters—Findley Reports and Directors Compass—and the California Banks Reference Guide, a gold mine of financial information on California banking institutions. Findley also conducts seminars on banking topics.

Finally, his Findley Group is an investment banking and consulting firm with primary emphasis on strategic and capital development, merger analysis, fairness opinions, and regulatory applications.

He started the law firm in 1979, fresh out of Whittier College School of Law. He did his undergraduate work at Occidental College. He's forty-eight. He and his wife Rebecca have three children—twenty, sixteen, and twelve years old.

More to the point of his banking expertise, his father, Gerry Findley, is illustrious in the annals of California banking, the "Dean of California Banking," a veteran independent banking consultant (since the early 1950s) widely recognized in Western banking circles, author of nine books, including *Get Richer, Own the Local Bank* (1978), and self-professed "good and loyal friend of the honest and forthright banker, but an enemy of the deceptive and crooked banker," says his son Gary.

Gary has assumed the father's role and is described today in the same terms. The father's books influence him. He acts on the same principles. For instance, like his father, he emphasizes the long-term nature of a bank CEO's job. "Some banks have a good year or two, but we must look to those who do it year after year. It's not a one-year gig but a ten-to-fifteen-year one." "Exceptional" California CEOs take five, ten, or fifteen years to build a bank. "There are ten to fifteen exceptional CEOs in California. They are consistent performers."

John G. Rebelo, for instance, ran Peninsula Bank of San Diego for twenty-seven years, 1973 to 2000, when U.S. Bancorp bought it. It had grown from $8 million in assets to more than $456 million in that time. Rebelo's philosophy, said Gary, was to strive for "consistent, even performance"—not, he added, to "take the last dime off the table."

Carrol R. Pruett, chairman of Mid-State Bancshares, in Arroyo Grande, took over Mid-State Bank and Trust in 1967, when he was twenty-nine, becoming the nation's youngest bank president. He can look back now on "achieving overall consistency as a premier performing bank," said Findley.

I asked about my friend John Eggemeyer, of First Community Bancorp. "I know John well," he said. "One thing about John is that when he gives his word, he performs."

Findley speaks in terms of "super premier," "premier," or "commendable" performing banks, per the rating and tracking system he uses for California and other western banks. Four very reliable performance ratios, modified for 2004, make a bank "super premier"—14.5 percent or better return on beginning equity capital of $8 million to $10 million (ROE), 1.75 percent on average gross assets (ROAA), lower than 0.6 percent net loan loss as a percentage of beginning gross loans and 6 percent or better growth in assets, deposits, or gross income. In 2002 more than 125 California banks, of 278, are rated as "super premier" or "premier." The others placed too high a value on short-term results, in Gary's view.

"Success calls for planning and the monitoring of the basic ratios," he says. "If a board of directors and a management do not know where a bank is going—in what direction, at what speed—and do not have some idea of what it is to look like at selected points along the way, they will flounder, and the bank will deteriorate and possibly go out of business."

"My dad was very straightforward," Gary recalled. "He got agitated when a board was not doing its job." Once his father walked in on a client bank's board gathered for one of his highly regarded seminars aimed at helping boards to develop their business plan and, as Gary watched, "laid the board out" for falling down on the job.

"I was embarrassed," Gary recalled. Young as he was, just out of law school, he intervened with a comment, trying to "soften the blows."

That was in 1979. Twenty years later, his father had to do the same thing at another board seminar. "It was his turn to calm me down, as I began to lay a board out," he said, chuckling. "The acorn didn't drop far from the tree, I guess."

STARTING A BANK

California, a state whose number of banks has been in steady decline, is bursting with new ones. One out of four in the Controller of Currency's fourteen-state Western District is under five years old. Twenty applications were pending in June 2003, in California alone.

Gary Findley helps start an average of two new (de novo) banks a year, investing $100,000 of his own money if a bank passes his "litmus test." The litmus test looks "primarily" at the character and quality of its directors and management team, whether they will produce a bank he "can be proud of in five, ten, or fifteen years."

Such promise requires a plan, needless to say. What's more, put it in writing, he says. "Without such a written business plan, a de novo venture will turn out to be merely a dream, a vision, maybe even a nightmare."

As for raising capital, he made an interesting observation: "We prefer that it is somewhat difficult to raise capital. If it's too easy, it could simply be a backup for mistakes."

Location? "Means nothing. I've set up really good banks in unpromising areas."

THE DIRECTORS

Directors are most important. "The board is the heart of the organization. CEOs come and go. The board stays."

He and his associates spend a lot of time with directors, last year alone to the tune of thirty-five meetings which he led personally. He tells them not to think like bankers, but like businessmen. The bottom line, he says, is to "make sense business-wise." Understand banking, he says, "but be businessmen first."

He tells them each to get close to five other directors, whom they meet at seminars, for instance, people to whom they can tell their problems. "One in five," he says, will have faced the same problem. Don't worry about confidentiality, he tells them, as long as the other director is not in their immediate marketing area. It's a matter of developing peer groups of successful banks they can relate to—"a stellar group."

"Most banks don't have CEOs who have been through tough times; so one or two directors of any de novo should have banking experience. Regulators prefer it, and de novo banks need it."

THE CEO

The CEO matters, of course. It's the first challenge a board faces. Supposed candidates are out there, but they are seconds in command, in their thirties or forties, not CEOs. The trick is to get a CEO, someone who has won his spurs. These are the ones regulators have come to prefer.

"We've had good luck finding a number two guy in a good bank, in his thirties or forties." He said, "These days it's getting more difficult finding a good guy because the regulators are now emphasizing getting a proven CEO of a CAMELS 1-or-2-rated bank." Rated, that is, according to capital adequacy, asset quality, management, earnings, liquidity, and (since 1997) sensitivity to market risk, on a scale from 1 to 5, with 1 representing the highest rating. Banks with ratings of 1 or 2 present few supervisory concerns. The others present moderate to extreme degrees of concern.

"Too many are 'transient bankers,'" says Gary, "people who want to participate without working." These bankers don't perform and "usually cause great harm to a bank." A new bank needs a worker, "someone who's always thinking about the job."

He points out Keith Robbins, for instance, CEO of Butte Community Bank in Chico, about $250 million in assets, a super premier performer with an average ROE of 20 percent. The market value of this bank's stock has risen a "whopping" 1,450 percent over its eleven years.

Robbins has done this while making no acquisitions and maintaining a "1" rating with regulators. He sends his people to leadership training classes as a matter of course and regularly solicits ideas from them. "He always listens," said Gary.

As Gary wants directors to mix with their peers, so does he want CEOs to do so, also with five others. Indeed, "The first essential for being a top bank CEO is to personally know and intensively communicate and relate with five other CEOs." That's how Gary feels about it. It's from *California Banking—In Pursuit of Premier Performances*, a book by someone he looks too often for guidance, his father, Gerry Findley.

Gary observes: "The average tenure of a new CEO is less than eighteen months. The directors/organizers find someone to get the bank open and too late discover they have a misfit. Their CEO doesn't perform and they get rid of him."

HEROES

He echoes his father in another respect: he considers himself "an enemy of the deceptive and crooked banker." Knowing it sometimes takes courage to do the right thing, he aims through consulting to supply what he calls "rented courage, the courage to ask tough questions and make hard decisions."

He's high on the importance of the annual meeting. "All high-performance banks take the annual meeting as a golden opportunity to communicate with shareholders and lay out a bank's vision, its business plan." It's a simple matter: "If chairman, board, and senior management know the vision and are comfortable with it," he asks, "why not tell people?"

He's proud of the industry. "There are some bad ones out there," he says, "but banking is a noble career and we want noble people in it."

Chapter 34

Steve Didion, Hoefer & Arnett:

The Bank with Working Investors

and Other Favorites

Steve Didion's model community bank is Central Valley Bancorp, parent of Modesto Commerce Bank, in Modesto, California, founded in March 1998, with $100,000 investments (no more, no less) of seventy-five Modesto-area people, each of whom had to bring in a million dollars worth of business, or their hundred thousand was no good.

Of the seventy-five, only a few became directors because of restrictions by regulators. The seventy-five, recruited with the help of a former Modesto mayor, comprised the "founders club," a congenial and active group that included Modesto's highest-profile people. The bank, instantly successful, was profitable in its second full quarter and at first year-end had almost $100 million in deposits.

It was sold in 2003, by then at $285 million in assets, to the $1.5 billion Bank of Stockton for $69 million cash, but with a proviso at behest of its directors and founders, that the new owners keep the bank's name and its employees. Bank of Stockton bought in, paying two and a half times book and eighteen times earnings.

Hoefer and Arnett, San Francisco, managed the sale, which is in part why Didion, H&A's president, knows it so well. He traced the creation and sale of Central Valley in a June 2003 conversation.

Jeffrey P. Burda, president and CEO of Modesto Commerce Bank, had been involved with a 1993 sale of his bank to California Bankshares and its subsequent sale to U.S. Bancorp. He did not like what he saw of big-bank service and in 1998 he went to Mark VanOverbeek, MD, a local physician, who joined him in starting Central Valley on its unique pay-and-play model. They gathered the seventy-five founders. VanOverbeek, the force behind the bank, became vice chairman, per his wish in the matter.

It's a great community-banking story. Didion, a veteran bank stock analyst and investment banker, is the one to tell it. He's been at Hoefer and Arnett since 1991, when he joined as a managing director from Salomon Brothers, where he was a senior research analyst with its Financial Institutions Group in New York, Los Angeles, and San Francisco.

For Hoefer, one of the top three of such companies in the United States, with Seidler Company and Webb Bush Morgan, he covers over thirty stocks (of seventy the firm covers) with emphasis on western regional and community banks. He manages its bank research group and is senior advisor to an affiliated entity that specializes in bank stock investments, heading a forty-seven-person staff. It's unusual for "a boutique analyst" such as he to be both president and analyst, said Brian O'Connell in *Wall Street Research Magazine*.

Didion's ideas are important here because of his and Hoefer's focus on community banks. Hoefer is a full-service firm offering the full-service mix of research, sales, market-making, investment banking, and money management. It has offices in San Francisco, Baltimore, Los Angeles, San Diego, and Austin, Texas.

It was in 1986 that Steve saw the advantage in making market in stocks of the many relatively unknown banks started a few years earlier, in days of "charter giveaway." When he came to Hoefer in 1991, he started its research department. Focus: community banks.

Raising capital for banks by selling trust-preferred (nonvoting, pure investment) stocks, which he considers "very cost efficient since the Fed made it tier I capital in 1996," has been important for Hoefer, which handled fifteen trust-preferred transactions in the last several years, ranging between $3 million and $25 million each.

Hoefer did a half dozen or so M&A deals in the same period, one of them the Central Valley-Bank of Stockton deal described above. Two others were purchases by John Eggemeyer, of First Community Bancorp, of two California banks, Verdugo Banking Corporation, in Burbank, and Bank of Coronado. John Eggemeyer, said Didion, is an investor who looks primarily at a bank's management before he buys. He "buys management."

Central Valley Bancorp remains the model supreme. Those seventy-five investors receive convertible preferred stock for business they bring in after the initial $1 million required at the start. They are rewarded by conversion in proportion to the amount of business they bring. The idea was Sterling Bank, of Houston, that operates with a fifty-member advisory board.

As to banks in general, the most critical factor for some is the board. For others it's the CEO. American Business Bank, in Los Angeles, is a case of the latter. Its chairman and CEO, Bob Schack, is a *de novo* banker who made his move when his former bank was bought out by a bigger one. Starting American Business in 1998, he took his managers with him "across the street," recalled Didion.

As for location, Didion could think of no successful community banks in urban areas. Instead they have been built in what he calls "self-contained towns."

Didion considers bank stocks in general "quite safe investments," thanks in large part to the regulators, whose oversight protects investors' interests. He knew of only one bank that has recently failed, the $1.5 billion Hamilton Bank in Florida in January 2002.

Chapter 35

Kathy Smythe, Keefe Bruyette & Woods:

Community Banking Today

Today's community bankers face squeezed margins, but it's not a "rough" environment, says Kathy Smythe, managing director of investment banking in San Francisco for Keefe, Bruyette and Woods, one of the country's top investment firms specializing in banks, with sixteen third-quarter 2003 M&A deals worth $21 billion, ninth among investment firms worldwide.

Community banks have "very few" credit problems, for instance, and are raising capital, she said in a July 2003 interview. And being community banks and therefore "much more responsive to customers," they are "running circles around" big banks. All in all, it's "a charming industry," in which "the friendly mixture of community and shareholder is critical."

Community banks do well because they are people-oriented. They have to be. It's "crucial" for them, as it's crucial for their CEOs to be a "persuasive" sort, "tied to their communities," and fully cognizant of their niche, which is to operate "below the radar of the big banks."

She has watched these CEOs at work, on the road with them at analysts' and investors' dog-and-pony shows, where their banks' health is at stake. They are "phenomenal" sales people, "cheerleaders, always upbeat." Everything's fine with them. They believe in what they're doing. They give lessons in positive thinking.

For instance, John Eggemeyer, of San Diego-based First Community Bancorp, "the quintessential people person," is a "highly sophisticated big-picture strategist, alert to performance," with "a great sense of market timing."

Another, whom she calls "an Oregonian John Eggemeyer," is Ray Davis, CEO of Umpqua Bank, in Portland. He's a "phenomenal" salesman who has been making "lots of acquisitions." (Innovative too. His bank has a store-coffeeshop-cybercafe that *Christian Science Monitor* said reminds you of "a Hard Rock Café as much as it does a financial institution." It has its own coffee blend, T-shirts for sale, and employees roaming and hawking products.) His bank has $2 billion in assets, she said, "built from nothing!"

Another, back in California, is John Rebelo, who "dominated" San Diego before he sold his Peninsula bank to U.S. Bancorp. This became "a collar" deal because of declining stock prices, for which Rebelo had to guarantee a price. It was also a "fill or kill" deal for U.S. Bancorp, which had to buy right away or not at all. To make the purchase, U.S. Bancorp had to pay more, in its own shares, when the Rebelo bank stock went down. Smythe worked the sell side. John Eggemeyer might have been her buyer, but his stock "cratered at the wrong time."

Kathy knows Eggemeyer from that experience and also from her sell-side work in 1999 and 2002 respectively in sales to him of Santa Monica Bank and First National Bank of San Diego. She also worked the sell side in the 1992 sale of Chico, California-based Sierra West to the Walnut Creek, California-based Bank of the West.

A community bank's board makes a huge difference, of course. In this lies another reason for community banking's good record: boards in general have gotten better. Once you had the "butcher, baker, and candlestick maker" on your board. Now, she said, you have "much more sophisticated" directors.

How have these banks done so well in raising capital? One very important, indeed "huge," source of capital has been the trust-preferred security, with its similarities to debentures and preferred stock, a generally longer-term investment which matures at a face value and has early redemption features for the issuer and fixed interest quarterly payments. These trust preferred securities enjoy favorable accounting treatments and have more than ordinary flexibility. They are taxed like debt obligations by the IRS while keeping the appearance of equities in GAAP-style accounting statements.

Smythe finds it all very interesting, since IRS and regulators, including the Federal Reserve, used to rule out the trust preferred security as Tier I (core) capital. Once they ruled it in, in 1996, the trust preferred business went "gangbusters!"

Keefe, Bruyette and Woods was doing $500 million to $600 million per quarter in trust-preferred work. It had done fourteen or fifteen such deals by mid-2003. It was the biggest player in the country in this work, in which it collaborated with First Tennessee Bank.

The trust-preferred option put the brakes on M&A deals, as banks had seen they could raise capital without selling.

The equity part of trust-preferred sales was yielding up to 25 percent, with a pretty good floor of 20 percent, down from a floor of 24 percent. There was no liquidity yet, but no credit problems either. Maturity is usually at thirty years.

Questions remain, however. Is it debt or equity? And how long before IRS says the interest no longer qualifies as an expense?

But trust preferred securities have had "a real party" in the last several years.

The current rate for the debt side of trust preferred securities is between 4.75 and 5 percent, or about 3.05 percent over the three-month LIBOR rate.

THE BANKER-SCHOLAR

Kathy Smythe's education is unusual if not unique for an investment banker: three master's degrees—two from Harvard and one from New York University, the one from NYU in international business. Her PhD is from Harvard in seventeenth-century drama.

In 1986 she began her business career, joining a San Francisco investment firm specializing in community banks, Montgomery Securities, where she reported to the well-known banker and later ambassador to Switzerland, J. Richard "Dick" Fredericks, then senior managing director in Investment Research. She spent eleven years at Montgomery, developing a research magazine covering top western banks, *The Western Bank Monitor*. Montgomery sold to Bank of America in 1997, and Kathy went to KBW, bringing *The Western Bank Monitor* with her.

At KBW she has dealt with larger banks—twenty-five in California, Washington, Oregon, and Hawaii, mostly of $300 million or more in assets. In the last few years, KBW has been in on ten to fifteen M&A deals in the West and approximately one hundred nationwide, serving either buy or sell side. They have not done much in the West lately, however, as sellers are more cautious.

The office has twenty-five people, including eight in corporate finance and five in research. The rest are traders, equity sales people, and bond sales people. They help banks in growth strategy and advise on poison pills and the like and on security sales and bond transactions. They also help raise capital, in public offerings and private placements, as recently for a California bank which completed a $10 million private placement.

Tragically, the firm lost seventy people, mostly researchers, in the 9/11 attack on the Twin Towers in New York City, including the son of the chairman, John Duffy. Some Morgan Stanley people were hired to rebuild their research department.

Chapter 36

Mike Sammon, Friedman, Billings, Ramsey:

Community Banking in the Midwest

New markets are opening up all the time as big banks acquire community banks, and community banks get the best people because many don't want to work for the big ones. That's a major advantage. Community banking has a great future.

Community banking is in "a de novo era," says investment banker Mike Sammon, who helped us go public at First Colonial Bankshares in 1984. "In the last ten years there has been a tremendous increase in de novo banks," he said. "The increase comes from larger banks' doing a bad job of assimilating the smaller community banks which they buy. There have been one thousand new bank charters because of the five thousand that have been acquired. There will be more."

Mike has worked thirty years in community banking in the Midwest—in underwriting, stock analysis and sales. He currently works for Friedman, Billings, Ramsey and Company in its Chicago office, where he is a senior vice president. I have known him since 1978, soon after I formed First Colonial Bankshares as a three-bank group in Chicago. He was establishing a banking department at Chicago Corporation, a banking-specialist investment firm, where during ten-plus years he worked on dozens of merger and capital-raising assignments, in addition to research and trading activities.

When we went public in 1984, I turned to Mike and Chicago Corporation. It was a difficult period. Chicago's failing Continental Bank was being taken over by the FDIC. Mike, Chicago Corporation, and Dean Witter brought together several Midwestern investment banking companies as a selling group, including the firm I had started with, Robert W. Baird and Company, in Milwaukee, selling $10 million of our stock. It was excellent work.

Mike had started in the business at Bacon Whipple and Company—later acquired by Stifel Nicolaus—after Notre Dame, Loyola of Chicago law school, and service in Vietnam as an army captain and platoon commander. In twelve years at Bacon Whipple, he started a banking department specializing in research, trading and corporate finance work for Illinois banks.

He'd come from a banking family. His father, long-time Illinois banker Howard Sammon, was president of the Illinois Bankers Association. Mike has headed his law school's alumni and belongs to the Chicago, Illinois, and American bar associations.

Then came his Chicago Corporation work. In 1992 he went to Howe Barnes, where he headed its new banking department, with its concentration on small and medium-sized Midwestern banks and thrifts. In this capacity, he structured five community-bank unit investment trusts (UITs) whose units were sold to the public.

The performance of these five UITs in aggregate exceeded the NASDAQ Bank Index by 4 percent annually over their life.

He also supervised research and trading in more than one hundred bank and thrift stocks and worked in providing corporate finance services to banks and thrifts, substantially raising Howe Barnes's profile as an investment banker.

In 2000 he went to Stifel, Nicolaus and Company, where he primarily marketed trust preferred securities of community banks to institutional and retail accounts. In November 2002, he joined his present firm, Friedman, Billings, Ramsey, an investment banking heavyweight, though largely unrecognized as such.

In truth, FBR led twenty-four IPOs and secondary issues in the first half of 2003—second only to Citicorp, with twenty-six, and ahead of the widely recognized Goldman Sachs, Merrill Lynch, and others. In the same period, FBR raised $2.5 billion—fifth among all firms, more than headliners Morgan Stanley and Credit Suisse-First Boston. Aftermarket performance of FBR's IPOs and secondaries had a weighted average of +32.9 percent from July 1, 1998, to June 30, 2003—far higher than any of its nineteen peer firms, fifteen of whom had negative numbers.

This is a de novo era? "Yes. Twenty years ago new banks were started only in big growth areas and only occasionally. It would take three years to become profitable, because it was not easy to get loans, which you need to make money.

"That changed. Now all it takes is to start a bank across from a big bank that just bought a small one. Do that, and big dollars flow to your new [community] bank. Now it takes not three years but eighteen months to become profitable, half what it used to take, because new smaller banks regularly take loans from big banks who don't give comparable service. Business develops quickly, so do profits. It's not unusual these days for a new bank to become profitable in a year."

Lending is at the heart of banking success. "The best community banks are good lenders. The successful CEO has a good lending background, good connections, and good community relations. He understands local businesses.

"The bank investor should look for a history of success. It's a sign of success to come. The investor should not bet on people *without* a history of success. For instance, the successful chief financial officer of a large bank is not by that fact qualified to be CEO of a new bank."

As examples of highly successful de novo organizations, he offers a Chicago-area bank, Wintrust and two Michigan banks, Macatawa Bank and Mercantile Bank. Wintrust, based in North Suburban Lake Forest, is run by Ed Wehmer. It was started twelve years ago by Howard Adams, a banking executive, who several years ago fell out with the directors over governance issues.

Wintrust, now with $4.3 billion in assets, opens two or three banks or branches a year, in none but the most affluent suburbs. Starting de novo banks has always been their strategy. First came Lake Forest Bank and Trust. Seven banks followed, each with its own board answering to no holding company, as First Colonial boards answered to no company. Wintrust banks' directors, twelve to fourteen for each bank, constitute a who's who of their communities. Wehmer keeps pressure on to produce business. Each director has a quota.

Among Wintrust subsidiaries is a premium insurance company—one that finances commercial insurance premiums—FIRST Insurance Funding Corporation, the country's largest independent premium finance company. Through FIRST Wintrust lends to small businesses to pay their commercial insurance premiums. The policy holder pays a monthly fee, the bank pays the premium. These loans, which are low-risk, are 15 percent of the bank's portfolio.

In February 2002, Wintrust bought out the Chicago brokerage and money management firm Wayne Hummer. It was "a great move," said Sammon.

Yet further departing from the de novo strategy, this time more radically, in 2003 Wintrust bought several existing (but recently established) suburban banks in affluent markets. Better own them than have them for competition, they figured. They had the wherewithal to buy them in their (highly valued) stock—worth $45 now, down from $60 because of splits, but up six times in eight years, with $13.50 book value. "Wintrust is hard to value, because it's constantly coming back to the market for more capital. As of December '03, they had $350 million in total equity."

Two other banks make great stories, Macatawa and Mercantile. Both are in Michigan and both are successful because of how well they pursue community banking goals and how poorly Huntington Bancshares absorbed the First Michigan Bancorp banks it bought in 1997, in Holland, Zealand, and Grand Rapids.

"Ben Smith started Macatawa in 1997, and it's up to about $1.25 billion now. They're making about 1 percent on assets. It's a retail bank with fifteen to twenty branch offices. In their first year, capitalizing on tremendous loan demand, they reached $200 million in assets. The regulators saw a lot of what seemed to be new loans and were concerned about it. But they weren't new. They were seasoned loans brought over when most of the loan department left their old bank—one of the former First Michigan banks—and came to Macatawa.

"Macatawa stock came at $10 a share in 1997; it's up to $25 now, 150 percent higher.

"Mercantile of Grand Rapids is another 'spin-off,' you might say, of the First Michigan purchase; but unlike Macatawa, it's a business bank, not retail. It has five offices, all in greater Grand Rapids. It is up to $1 billion in assets with a deposit base of $350 million. It concentrates on commercial loans and small business lending. Their position is that it doesn't pay to seek out retail deposits; so they buy theirs. Theirs was the standard de novo choice: going retail or commercial. It's a choice that depends on the community.

"The Mercantile CEO, Jerry Johnson, had run the First Michigan operation in Grand Rapids. Mercantile has exceeded its organizers' wildest expectations. The stock came out at $10 a share; now it's $34, five and a half years later."

Mercantile had a double helping of big-bank aftermath benefits: Huntington bought First Michigan; and Fifth Third bought Old Kent, another company with high concentration in the area. Fifth Third did it right, but pockets of opportunities still turned up for Mercantile and other community banks.

"In general, this is an incredible market. Community-bank

stocks did well throughout the '90s; 1997 was spectacular. Stocks rose 50 to 60 percent, peaking in April 1998, then declined quickly, hitting bottom in early 2000. But by March 2000, the market was rallying, and recovery got under way in April and is now in its third year. Prices are getting a little full, but there is still demand out there.

"This market has risen so fast, so far, it risks dropping like a rock, like Wile E. Coyote chasing Roadrunner, who runs off a cliff with his legs still going until he looks down. Then he falls.

"But in the recent recession, not many bad loans cropped up, and that's a pleasant surprise. Asset quality has remained quite good.

"The merger and acquisition business is picking up because the currency of acquisition, namely stock, is worth so much. For instance, Wintrust at $45 can pay twice book for a purchase, and the deal will be accretive"—this will immediately increase earnings. "It's like the days when Bank One stock was at a very high multiple, with stock priced at 250 percent of book value, and Midwestern banks were selling at 175 to 200 percent of book value.

"It's said that two emotions drive the market, fear and greed. We're in the greed mode now. The 'greater fool' theory is at work" (when you make a questionable investment, assuming you can sell it later to a bigger fool). "People are telling themselves, 'I don't want to be left behind. What can I buy?'

"There's a lot of liquidity, and a lot of it is going into bank stocks. But eventually the appetite will be satisfied. However, the long-term increase in prices will parallel the earnings-per-share growth rate.

"As for prices paid for banks, at year-to-date September 30, 2003, deal prices were 216 percent of book nationwide, 196 percent in the Midwest. They were 22.3 times earnings nationally, 20.2 times in the Midwest. These are the highest prices and multiples since 1998 and 1999."

As for who's more important, board or CEO, it's the CEO.

"A poor CEO and a good board won't cut it, but a good board usually won't get a poor CEO, and a good one is the key. One of the best CEOs I know of is Jerry Francis, president of City Holdings, that has City National Bank in Charleston, West Virginia. Jerry came from the People's Bank in Indianapolis, which he grew from $400 million to about $700 million, then sold to Fifth Third for over four times book.

"Then he and his four or five top guys, out of a job, went to City National, which was having problems. By their second quarter there, it was profitable. In 2002 it made 1.89 percent on assets and 22 percent on equity. Its stock went from $8 a share to $37, and Jerry was named banker of the year by *American Banker*.

"Why did he do so well? Mainly because he believes in what he's doing, in his case retail banking. 'You can make a lot of money in retail banking,' he says. He also runs a very efficient operation. He controls costs and does a great job growing the revenue side. In general, he gets into things that make money."

Chapter 37

Murray Bodine, Investment Banker, San Francisco: Tips for the Community Banker

The first key to community-bank success is to pick the right market, says San Francisco investment banker Murray Bodine. Beware the market dominated by large banks.

The second is to have a board of directors with a reputation for prudence and integrity that understands and relates to the community. Too many try to enrich themselves at the expense of shareholders.

The third is to be careful how quickly you grow. Forget hitting some magic $100 million mark. Forget growth for growth's sake. This means you want a sensible credit policy. Credit quality is key. Bad loans can destroy the shareholders. Score one for the loan committee as extremely important.

Fourth, be sure your leader is experienced and competent, then let him lead. Don't micro-manage.

Bodine's work has been mostly in banking, where he got to know community banking. In recent years, as a member of the venture capital firm JGE Capital Management, he brokered sales of two important Napa community banks, Napa National to Wells Fargo and Napa Valley to West America.

His own career began at Bank of America, which he joined as a trainee in 1978 after gaining a finance degree from Babson

College in Boston. His first job was in small-business lending. In due time he headed the bank's SBA loan division, gaining valuable experience in a job he says "nobody else wanted."

Then he moved to the other end of the business spectrum, handling Fortune 500 accounts in Bank of America's world banking division. He specialized first in food products companies, then in lumber and paper, taking over Utah and Idaho clientele—large lumber and paper companies such as Boise Cascade. Then he worked in investment banking, including on mergers and acquisitions.

Then he abandoned the big-bank regimen and joined a small San Francisco firm, Hoeffer and Arnett, a broker-dealer that became a market-maker of small-bank stocks. These were days when bank-stock trades were so minor a consideration that they were made out of the bank president's desk and were sometimes announced on "pink sheets" of paper.

Hoeffer and Arnett turned to researching community banks and making markets in their stocks, and then to investing in community-bank funds, raising capital for them, and handling mergers. Bodine was in on all of it.

In 1997, after several years at Hoeffer, he moved to another San Francisco investment firm, Van Casper and Company, which was bought by First Security Corporation (of Utah) a year later. He promptly joined Dain Rauscher, a Minneapolis firm, running its western division until that firm was bought out by Royal Bank of Canada. In March 2002, he went with JGE Capital.

By now, he had his spurs on the investment side of community banking. He had seen the good and the bad and had learned what makes the difference. Hence his advice as above, based on years of experience.

What about two important options that present themselves to the successful community bank? One is to partner with another bank, usually for the capital involved, which is admittedly "enticing." Just remember, he says, "you need the right partner," one with goals like yours and the same ethical perspective.

Another issue is the nature of the partnership. A 20 or 25 percent partner may be like having a 250-pound gorilla on your team; just know what you are doing, and have a very good reason for taking him on. But a 51 percent partner, no matter what he brings to your bank, is a bad idea. "Don't give up control for book," Bodine says pithily. "When you sell, get a premium."

As to finding a big-bank buyer for 100 percent of your bank, there are problems with that too, for the buyer, who loses value if he loses your key people, and for you, the seller, who must be alert both to price and to the character of the buyer, who has to be the right one for you. Keep your eyes and options open until the ink is wet on the page.

PART IV-B

OUTSIDE EXPERTS: REGULATORS

Chapter 38

Conrad Hewitt, Former Commissioner of Financial Institutions, State of California

The first thing Conrad "Con" Hewitt did as superintendent of banking for California was to consolidate the credit unions, thrifts, industrial loan companies, and banks under one supervisory body, which he named the Department of Financial Institutions (DFI), of which he became commissioner. Thus he became California's first DFI commissioner by becoming its last superintendent of banking.

He spent four years in that position, retiring in 1998. He was the only nonlawyer CPA to be a California commissioner. Before he took the position, he had been managing partner of northern California for Ernst and Young, from which he retired. "It was an easy adjustment" for him. He had twelve lawyers on staff and other "very good" staff people. It was a "rewarding" experience.

He was offered the job of Inspector General of the Government Printing Office in Washington, DC, when he left the DFI but turned it down. He did not want to move to Washington.

He had served California's financial industry well by bringing a businessman's approach to the banks commissioner position and consolidating oversight of financial institutions. As a director of North Bay Bancorp, the holding company for Vintage and Solano banks, since retiring as commissioner, he is also as good an example as one will find of a highly qualified community-bank director. As head of North Bay's audit committee, he has been "an enormous help to the banks," says North Bay CEO Terry Robinson.

He grew up in the Midwest. A native of Sheffield, Illinois, he received his BS in Finance and Economics from the University of Illinois. During summers he worked at the Commercial National Bank in Peoria, Illinois. He joined Commercial National full time when he graduated in June 1958.

He was with the bank until October 1958, when he received his air force commission and went off to Lackland Air Force Base in Texas. After that he went to Strategic Air Command headquarters in Omaha, Nebraska, where he was assigned to the air force's auditing service, though he had not majored in auditing.

Out of the air force in three and a half years, he joined Ernst and Ernst in Los Angeles in 1962. In 1989 he became managing partner for northern California of Ernst and Ernst, newly merged with Arthur Young and Company.

He retired from Ernst in 1995, and he and his wife moved to Napa. While DFI commissioner, he addressed the Vintage Bank board at Terry Robinson's request. When North Bay Bancorp was formed in 1999, he was asked to be one of two outside directors.

I asked him where a board comes in. "I sit on a number of

boards and am surprised at how few keep up with continuing education. Directors have to keep current, there are so many things going on!"

He has helped North Bay in strategic planning and has educated its board about the "very competitive" financial industry.

Regulators? Don't take them on, he said. "It's the wrong approach." He was the Ernst and Young partner in charge of Bank of America, working with Tom Clausen, CEO, and Dick Rosenberg, chairman, when they bought Security Pacific. A member of the new audit committee from Security Pacific said they had relied heavily on senior management, internal auditors, and external auditors, but not regulators. They had not paid regulators enough attention. It had been "a big mistake."

"Pay attention to regulators. Do not fight them," Con said. "I speak from experience. They can tell you things your staff does not see."

When he became Superintendent of Banking, the examiners were into everything, "even controlling the architecture and furniture of new banks and branches." That stopped, as did enforcement of many other "outdated and cumbersome" regulations, which were eliminated and consolidated. These reforms "made banks more competitive with nonregulated financial institutions."

As for starting a de novo bank, he rates board and CEO equally important, with the board's audit committee very important. As for regulators, DFI would ask some "important questions" on the application:

1. Where are the deposits coming from?
2. What is the three-year forecast? (Most community banks have not worked up good profitability models.)
3. How confident are the applicants with their marketing-feasibility study?

And branches? "Branches are dinosaurs. Baby boomers

never enter branches. Traffic in branches has declined significantly in the last ten years."

In the last ten years there has been a 32 percent decline in the number of banks, but a 15 percent increase in the number of branches. Meanwhile, however, the size, nature and purpose of a branch has changed,

Grocery store branches he finds interesting. "The concept is good, but the needs have changed. Banks have tried putting full-time people in these branches, but many are not profitable. But grocery store branches have attracted new customers and do serve present ones."

Internet banking has not taken off, contrary to his expectations.

A board for a de novo community bank should be leaders in the community, "with excellent financial, business, and commercial-organization reputations." They should be of a variety of age groups, not all fifty-to-sixty-year-olds. There should be "a diverse ethnic blend" if possible. "But it's difficult here [in Napa Valley] to get a good Hispanic board member. You hope you can find several directors with banking experience, but they are hard to find. You want a CPA for audit, asset-liability, and loan committees."

What about the North Bay loan committee, which must be a good one, because of their extremely low charge-off history? "We might be *too* conservative and strict," he said. When he joined the board, most of the directors were on the loan committee, and they met every week. They cut the committee to three or four but continued to meet weekly. The only loans that go to the board are Regulation O loans, which are loans to directors.

Credit review is outsourced to a San Francisco company, which reports to the audit committee in executive session, with no management present. EDP is done in-house, because they are "big enough" to do it for themselves.

Which regulatory agency does he prefer? Never a national-bank agency. The fees are too much, half again as much as being a state bank. More importantly, the state agency knows the state's businesses better.

Four out of five California banks—mostly medium-size and smaller—are state banks.

Regulators of the Federal Reserve, of which Vintage is a member bank, are "very open and easy to work with," filling Vintage people in on "best practices" of other banks, which they find "very helpful."

The major pitfalls for a community bank? "The first is acquiring a low-quality loan portfolio, which does not become clear for two to three years. Second is a reluctance to invest in technology. Third is expansion for its own sake, without a plan. Fourth is reluctance to invest in top people."

That said, how do you find a top CEO? "Quite a few" are available, because of the many acquisitions and mergers over the last five to six years which have left "good officers" out there who lost jobs in that process. Use a head-hunter, he said. It's "the quickest way."

What are you looking for? An excellent track record as a CEO or chief operating officer, excellent communication ability, a vision of where the individual wants to go, and strong "customer-relationship drive."

What's to come? "There will always be a place for community banks, but the competition is tremendous, and not just with other banks, but with nonbanks such as Merrill Lynch and mutual funds."

As of the fall of 2003, he was serving on boards of three public companies and three private ones and was a trustee, one of three, for a large private charitable foundation. He's happy in all this, but happiest in his work with North Bay Bancorp, whose May 1999 decision to start its de novo bank in Solano County he praises as excellent strategy, largely because the county had no community banks.

Chapter 39

Don Meyer, Former Commissioner of
Financial Institutions, State of California

Don Meyer is optimistic about community banking. "It's been growing. It shows resiliency. Community bankers are facing their problems. They can compete well with the big banks."

He has the evidence. Since he took office in April 2000, as California's commissioner of financial institutions, twenty-eight banks have opened; several applications are pending. In 2003 alone, as of early fall, California had licensed six de novo banks, losing just one, Comerica, which left for Michigan, where it chose to consolidate its banks.

Capital is on the rise. Three years ago capitalization of de novo banks was $6 million to $8 million. Recently a number of banks have capitalized for $12 million to $20 million. It shows that investors are willing to put more capital into banks. It's a sign of confidence.

The important issue for him as a regulator is annual CAMELS ratings—measuring capital adequacy, asset quality, management, earnings, liquidity, and sensitivity to market risk. Of California state-chartered banks, 90 percent have (high) CAMELS ratings of 1 or 2, in contrast to only 60 percent of them in the 1989-1993 period.

The improvement, he said, stems almost entirely from higher

asset quality, which has been achieved even with a slight increase in management problems. There has also been, recently, a rise in interest-rate sensitivity, "which means some banks are making bad guesses."

This major banking improvement has happened in a time of low interest rates that depress the value of a bank's investment portfolio, in part because of the effect of low rates on bond prices. This developed when bankers had to sell their longer-term investments in 1993 and 1994, when rates jumped one hundred basis points in a very short time. As bond yields went up, bond's value went down.

Banks had to price per market directions, and there were big losses. The lesson is, don't chase yields. Rather, turn to other investment strategies using derivatives and hedging and stay short. This minimizes potential portfolio loss. This is how community banks have been increasingly able to avoid losses from low rates.

Another low-rates fallout has been a squeeze on margins. When the net interest margin drops below 3 percent, it's hard for a bank, especially a new one, to be profitable.

Yet another, stemming from the wider availability of lower rates from other sources, is the considerable migration of borrowers away from banks.

DON MEYER AND I

I met Don Meyer in 2000, a few years after I had moved to Napa and shortly after I had been asked to help organize a bank there—by Congressman Mike Thompson. Don was the first regulator I met in California. We got to know each while the bank was being organized and during my time as its chairman, March 1, 2001, to November 2002. We've stayed in close contact since then.

He had come to the commissioner's office after twenty-two years in banking—as a general counsel, all but two of the twenty-two with Union Bank and its parent, before and after stints of several years each with first one, then another San Francisco law firm.

As a banker, he received the Almon B. McCallum Award in 1989 for outstanding service to the industry from the California Bankers Association, on whose Legal Affairs and Federal Government Relations Committees he served. He was California state vice president for the American Bankers Association and a long-time member of the ABA Government Relations Council.

He had his law degree from Berkeley, his MBA from Harvard. Between school and career, he put in two years in Seoul, Korea, with the Peace Corps, 1968 to 1970. Years later, he became probably the only state banking commissioner who speaks fluent Korean.

In extracurricular matters, he covers the waterfront with multiple memberships: the World Affairs Council of Northern California, the Society of California Pioneers, and the Sierra Club. He's on the American-Asian Cultural Exchange Advisory Board, is past president and current chairman of the board of directors of the Korean-American Chamber of Commerce, and serves as trustee of the Asian Art Museum Foundation.

As commissioner, he has won the glowing approval of Consultant Gary Steven Findley, who has seen commissioners come and go for twenty years. Findley calls Don Meyer "a gentleman and a peace maker" who "sees the whole picture." It's a complex picture, and he has done well while heading an inadequately budgeted agency. Be that as it may, as commissioner he oversees one of the largest groups of financial service institutions in the country:

Total Assets

	Number	June 30, '03
State Chartered Commercial Banks	184	$133 bil.
State Chartered Credit Unions	219	54 bil.
Industrial Banks	17	11 bil.
Trust Companies	12	.5 bil.
Savings and Loans	1	.4 bil.
Foreign Banks	42	16 bil.
Premium Finance Companies	71	322 bil.

THE DE NOVO STARTUP PROCESS

Of these 184 state banks, about six start new every year, or have done so during Meyer's time at the helm. What's the startup process? What advice does he have?

Regulators usually start with a meeting with the lawyer or consultant, some of the investors, and the proposed CEO. They identify key issues to be addressed by the applicant and suggest how to strengthen the application—in hand in draft form—for delivery.

They ask for a list of proposed directors and credentials of the proposed CEO and chief financial officer. They say two of the officers must be experienced in their proposed position, preferably the CEO.

Then they interview the proposed directors, one by one. Then they go to the community, sometimes meeting with the mayor and the Chamber of Commerce. They gather feedback from other sources, checking with other agencies and doing criminal and noncriminal background checks.

They study the business plan and the proposed management plan. These are the two most important factors. They consider the adequacy of proposed capital, which is a close third in importance.

They want a realistic plan, "pragmatic" is the word. A group of pharmacists with limited banking experience offers too narrow a scope, for instance. A bank has to serve the whole community, not just a segment.

Neither do they like one-note banks specializing in leasing or credit card issuance, for instance. These they leave to the U.S. Controller of Currency.

WHERE A BANK'S BOARD COMES IN

A bank's board must know where it fits in. Its main task is to hire the chief executive, financial, and credit officers. But that's not all. It has to give a bank direction, so that it promotes shareholders' interests and serves the community properly.

In short, says Meyer, "The buck stops with a bank's board."

At least one director should have bank board experience. Each director should have "some financial experience."

No director should have more than 10 percent of a bank's stock, 10 percent being a control position in his view, and no individual should control a bank.

A director should bring business. Meyer's regulators evaluate each according to net worth to decide whether it's adequate to support proposed investment and be a source of capital.

Location matters but is not as important as the business plan, assuming adequate capital. They leave location up to organizers. "We test investors' assumptions," he said, "but we do not substitute our own judgment."

However, an area can be overloaded with new banks. Over $60 million in new bank capital has come into Orange County in the last three years, for instance, according to a recent Findley newsletter. That $60 million will call for $600 million in loans to justify it, Meyer said, calling it "a heavy concentration of new banks and new capital."

Finally, directors take note: Don't fight with bank examiners. "It's too much like wrestling in the mud with a pig. Eventually you figure out that the pig enjoys it."

As for being a commissioner, for Don Meyer it hasn't been wrestling in the mud, but he enjoyed his four years in the job. It's been "intellectually challenging," he's been in on "a fair amount" of public policy, and all in all he's found it satisfying.

He's been able to watch financial services grow and flourish in California. Such a different experience it has been from that of his predecessor James E. Gilleran, who in 1989 as superintendent of the California State Banking Department had to close more than sixty banks. He has had to close just one bank and one credit union while licensing twenty-eight new banks. Quite a difference.

He is high on his staff. Coming from the private sector, he did not expect much and is happy to report he was wrong, and this with staff that is paid 35 percent less than comparable federal staff. What keeps many of them around is his department's "non-bureaucratic, pragmatic, approach."

The chief state examiner, David Scott, was retiring in March 2004, after more than ten years in that position. "Unfortunately," said Meyer, "because he's so good at it."

None of which means he's happy about state-imposed spending constraints that keeps them from hiring people ready to take on the work at hand. For the most part, they train them, only to see some leave after five to eight years for the FDIC and Federal Reserve, where salaries are better.

It comes down to finances. DFI, funded by assessments on the industry, depends on legislative and gubernatorial approval to spend anything. The state's Credit Union Advisory Committee, on the other hand, spends as it wishes, so that in 2003 it has twice its income of 1996, when both it and DFI were established, but still a staff of twenty-seven. This happened while credit-union industry's assets doubled in size, it should be noted.

As for banking today, Don Meyer likes to quote FDIC Chairman Don Powell from an August 2002 speech to the American Bankers Association in which Powell chided bankers for not innovating more, even as he critiqued a funding innovation, namely the recent proliferation of trust preferred issues. "Is this the time to leverage your balance sheet?" he asked. Is this the time "to add more capital"?

As for neglected innovation, he urged them to "take advantage of a time of unprecedented industry strength to purge unprofitable revenue streams, overhaul balance sheets, weed out weak employees, and upgrade boards."

Now is the time, he said, "to focus on your employees . . . rid yourselves of those bad directors . . . build relationships with your regulators." If you don't do that, he warned, your "complacency could bring unpleasant consequences."

The Powell message is one that Don Meyer wants to pass on to bankers everywhere in 2003, as in the Powell speech title, "Welcome to paradise," he says, meaning banking's golden age of opportunity. "Now shape up!"

POSTSCRIPT

In early February 2004, Don Meyer was replaced as commissioner by Howard Gould, of Los Angeles, an appointee of the new governor, Arnold Schwarzenegger. Meyer was an excellent commissioner. The industry will miss him.

Chapter 40

FDIC Regulators, Chicago

In my chapter "Starting a Community Bank," I say, "Work and cooperate with regulators. They are there to help. Always be honest, never try to hide anything, and prepare well for examinations. Your life will be a lot easier if regulators and examiners like and trust you. They are not antagonists. They want you to succeed."

Steve Didion, president of Hoefer Arnett, says, "Bank stocks are safe investments to a large extent because of oversight by regulators."

Joe Stieven, of Stifel Nicolaus, in another chapter agrees and puts it in a different perspective, as a top bank analyst: "The beauty of banking is that we have the most independent set of bookkeepers out there, the regulators. They are investors' best friends . . . . Banking is the most regulated industry in the world. The regulators are fabulous for us . . . . If you earn the respect of the regulators, you have much greater flexibility . . . . I can't recall any CEO of the banks in our coverage complaining about the regulators."

Joe and I agreed it's a fool's game to battle regulators on aggressive accounting practices or arguing loan classifications. He said there are only a few banks in the Midwest who do, and investors in those banks should be wary.

I remember when Silas Keehn became president of the

Chicago Federal Reserve in the early '80s. The Chicago Fed had been notoriously bureaucratic. He called a meeting of CEOs of Chicago's top banks to introduce himself. He told us, "We're here to help you succeed . . . to help you, not to be antagonists." He brought a refreshing businesslike approach to the bank, and he performed as he said he would. He and his senior vice president, Frank Dryer, were great to work with.

Bill Harris, Illinois banking commissioner during that time, also helpful, cooperative, and resourceful, transformed the state commission into a banker-friendly organization.

Don Meyer, until recently commissioner of California's Department of Financial Institutions, is the ideal banking commissioner—bright, an experienced lawyer, banker-friendly—an administrator who understands his role well. Bankers in California respect him for his evenhandedness, his forthright manner, and his enthusiasm and dedication.

Thanks to his stint with the Peace Corps, he also speaks fluent Korean, which makes him a truly unique banking commissioner!

In my ongoing pursuit of regulators, I interviewed two Chicago-office FDIC case managers in June 2003. The Chicago office oversees several Midwestern states including Michigan and Illinois. One of the two had been an examiner of some First Colonial Banks. The other I have known for a number of years. We had and still have a great deal of respect for each other.

Their insights were helpful.

I laughingly told them the banker's interpretation of the acronym FDIC—"Forever Demanding Increased Capital." They said, "The driver of a well-run bank is management. Capital is king, but management is the key."

In reference to their CAMELS ratings—capital, assets, management, earnings, liquidity, sensitivity to market risk, on a descending scale of one to five, they said they see "more composite 1s during strong economic times" but where seeing fewer "because of the [then current] more difficult economic times."

They "focus more on the loan portfolio in [their] risk management assessment, but now with the interest rate decline and the interest rate compression, [were] looking more closely at that area. Funding is becoming more of a factor. Banks need more forethought in funding strategies."

I asked about the seriousness of a 3 in their CAMELS ratings. They said it means they have "some concerns, frequently in the asset quality area, [that] management has to be proactive but usually can correct the deficiencies. The bank needs extra work but is not an imminent risk to the insurance fund."

In such a case, they issue "a memo of understanding, an informal enforcement action," seeking "a binding agreement to address specific areas of concern."

A 4 rating means a bank is getting into areas of "imminent risk." A 5-rated bank "has lots of problems . . . obviously poor management. It is losing money and there are liquidity problems."

As for denials on de novo bank applications, there are "not many, but we saw a brief rise in de novos' composite ratings of 3s and 4s a couple of years ago."

Regulators are looking much more closely at a CEO's experience as an approval factor, according to Ed Carpenter in California, who does the majority of de novos in California. The FDIC pair confirmed that. "We are looking a lot more closely at a president/CEO's qualifications. We are requiring some significant experience."

This translates to a CAMELS (management) rating of a 2 or a 1, "as if the new bank had already been in business," as a requirement for approval.

I asked how important a board of directors is to a bank's success. "We want a business plan showing the board plans to stay on with the bank, not sell in three or five years. We look for intent of continuity. We don't want a group that is getting into business just to make some money quickly. We want a long term commitment.

"As for the relationship between the board and the CEO,

we like a balance. We don't want the CEO to be dominant. We want several board members to have banking experience. The board can't rely completely on the CEO."

I asked about stock options. "We must approve all stock option plans in de novos, in fact anything to do with compensation. Plans have to conform to FDIC policy.

"We also look closely at insider activity, such as ownership and leasing of the bank building. All affiliate relationships must be disclosed."

They were at a point of "pretty high [de novo] activity." They had fifteen applications in their office and were expecting to hear "soon" from six to ten other groups.

I asked about recent bank failures in their district. They mentioned the Blanchardville (Wisconsin) Bank, a small national bank in a town of eight hundred people; a small Illinois bank twelve to eighteen months previously; and the New Century Bank, in Southfield, Michigan.

The biggest recent failure was the Pritzker family's bank in Oakbrook Terrace, Illinois, in July 2001, a $2 billion bank "with problems of accounting, mortgage servicing rights, and bad loans."

Organizers of de novo banks will find regulators helpful and cautious. A positive relationship will help them greatly. As for these two case managers, they "do not want an adversarial position with a banker." They consider it "very counterproductive."

Chapter 41

Richard C. Houseworth,

Superintendent of Banks, Arizona

Sitting with Richard C. Houseworth, superintendent of banks for Arizona, in April 2003, I asked him what he considered a de novo bank's biggest challenge.

Its leadership, he said. "Who is the CEO? Who is the credit officer? Who is the chief financial officer? These are the questions I ask first."

Directors are crucial. "A bank's directorship has to be committed to find a competent CEO who will manage the bank the way they want it managed. Unfortunately, many CEOs do not have management experience," he said.

So important is leadership that his office must give its approval when a CEO or director wants to leave a bank in its first three years of being chartered. "When it happens," he said, "I call the individual and ask why."

Dick Houseworth came to his present position in 1993 after extensive private and government experience—thirty-three years with the Arizona Bank, now Bank of America, after beginning in banking in his native Kansas in 1955, and seven years in Washington, 1988 to 1993, as a director of the Export-Import Bank and then as a U.S. alternate to the Inter-American

Development Bank, followed by four months as a consultant to the Treasury Department.

Arizona has thirty-seven banks, twenty-seven with state charters and ten with national charters. Six had started in the seven months previous to our conversation in April 2003. It's his job, he said, "to help people do what they want within confines of the law."

When a group wants to start a de novo bank, what does he do? First, he "sizes them up" in a meeting, to see if they belong in banking. "Not everyone does." He looks over their business plan and asks how much capital they think they will need.

"A good bank is like a three-legged stool," he said. "In addition to a good directorate and a good CEO and staff, you need adequate capital."

How much is enough? "Between $6 million and $10 million, depending on the kind of bank you want, a one-office branch and in a city or not."

In any case, organizers should raise enough capital so that it is not outrun by the business at the crucial three-year point, when "the feds" want it to be at least 8 percent of assets. His point was that it's a mistake to undercapitalize because you underestimate coming growth. If at the two-year point you see you are falling short, he said, it's too soon to go back to the market for more.

Arizona's audit committee requirements for state banks? "The audit committee must have three independent directors. There must also be a compensation committee."

Taking loan fees up front, in violation of FASB 91, as at least one Arizona bank does? Banks "had better assess the risks" of this.

Epilogue

What Is My Bank Worth?

Investors in de novo banks like to know what their banks are worth on the open market, even if they are not looking for a quick profit. They are right about quick profit: community-bank investing is a long-term proposition, with few or no dividends for a while. In fact, many people invest in a community bank to have part of an institution that is important culturally as well as financially. This was our experience when we formed Napa Community Bank in 2002. Many of our 477 local investors invested $1,000 each, more to be part of the bank than to make money. We raised $4.2 million in all, but set a low minimum investment to attract such wide participation.

Nonetheless, the return on a community-bank investment can be substantial, as you know from reading this book. And safe. Banks rarely fail. No major bank has failed in the United States since 1991, none of any size since 1995 in California, where four out of five have FDIC safety ratings of "1" or "2," says Ed Carpenter.

This is no accident. "The beauty about banking," says Joe Stieven of Stifel Nicolaus, "is its independent set of bookkeepers, the regulators"—from Federal Reserve, FDIC, Office of the Controller of Currency, and state banking commissions. They are bank investors' "best friends." He calls banking the world's "most regulated industry, policed by these patrolmen on the banking highway. They are fabulous for us."

The highly successful Ed Wehmer, CEO of $4.2 billion Wintrust Financial Corporation, says the same thing. "We like regulators. They're watching my net worth, and that's comforting."

So the failure of the bank you invest in is almost never an issue. Performance is, however; and sale price depends on performance. Investors can be optimistic on this score. In four of the last eight years, banks in the Stifel Nicolaus regional bank index have outperformed the S&P 500 by more than 50 percent. In the last three years, small-cap bank stock—under $500 million—averaged a gain of 157 percent.

Sale-price figures further support optimism. Consider the high price-to-earnings and price-to-book-value ratios for banks of less than $500 million in assets in twenty-two Midwest states as of November 28, 2003, according to Stifel Nicolaus:

Price to last twelve months' earnings (LTM):
2001   17.8x
2002   19.6x
2003 (YTD)   21.5x

Price to book value:
2001   1.65x
2002   1.68x
2003 (YTD)   2.13x

Banks of less than $1 billion in assets enjoy comparable ratios. So do ratios for California banks of all sizes sold from the start of 2001 to the end of October 2003, as supplied by Gary Steven Findley and Associates:

Price to last twelve months' earnings:
2001 Average 13.9x
2002 Average 17.1x
2003 Average 23.6x

Price to book value:
2001 Average 1.77x
2002 Average 1.89x
2003 Average 1.90x

Comparable ratios are found in 2001-2003 bank sales in the United States, according to Friedman Billings Ramsey:

Price to last twelve months' earnings:
2001   18.5x
2002   18.3x
2003 (YTD 10/30/03)   22.3x

Price to book value:
2001   1.77x book
2002   1.69x book
2003 (YTD 10/30/03)   2.16x book

The following are bank-by-bank results. Note that most of these banks were ten to twenty years old at time of sale. The youngest, Modesto (California) Commerce, was five years old. Figures are from Stifel, Nicolaus and Company and Gary Steven Findley and Associates. All are 2003 sales. "DA" following the bank's name stands for definitive agreement.

	Assets	Sold	Book Multiple	Earnings Multiple
Central Sierra Bank, CA	$137 mil	7/14/2003	1.94x	22.5x
First Continental Bank, CA	$334 mil	7/11/2003	2.34x	25.5x
North State National, CA	$144 mil	4/4/2003	2.36x	16.3x
First Western, CA	$214 mil	5/13/2003	2.56x	18.3x
Harbor Nat'l. Bank, CA	$177 mil	12/1/03 (DA)	2.60x	29.0x
Modesto Commerce, CA	$300 mil	12/1/2003	2.73x	20.0x
Lakeland Financial, IL	$171 mil	11/24/03 (DA)	2.48x	33.3x
Reunion Bankshares, TX	$214 mil	10/27/03 (DA)	2.95x	30.2x
Alliance Bancorp, AR	$139 mil	10/8/03 (DA)	2.47x	21.3x
Caledonia Financial, MI	$206 mil	12/1/2003	2.67x	17.1x
Round Lake Bancorp, IL	$104 mil	9/11/03 (DA)	2.16x	20.3x
Pioneer Bankshares, TX	$ 73 mil	8/18/03 (DA)	2.35x	29.4x
Beltline Bankshares, TX	$177 mil	8/8/03 (DA)	2.42x	34.8x
Lake Region Bancorp, IL	$ 83 mil	6/20/03 (DA)	2.12x	31.2x
Commerce South, AL	$312 mil	5/28/03 (DA)	2.34x	23.3x
Secured Trust, TX	$ 53 mil	8/15/2003	2.69x	20.3x
ANB Financial, TX	$ 93 mil	9/30/2003	3.29x	24.3x
WB&T Bankshares, TX	$154 mil	8/15/2003	2.37x	18.3x
Founders Bankshares, MO	$122 mil	6/13/2003	2.99x	28.6x
Marion Financial Holdings, TX	$321 mil	7/1/2003	2.20x	20.1x
First Central Bank, TN	$150 mil	4/1/2003	2.39x	22.7x

Bank sale prices such as shown here are based not just on the multiple of earnings, as in other industries, but also on the multiple of book value, which is determined in part by its assets, that is, its loans, which drive earnings. A forward—looking bank board limits dividend payouts for the sake of book value, which is a very important part of the sale equation.

It is interesting to note that of thirteen banks sold in California in 2003, five had lost money in the previous twelve months. But book values ranged from 1.22 times to 2.14 times. So these banks all sold at a book-value premium, even the ones that were losing money.

"Most sales—about 65 percent—are of banks of $100 million to $200 million in asset size," says Ed Carpenter. "And competitors pay the highest prices." These are banks attracted by location, which they consider a prime factor. They also pay close attention to quality of loan portfolio, strength of earnings, and quality of staff.

Ample return on investment does not always require selling, notes Mike Sammon, of Friedman Billings. He cites Lake Forest-Illinois-based Wintrust Financial, whose stock rose six times in eight years; Macatawa Bank of Holland, Michigan, whose stock rose 150 percent in five and a half years; and Mercantile Bancorp, of Grand Rapids, whose stock went from $10 a share to $34 also in five and a half years.

Another fast-earner is seven-year-old Community Bank Oak Park & River Forest, in Illinois, whose stock is closely held. Its earnings are strong—1.6 percent ROA and 22 percent ROE—and it is in the highly competitive Chicago area; so it could be sold at a good premium. If it could be sold for 2.25 times book, for instance, the selling price would be $27 million. If for fifteen times earnings, it would be $30 million. On this bank's original investment of $5.25 million, that comes to an approximately six-times overall return and 26 percent to 28 percent annual return.

Yet another fast earner was Auburn Community Bancorp, a de novo sold after only five years to Western Sierra of

Cameron Park, California, for cash and stock at approximately 2.6 times book. Auburn had opened with capital slightly in excess of $4 million. Five and a half years later, its assets were $89 million, its total capital $8.6 million. It sold in August 2003, for approximately $19 million. But Western Sierra's shares increased significantly in the next few months, from the low $30 to $47 a share, adding $4 million to the sale price—up $45 a share to more than $350. So the beginning investment in Auburn Community, valued at $100 a share, had more than tripled in five and a half years.

Modesto (California) Commerce Bank is another fast-earning community bank. It opened in March 1998, with $13.5 million in capital and sold in 2003 for $61.5 million—2.73 times book and 20 times LTM earnings. Its assets were $308 million. Modesto investors made nearly five times their investment in five years.

You can't rush these things, however. If Modesto had sold in three years—at 150 percent of book when earnings were $2 million and shareholders equity $17 million—the sale would have been at only $25.5 million, well below half the five-year price.

If you can avoid it, wait, says Ed Carpenter. "A bank doesn't hit its stride for five or six years, or when it hits $250 million in assets."

It takes three years to recover starting costs and recoup book value. Your return should begin to look good in the third year and will increase yearly. Two or three years of increasing earnings drives book value up, so that in five or six years you can command the higher premium, the hoped-for double book or more—your "double play," as it's known. But you needn't sell, of course. If you're running your bank well, your investment should continue to increase in value.

The question will arise whether to sell for cash or stock. A stock sale has the advantage of deferring taxes until you sell the stock you receive. But you may not like the buying company's stock. If you can't tell yourself, "I'd buy that stock as an investment today," you may want to make it a cash deal, paying your taxes and investing in something else. Or if you have no choice in the matter, just sell the stock, pay the tax, and reinvest.

Finally, there is something else to consider in the cash-or-stock question—the possibility of selling your bank for stock to someone who may then sell to a larger bank. We sold our Chicago-based $2 billion First Colonial Bankshares in 1995 with that in mind. Our buyer was $20 billion Firstar Corporation, of Milwaukee, which looked good partly because of its apparent salability to a larger bank at a good premium. This would be in addition to the very good premium—near triple book, twenty times earnings—and with a 50 percent dividend increase, that we realized for First Colonial.

We were right about Firstar. In two years it was purchased by Jerry Grundhofer's StarBanc, of Cincinnati, for a good premium—our "double dip." Shortly thereafter Grundhofer merged StarBanc with his brother's bank, U.S. Bancorp. For First Colonial shareholders, acquiring new stock at a premium with each transaction, this was a very profitable "triple dip."

Appendix

What Is a Community Bank?

In the conduct of their business, large banks "often rely on hard financial information, computer models, and centralized decision making"; but small banks rely on "personal knowledge of customers' creditworthiness and a keen understanding of [local] business conditions," reports the Federal Reserve Bank of Kansas City in a 2003 economic review, "The Role of Community Banks in the U.S. Economy."

These small, that is, community banks "hold only a small share of the nation's banking assets [but almost alone] provide important financial services . . . to some key sectors of the economy." They will continue to do so, "even as technology and market conditions change" and even if they "account for a much smaller share of total banking activity than they did twenty years ago."

The Kansas City Fed claims "no single definition" of a community bank but cites two essentials: They are small and do most of their business where they are located. Size and local banking usually go together and size is easy to measure; so community banks are commonly identified by their size, under $1 billion in total assets.

Almost half of them at year-end 2002, of more than 6,900 total, were under $100 million in size and accounted for less than a fifth of total community-bank assets. Well over half of all community-bank assets are held by the two-fifths of community banks with between $100 million and $500 million in assets.

Share of community banks in total banking activity over time.
Community banks account for a very large share of all banks, but a much smaller share of total banking activity. Community banks represented 89 percent of all banks at the end of 2002. In sharp contrast, they accounted for only 34 percent of banking offices, 19 percent of bank deposits, 16 percent of bank loans, and 15 percent of bank assets. The reason community banks hold a smaller share of bank assets and loans than of bank deposits is that they have less access than larger banks to nondeposit sources of funds such as federal funds, repurchase agreements, and subordinated debt.

These measures of community banks' importance are down considerably from 1980. Since that time, community banks' share of banking offices has fallen by eighteen percentage points and their share of bank deposits, loans, and assets by about fifteen percentage points. The decline in community banks' market share has been continuous. However, the pace of decline moderated somewhat in the 1990s, with community banks losing only half as much market share in that period as in the previous decade.

Community banks have not been the only group of banks to lose market share over the last twenty years. The deposit share of organizations between $1 billion and $10 billion in size, often referred to as "regional" banking organizations, has declined by roughly the same amount. The big gainers during this period have been the "megabanks," those over $100 billion in size. These organizations held only a tenth of total deposits in 1980 but now account for two-fifths.

The reduction in community banks' role in the banking system has been due mainly to absorption by larger banking organizations, and not to below-average growth at those community banks that remained independent. Community banks that have survived consolidation have had little difficulty competing for customers.

Importance of community banks in key sectors: While community banks account for a relatively small share of total banking activity in the United States as a whole, they remain highly important in some types of communities and in some parts of the country. Community banks are especially important in rural communities, accounting for 58 percent of all banking offices in such communities and 49 percent of all deposits.

It's interesting to note the Federal Reserve districts having the most number of community banks (June 2002).

	# of Branches	% of All Branches	Deposits
Chicago	3,642	39.3%	$126.4 bil.
Atlanta	3,357	32.4%	106.6 bil.
Kansas City	2,968	58.3%	84.0 bil.
St. Louis	2,493	50.0%	76.6 bil.
All U.S.	23,565	34.1%	737.9 bil.

The importance of community banks by state (June 2002) is also interesting.

	# of Branches	Deposits
Texas	1,793	$58.7 bil.
Illinois	1,543	63.7 bil.
Missouri	971	29.5 bil.
Minnesota	923	27.9 bil.
Iowa	922	22.3 bil.
Pennsylvania	916	28.6 bil.
All others less than 900		
All U.S.	23,565	$737.9 bil.

Importance of community banks as financial service providers:
Besides providing a substantial share of banking services in rural areas, smaller cities, and the middle of the country,

community banks perform highly important roles as providers of relationship-based and information-intensive banking services. These services are consumed mainly by smaller customers such as small businesses, family farmers, and depositors of low to moderate wealth.

Small business lending. Community banks' role as small business lenders is important because small businesses account for a significant share of total output and employment growth. While there is no single definition of a small business, the most common one is a firm with fewer than five hundred employees. According to this definition, small businesses account for just over half of private sector output and employment and provide two-thirds to three-quarters of net job growth. In fact, half of net job growth in the country is provided by even small businesses—those with less than twenty employees.

Community banks have some important advantages over larger banks in making small business loans. Loan officers at small banks can take into account a wide variety of factors in reviewing applications for small business loans, including the character of the borrower and special features of the local market. Loan officers at large geographically dispersed banking organizations are usually not given so much autonomy in making small business loans because it is not feasible for the top managers of such organizations to review every small loan decision.

Community banks are also important providers of another form of small business credit—bank loans backed by nonresidential real estate. In June 2002, community banks account for 42 percent of all nonresidential real estate loans of $1 million or less held by banks and 61 percent of all loans of $100,000 or less held by banks.

Two other forms of evidence support the view that community banks have an inherent advantage over larger banks in making small business loans. First, some researchers have found that small banks earn higher rates of return on their small business loans than large banks, even after adjusting for loss rates. Second, although far from unanimous, studies of the impact of bank mergers on small business lending have generally found that small business lending declines when the acquiring bank organization is large.

Retail deposit services. Relationship-based services are not only important to small businesses but also to many depositors. Some analysts argue that community banks are more interested than large banking organizations in providing personal service to depositors of low to moderate wealth. One possible reason for the difference in focus is that community banks depend more heavily on retail deposits for their funds than large banks. Another reason is that large banks often prefer specializing in impersonal, transaction-based deposit services, where they tend to enjoy a comparative advantage over community banks due to their size and access to technology.

The limited data available suggest that community banks do focus more on small depositors than larger banks.

SUMMARY

Community banks have declined in importance over the last twenty years but continue to play a key role in the banking system. There are still over 6,900 community banks, defined as those belonging to organizations under $1 billion in size, but they account for only a fifth of total deposits and an even smaller fraction of total assets and loans. Furthermore, these shares are down significantly from twenty years ago, as mergers have reduced the importance of community banks and increased the importance of super-regional banks and megabanks. Despite these declines, though, community banks still provide a significant share of banking services in smaller communities and in the middle of the country, where branching restrictions have limited the size of banks. Furthermore, in both rural and urban areas across the country, community banks continue to be important providers of relationship-based banking services, especially to small businesses and farmers but also to small depositors who place a premium on personal service.

II. THE OUTLOOK FOR COMMUNITY BANKS

Community banks still play an important role in the banking system. But can they continue to do so as technology and market conditions change? This section begins by pointing out that banking industry observers expect the number of community banks to decline further but remain in the thousands. The section then points out that community banks *as a group* have performed well relative to large banks over the last decade, but that very small community banks—especially those in declining areas—have not fared as well and face a more uncertain future. Finally, the section argues that contrary to the popular views, advances in information technology and the spread of online banking are unlikely to eliminate the demand for relationship-based services from community banks.

Future structure of the community-banking sector

Some analysts have used complicated statistical techniques and data on past changes in banking structure to predict how many community banks will remain in operation over the long run. These studies generally conclude that the number of community banks will shrink further but that thousands of banks will survive as independent organizations' areas. Thus, while the number of very small community banks may dwindle, the recent record suggests that community banks located in more prosperous areas should continue to thrive.

Deposit and asset growth and new entry

One indication that community banks as a group performed relatively well during the 1990s is that they enjoyed faster growth in deposits and assets than larger banks. The reason small banks were able to pay higher deposit rates was that they also earned from 70 to 150 basis points more than large banks on their loans. The high loan returns not only enabled banks to pay higher deposit rates than large banks, but also allowed them to maintain higher net interest margins. Indeed, during most of the 1990s, the net interest margin of small banks held steady at over 4.5 percent, while the net interest margin of large banks trended down from 4 percent to 3.7 percent.

A related piece of evidence that small banks are still viable is that many new banks continue to be chartered. After declining steadily since the mid-1980s, the number of new bank charters in the United States increased sharply during the second half of the 1990s, surpassing two hundred at the end of the decade before falling back to ninety-one last year. Many of these new banks were started in markets in which large banks had been actively acquiring smaller banks, suggesting that a substantial number of depositors and borrowers still prefer the personal service that community banks tend to provide.

III. CONCLUSIONS

Community banks play an important role in the financial system of the U.S. economy. They complement large banks by specializing in relationship banking and providing credit to small businesses—a sector that is arguably under served by large banks. In addition, community banks serve customers in rural areas and small metropolitan areas that are not served by large banks. Community banks are also important lenders in the farm economy, and they serve the retail deposit needs of many depositors. Although the number of community banks will continue to decline because of merger activity, they will continue to play an important role for the foreseeable future.

INDEX

About the Authors

C. PAUL JOHNSON has had an interesting and varied entrepreneurial life. His first job, at six years old, was working at his grandfather's Chevrolet dealership in Detroit, Michigan. His job was swatting flies in the dealership's showroom, with a going rate of 1 cent per fly. His grandfather, a lifetime entrepreneur, knew the importance of finding loyal, dedicated employees...no matter how young! Losing his father when he was ten years old, Johnson learned independence and responsibility early. Two years in military school and two more at Denison University in Ohio prepared him for a finance degree at Michigan State University and advanced U.S. Air Force (USAF) ROTC.

Johnson earned his fighter pilot wings and served in the USAF for three years, most of this time in Japan, becoming fluent in Japanese. It was just one of the things he learned while in the Air Force. He also became comfortable with risk-taking and decisiveness under pressure, both of which have served him well in the air and in business.

At twenty-nine years of age, Johnson formed a venture capital company that helped to familiarize him with a variety of entrepreneurial pursuits, such as the production of a full-length feature film. He also oversaw investment in and marketing of the largest hotel in Jamaica, which he sold to the Playboy Club in 1964.

In 1972 Johnson purchased his first bank, the $60 million

Colonial Bank in Chicago, Illinois. He developed the company into First Colonial Bankshares Corporation, a $1.8 billion company comprised of 17 banks with 36 locations, and four financial services subsidiaries. During his years as a banker, Johnson served as president of the Illinois Bankers Associations, Chicago district, and worked tirelessly and successfully for the passage of multi-bank holding company and branch legislation.

Among Johnson's consuming interests is Western art and history. His cattle ranch in Wyoming is a magnet for his friends and family. Another of his interests is astronomy, which led him to many happy years taking classes at Chicago's Adler planetarium. Johnson now serves as a life trustee of the planetarium. His family foundation recently contributed a gallery dedicated to archaeo-astronomy.

Johnson has also made a study of archaeology and paleontology. This led to his chairmanship for eight years of the Crow Canyon Archaeological Center in Cortez, Colorado, and his current position as a trustee of the Leakey Foundation in San Francisco. He has sponsored archaeological excavations in both Israel and Jordan for more than fifteen years. He also serves as trustee of Roosevelt University, Chicago.

Moving to California gave Johnson the opportunity to purchase a winery he named Astrale e Terra (meaning "heaven and earth"—encompassing two of his favorite areas of study) and once again to establish a de novo bank. He lives in Napa with his wife Debbie and their two sons, seven and three years old, and keeps in close touch with his three daughters and six granddaughters.

Johnson intends this book to demonstrate, in spite of widely known examples of deceit and ruthlessness in today's business world, that good guys really do finish first.

JIM BOWMAN has written six books, including *Booz, Allen & Hamilton: Seventy Years of Client Service, 1914-1984; More Than a Coffee Company: The Story of CFS Continental; Good*

Medicine: The First 150 Years of Rush-Presbyterian- St. Luke's Medical Center; and "Waste Not . . .": The Safety-Kleen Story. A former *Chicago Daily News* reporter and Chicago history columnist for the *Chicago Tribune*, he specializes in corporate history. He has also written about the telephone industry, shoe and candy making, investment banking, and the practice of law.

He and his wife Winnie live in Oak Park, Illinois, where they raised their six children.